BRIAN DAVIS

The Confident Gardener

THE KEY TO SUCCESSFUL GARDENING TECHNIQUES

PENGUIN BOOKS

PENGUIN BOOKS

Published by the Penguin Group
Penguin Books Ltd, 27 Wrights Lane, London W8 5TZ, England
Penguin Books USA Inc., 375 Hudson Street, New York, New York 10014, USA
Penguin Books Australia Ltd, Ringwood, Victoria, Australia
Penguin Books Canada Ltd, 10 Alcorn Avenue, Toronto, Ontario, Canada M4V 3B2
Penguin Books (NZ) Ltd, 182–190 Wairau Road, Auckland 10, New Zealand

Penguin Books Ltd, Registered Offices: Harmondsworth, Middlesex, England

First published 1995
1 3 5 7 9 10 8 6 4 2

Filmset by Datix International Limited, Bungay, Suffolk
Printed in England by Clays Ltd, St Ives plc
Set in 11/13pt Monophoto Sabon

Contents

List of Illustrations

All photographs copyright © the author

Introduction

It is a strange feeling to be setting down on paper the gardening techniques that have become second nature to me over the last forty years or more of my gardening career. Many of the techniques that you will read about in the following pages were taught to me as a garden boy by a head gardener, and they have remained constantly in use in the work which I have done and continue to do today.

There have been times of course when I have been tempted to shortcut, adapt or even omit some of the procedures that I describe, and each time it has proved to be a mistake. Sometimes the proof has been seen in a matter of a month, sometimes it has only shown up several years later.

Slowly, over the years, I have come to understand how these techniques are linked to the ways in which plants grow and to the effects of soil type, weather conditions, aspect and geographical location on overall performance. I remember well, some twenty years after starting work, walking down through the nursery gardens and literally stopping in my tracks when I suddenly realized that I did, at last, understand what it was all about; from that moment I could see the reasons for every operation, every problem and every success or failure.

It is not enough to gain experience in a single location; I have been lucky in that over the years I have worked in a wide range of different environments and geographical locations, and in both the amateur and the commercial gardening worlds. Talking to other gardeners at all levels has added to my knowledge. Observing and recording the growth of plants in so many differing conditions has given me an understanding of how they react and respond to their environments and to the various techniques we practise for their well-being.

Being able to observe and understand small changes and

how these changes can affect success or failure gives one the ability to pick the right plant for any particular purpose and the right plant for the local conditions, and to understand the continuing needs of the plant once it is established in the garden.

There can be no operation so intimate with the plant as propagation; once you have handled many thousands, if not tens of thousands, of the offspring of a single plant, they start to communicate and identify their own particular requirements.

There is always room for experiment, but the established rules and procedures nearly always indicate the best way to handle any particular garden operation. In the following pages I have tried to record as many of these techniques as possible, in such a way that the reader will be able to shortcut the years of practical experience through which I learnt.

As well as saying what should be done, and when, I have attempted to say why it should be done. There is so much information that I have tried to stick to the facts, without wasting time on irrelevant chat: my aim is to use the space to the maximum effect to pass on the information and knowledge I have been privileged to absorb.

It is never too late to start gardening and it is never too late to learn; I learn more every day. There are exceptions to every rule, and you may find that what I say in a particular case does not work for you – that's gardening – but I have tried to make sure that if you do follow the methods described, you will normally succeed.

If you bring in outside assistance, it is important that you know what you want your helpers to do and that you are able to explain it well, otherwise they may do more harm than good.

A great deal of money and effort may be wasted if a garden is not well cared for after it has been planted. It is worth waiting to do things at the right time, even if it means waiting three months, six months or a year, rather than pushing on regardless. Waiting, managing the work programme, is one of the most important considerations for the gardener.

Many garden techniques are interconnected – soil preparation leads to planting, planting leads to staking and tying, staking and tying leads to pruning, and pruning leads to feeding – so it has often been necessary to refer the reader from one chapter to another.

Sometimes it is impossible to describe in words all the detailed operations of a particular technique, and in these cases line drawings have been used to elucidate the text.

I see this book being used in two ways: if you read it initially from start to finish you should gain a good knowledge of the subject, but you will also need to dip into it from time to time to extract specific information as you require it.

I can truly say that I have enjoyed my forty years of gardening, and I hope to enjoy many more yet – watching a garden develop and flourish over the years gives unfailing pleasure. I hope that you, like me, can say that gardening is not work, but rather a way of life.

Many thanks to Capel Manor Horticultural and Environmental Centre, England, for their help with the illustrations.

CHAPTER ONE

Soil Preparation and Management

In soil management lie most, though not all, of the secrets of gardening success; the understanding of the role played by the soil must never be underestimated. So often it is suggested that there are short cuts in soil preparation and improvement, but these may lead to failure. There are those who are lucky and have all of the elements of good garden soil in their gardens, but even good soil can quickly become depleted or even destroyed. Poor soil management can too easily diminish the eventual results; planting, pruning, feeding, and pest and disease control are all affected by the preparation, management and final condition of the soil.

To understand the soil's requirements, it is necessary to enter a microscopic world of interlocking environments, where, if all is well, success is assured but, if not, disaster is only a moment away.

What is soil?

Soil is an interactive mixture of mineral or rock, organic and animal material, most of it dead, but some alive and active, that has been brought together over many millions of years by the action of glaciers, wind, rain, frost and many other factors.

Soil temperature

Each and every variety of plant responds differently to soil temperature, and no two varieties are the same. This explains why *Narcissus* (Daffodil) 'King Alfred' flowers before *N.* 'Cheerfulness' and *Clematis montana* before *C.* 'Nellie Moser'; and of course it is the reason why *C. montana* is spring-flowering and *C.* 'Nellie Moser' summer-flowering.

As we will see, when the optimum soil temperature for a particular plant is reached, it allows the soil moisture to enter into the roots. If the soil is slow to warm up in the spring, we observe our plants starting into leaf and growth later than usual, and we call the spring 'late'.

The temperature rise and fall also controls the *amount* of moisture entering the root system, so if there is a slowdown in growth and possibly of overall size, there will be an effect on flowering and fruiting as well. The soil temperature also sets the time for the storage of plant food for the following spring, and so the autumn and winter rest from feeding with fertilizers is linked in too. In fact it is the plants' clock and growth is controlled by it.

Soil moisture

We will discover shortly that the soil moisture is nature's clock controlling every growing process, but first we must understand a little more about it.

The moisture we are talking of is not water that can be seen, but a microscopic film that surrounds, when present – as it must be if plants are to survive – each of the mineral particles of the soil and infiltrates the organic material as if it were a sponge.

This moisture film is the storage and supply source of most plant foods, and it is from here that almost all plants obtain the bulk of their food; these foods enter as a liquid cocktail into the plant's roots, and then into the shoots and leaves, to be processed into new growth. But before any food enters the plant, nature's spring clock has to be set in motion by the sun, as it becomes stronger and higher in the sky, raising the temperature of the soil moisture. When it reaches the right temperature for each individual plant variety, that variety will begin to respond. Excessive soil moisture caused by heavy winter snow or rain and cold spring frosts, or poor drainage and management, all slow down the warming action of the sun.

The size of the soil particles will affect the amount of moisture retained and gardeners often refer to soils being 'cold' or 'warm'. If the aspect is sheltered or south facing, the soil moisture will be warmer. The amount of organic material it contains will also affect the spring temperature, for a high organic content means that more of the sun's heat is retained by the soil.

Now that we know something of how the soil's moisture and its seasonal temperature control the plants' clock, we can begin to see how our efforts can affect this rise and fall in temperature of the soil moisture.

Types of soil

Minerals

Minerals in the soil originate from rocks such as granite, sandstone, limestone and chalk, to name just a few, continually broken down and eroded by geological processes and the action of the weather until they are no more than a collection of small individual particles. These particles are then sorted, principally by flowing water in seas, lakes and rivers, into different sizes, and deposited in layers, often after having been transported vast distances over many thousands of years.

The action of the water also releases, by dissolving them from the rocks, some of the main plant foods as well as trace elements that plants require, and we ourselves also need, such as nitrogen, phosphates and potash, as well as iron, magnesium, manganese, calcium, etc.

Gardeners classify soil types according to particle size: large particles form sand and the smaller ones clays and silts, with varying proportional mixtures in between.

Sand

Rocks and stones are broken down into particles, the largest of which are referred to as sand. When a soil is principally made up of these grains it is called a 'sand' or 'sandy' soil.

Because the grains are large they have a smaller surface area in proportion to their mass than other soil types, and therefore retain less soil moisture. This makes them quick to warm up in the spring but quicker to cool down in the autumn.

The large grains have many spaces between them so there is less chance of plant root suffocation due to the lack of oxygen from poor drainage.

The good drainage will lead to a leaching out of plant foods, and so we often refer to these soils as being 'hungry'. Because of the limited moisture retention this soil type is easy to work and prepare, and is often also called a 'light' or 'easy' soil. Plant roots will not be suffocated, but they may dry out, particularly the fine root hairs which we will learn about later. The roots will have to extend over a wide area to find the full range of foods they need for balanced growth.

Because this soil type cools quickly in the autumn, plant growth stops promptly and autumn leaf colour is usually very good.

Clay

Clay soils are laid down, both historically and in the present time, in river estuaries and lakes. The smaller, lighter grains are transported in suspension in the water of fast-flowing rivers until wider, slower-flowing, shallower areas are reached, where they slow down and eventually settle out of suspension, forming vast layers of clay over many years.

Clay soils are the reverse of sand: the grains are small and so have a large surface area in proportion to their mass; the moisture content is therefore higher than for sand. The space between the grains is minute, if it exists at all, and there is a real danger of plant roots suffocating due to a lack of oxygen. Because of the high moisture content this type of soil is slow to warm up in the spring and we refer to it as a 'cold' or 'late' soil. In the autumn it is slow to cool down, as the high moisture levels retain the heat, and plants often go on growing and keep their leaves longer, but this may make them more susceptible to autumn and winter frosts and cold, and their autumn leaf colours may be less vibrant.

The high concentration of moisture makes the soil 'heavy' and difficult to work. Roots and root hairs rarely dry out but unless adapted for the purpose, or helped by the gardener, they find it difficult to penetrate the surrounding soil in the search for plant foods and can become stunted and inactive, leading to a decline in the plants' well-being.

Loam

In gardening, the word 'loam' has a number of usages, but when referring to soil type it means that the soil contains a mixture of sand and clay particles. This mixture is also often referred to as 'garden' or 'average' soil. If the mixture contains more sand than clay, we use the term 'sandy loam': likewise, if there is an excess of clay, we call it a 'clay loam'. The ideal balance of mineral grains is 50:50.

There is a third vital element of loam, organic material, and its presence greatly increases the productivity of the soil. Loam soils offer all the right conditions for the development of roots and root hairs as they retain plant foods and, if prepared and managed correctly, they are the ideal garden soils. Loam soils can be 'manufactured' by good garden techniques and management, and we will see how to do this later.

Silts

Silts are simply clay soils where only the smallest sizes of grains are present. They contain all of the good and bad points of clay but in higher proportions. Thankfully for gardeners, they exist in only a few areas, but even silts, with good management, can become very fertile.

Stony soils

With stony soils, the process of natural rock size reduction is not complete and, in addition to sand, clay and organic material, the mixture contains large numbers of stones or small pieces of rock. Stones may also be deposited in beds and can be found in both sandy or clay soil types in layers below the surface. Large concentrations are often produced by the action of rivers as they negotiate large bends; the stones break away from their parent rock and are then rolled along the bottom of the fast-flowing rivers until they are trapped on the outside of bends, where the water moves more slowly. Although they can make managing the soil more difficult when seeds are being sown or a lawn being laid, there is little need to remove them. In fact it is almost impossible to do so, for they just keep working up to the surface from below.

Chalk soils

Chalk – or, more correctly, calcium-based – soils have organic origins, being derived from the shells and skeletons of many billions of small sea creatures that once swam in the rivers and oceans that covered the earth millions of years ago. As the creatures died they were laid down in vast layers on the river and ocean beds; as the layers built up they became more compressed and eventually formed chalk.

Chalk is often referred to as lime in the gardening sense, but there is also limestone, which is laid down in the same way as chalk, but also contains a proportion of detrital material – sand or clay. Later we will see that both chalk and limestone have a major role to play in deciding which plants we can grow.

Due to their origin, chalk soils are very free draining and porous, but, as with sand, they therefore hold little plant food. Air is also trapped in large amounts and this keeps these soils cool in summer, sometimes to the advantage of certain plants. Due to their compressed nature, chalk soils are sometimes difficult to work and prepare; they cool down fast in autumn but quickly warm up again in the spring.

As chalk soils are associated with former oceans, they are often found together with clays that have settled in ancient river estuaries, and this combination of chalk and clay can be difficult to work. The mixture, however, contains high proportions of retained plant foods and can, with the right selection of plants and good management, be very rewarding from a gardening point of view.

Organic (peat) soils

Many organic soils began their life thousands of years ago, in the forests that existed before the dinosaurs. At that time, most of the world was covered by tropical or subtropical forests, with trees growing to great heights – in fact, relatives of the persistent garden weed, Mare's Tail (*Hippuris vulgaris*), were then substantial trees and can be found as fossil remains today. Leaves, and whole trees, died and rotted, and eventually formed deep layers of decomposing remains. In certain conditions this organic material eventually forms peat; these deposits may in the end become coal, oil or natural gas.

Organic particles, although they may look large to the naked eye, are in fact made up of many small particles grouped together. They differ from mineral particles in the fact that they were once alive – as animals, leaves, stems, flowers and fruits – and they are all in a state of decomposition, being slowly broken down by worms and soil bacteria, nematodes (roundworms) and soil fungi. The small, often microscopic, animals and plants, without whose presence decomposition would not be possible, need our protection and encouragement to do their work. As the decomposition and rotting takes place, plant foods are released back into the soil for future use by other plants, but not enough to sustain the whole galaxy of plants we grow in our gardens. Later, in Chapter 4, we will see how we can supplement these plant foods.

As the decay process continues, acids are given off and we therefore refer to these soil types as 'acid' soils. The process never stops – every year millions of tons of organic material is formed, and a visit to any woodland will confirm this.

Gardeners reproduce this process when they compost, in controlled conditions, the vegetable waste from the garden and farm. A well-constructed compost or manure heap is worth its weight in gold, and we will look later at this and other types of organic material we might use in the garden.

Organic soils retain moisture in their sponge-like tissue and this in turn retains plant food. There is plenty of air, so plant roots and root hairs do not suffer, and as the material is soft and easy to penetrate, plant roots can infiltrate it with very little effort. There are, however, drawbacks to very organic soils, the principal one being that in times of heavy rain they may become temporarily waterlogged, so that added drainage may be necessary or the choice of plants limited to those that can withstand these conditions. Another problem is that organic or acid soils contain very little of the trace element calcium and some plants resent this; the soil has to be limed to counteract the effect.

In fact all soil types contain a certain amount of organic

material – known as 'humus' – and it is the feather bed, larder and moisture store for the soil organisms, nemotodes and animals which continue the process of decomposition.

Alkalinity and acidity

Chalk soils are very alkaline; soils which contain a large amount of organic material may, as we have seen, be acid. Between these two extremes, all soils, whether they are loams, sand, clay, silts or stony, can be characterized by their level of acidity and alkalinity. It is important to know this level before selecting your plants, as many plants dislike growing in high levels at either end of the scale, particularly those which require an acid soil, such as Rhododendrons and Azaleas and ericaceous plants – we refer to these as 'acid-loving'. Plants we describe as 'lime-tolerant' grow happily on either alkaline or acid soils.

There is no way of telling the acidity or alkalinity of a specific area of your garden from the appearance of the soil, although if you see acid-loving plants growing in neighbouring gardens, this may be a clue, and of course on white chalk soils there is little doubt of the alkalinity.

Alkalinity and acidity is not controlled by the actual mineral or organic content of the soil so much as by the soil moisture and the effect on the moisture of the soil's constituent materials.

If you think of the amount of soil moisture and groundwater in the soil, you will realize that any attempt to change alkaline soils to acid or vice versa is almost impossible in the long-term. Even specially prepared pits or pots will return eventually to the acidity or alkalinity of the water in the local region.

Carrying out an acidity or alkalinity test will determine a soil's suitability for a specific plant; I feel strongly that to submit a plant, by growing it in the wrong soil, to a long, lingering death is wasteful, not only of finance but also of the effort that has gone into producing the plant in the first place.

Never be persuaded that acid-loving plants will grow on alkaline soil. They may survive for three or four years by using the energy stored within their roots and stems, but even if they flower they rarely grow well; they just survive.

From time to time it is suggested that particular acid-loving plants will grow on alkaline soils, but it usually turns out to be an isolated case of plants grown on limestone, which can affect plants less than chalk soils.

To carry out a soil test you will need to purchase a soil-testing kit. Always read the instructions, as kits may vary, and do not be tempted to purchase an unnecessarily elaborate kit or a costly electronic device. Divide the garden into small, logical areas, such as front garden, back garden, right side, left side, and from each area take small samples 6 in (13 cm) deep, 6 ft (2 m) apart, in a diagonal line from corner to corner.

When taking the samples try not to contaminate one with another by using an uncleaned trowel or spade. Also try not to touch the sample with your fingers as this can distort the readings. If more than one sample is being taken ensure that each is clearly labelled for future reference. Individual samples from each specific area are mixed together and a small quantity selected for testing. From this stage the instructions on the individual test kit should be followed.

The result of the test will show up as a colour-coded reading on a colour comparison chart supplied with the kit. The chart will represent the reading as a pH (phosphorus hydrogen) content. A reading of pH 4 to 6 indicates an acid soil, pH 6 to 6.5 is neutral and 7 to 9 is alkaline. Most gardens will fall into the range 5.5 to 8, and readings outside this are extremes.

Neutral is a difficult area to define and as the difference between success or failure is very fine it is prudent to stay on the side of caution when selecting your plants. Never cheat on the reading, whether acid or alkaline, because in the long run the planting of the wrong plant almost always leads to failure.

Soil structure

The proportions and arrangement of mineral and organic particles, together with moisture, oxygen and temperature, and microscopic animals and plants, make up a finely balanced cocktail. It is penetrated by an interacting arrangement of minute tubes and passages through which all of the different contents move and which the roots invade and use. If this structure is upset, plants will fail and the soil will be damaged, often beyond repair.

Topsoil and subsoil

We often hear soil referred to as topsoil or subsoil in gardening; in simple terms these names describe the locations of each type, but there is more to the story.

Topsoil

The word 'topsoil' pinpoints the location as the upper layer of soil. Almost without exception, plants produce the majority of their roots in a spreading, ever-increasing circle radiating out from the centre. Many would also like to send their roots upwards if we would allow them to do so and we will learn more about this in the section on mulching (p. 31). Far fewer than we think force roots downwards into the subsoil and those that do do it to find additional soil moisture and increased anchorage.

The reason for the roots spreading mainly in the topsoil is that this layer is the most fertile, containing over 80 per cent of the soil's renewable plant foods and 60–70 per cent of the available moisture. Air is also present and the structure of the soil is the least compacted, due to the action of many soil-burrowing animals such as earthworms – and of course it is this layer that we, as gardeners, are able to cultivate the most. The stronger plant roots themselves break up the structure so that finer roots can penetrate and when plants die or discard leaves, they rot down and form organic material which in turn improves the topsoil.

Earthworms and other soil animals pull down or bury all types of organic material, and gardeners, too, incorporate vegetable and organic waste into the topsoil, in the form of garden compost and farmyard manure and other organic material; we will look in more detail at these later. Again, this is the layer we feed with plant foods in the form of fertilizers. It is therefore evident that this layer is the more fertile of the two soil layers we have in our gardens and we should constantly try to protect and improve it.

Often the depth of topsoil is referred to as a 'spit deep', or the nominal depth is said to be 9 in (23 cm). The word spit is a historical term used to describe the length of the blade of a garden spade or digging fork. In fact topsoil depths vary from only 1 in (3 cm) or so to 2–3 ft (60 cm–1 m); it is geological accident how much there is in any particular location.

We can improve the structure, fertility and depth of the topsoil to ensure that the penetration of the roots and root hairs is as efficient as possible, thereby enhancing the growth of the plant.

Subsoil

Here again the name indicates the characteristics of this layer of soil, suggesting both that it is of an inferior grade to topsoil and that it lies, as it does, below the topsoil.

Its depth is very variable and there are few or no organic or beneficial soil animals living in it. It does, however, play a major part in the control and availability of soil moisture in the topsoil and to the plant. Should it be of a non-porous or compacted nature, as with clay and silt soils, drainage will be impaired and the air will be forced out by the rising moisture, possibly leading to plant roots being suffocated. So we may have to redress this situation by drainage and by adding organic material.

This layer is also directly in contact with the groundwater, and the many subterranean streams and rivers that rise and fall depending on the surface water supplies; this is either tapped directly by the deep penetrating roots (hence the name for these roots as tap roots) or it is filtered upwards by capillary action through the narrow cracks and passages in the soil.

Subsoils are also the basic material that we use to produce and increase the depth of the topsoil. If it is very porous, as in sand, stone or chalk soils, much of the plant foods we add to the soil will be leached out each time it rains, and we may therefore need to provide moisture-retaining organic material to conserve the soil moisture and the plant foods contained in it.

Soil pans

There is usually a soil pan of some form where a layer of compacted soil has built up between the topsoil and subsoil, or in some cases as a layer in the subsoil itself. It may be natural, caused by the unbroken nature of the soil, or it can be caused by the use of a shallow plough or, more likely, a soil rotovator for a number of years. The use to which the land was put before it became a garden, or building work carried out on the site, can also cause compaction of the soil; 'topsoil' may then have been spread over the top, hiding the compaction.

However the soil pan was formed, it can present the gardener with problems, not only at the time of preparation – some require great effort to break – but even at a later date, when a hedge or lawn, say, passes across it. This prevents the roots of the plants from spreading and causes poor growth or death in a specific area.

The soil pan caused by a rotovator is worst of all on a clay or silt soil, because as the blades rotate they glaze the bottom of the cultivated soil by the pressure they place on the soil each time they turn.

We will see later how to break up pans to prevent current and long-term problems.

THE SOIL AND ITS RELATIONSHIP WITH THE PLANT

Before we look further into soil management, we must spend time understanding how a plant works in relation to the soil. The contact is through the root system, so it is here we must start, but we also need to follow the subsequent action through the whole plant structure of shoots, buds, leaves, flowers and fruit.

Roots and root hairs

Most of us can recognize a section of root, and little effort is needed to locate them in the soil: the long white, grey or brown threads or branch-like structures are easily seen.

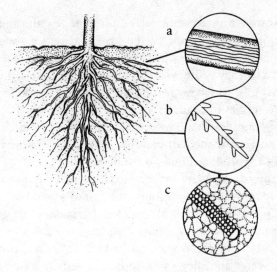

1. Root system
(a) Transporting tubes within the root   (b) Main and secondary
shoots   (c) Microscopic root hair positioned between soil grains

These visible roots have the functions of exploring the soil, transporting, storing food, and anchoring the plant in the soil, but they have only a very limited, if any, capacity to absorb the soil moisture and the plant foods it contains. The real work of food absorption and intake is carried out by microscopic root hairs, so small that in most cases it is impossible to see them with the naked eye. Each plant has tens of thousands of them, and they are constantly being lost and replaced. They start to work in the spring when the rise in temperature of the soil moisture has reached a specific level, which is different for each individual variety of plant.

Once this temperature level is reached, cells in the outer wall of the root hair open and allow a one-way passage of moisture from the soil particle through the cell wall into the root hair. In very simple terms, what happens is that the central cells of the root hairs contain a thick soup-like solution into which the soil moisture is absorbed.

These minute root hairs need to be constantly spreading and expanding out from the centre of the root system in a never-ending search for the cocktail of plant foods the individual plant requires. This is one of the principal reasons why most plants present their leaves in an overlapping pyramidal formation and why they grow wider every year: they are sending out their roots to cover new ground and opening up the potential for fresh supplies of plant food. Moisture is the key to feeding, and the pyramidal shape means that moisture is shed around the outer edges of the leaf canopy, where the majority of the root hairs are produced and positioned.

If for any reason root movement is obstructed due to difficult or unprepared soil conditions, the plant's growth will be retarded or stopped, with a resulting detrimental effect on its well-being.

The root hairs are always at risk from suffocation from excessive water and they can also be easily dehydrated by lack of soil moisture. Poor soil management and plant handling are also causes of damage. On the other hand their activities can easily be enhanced by attention to drainage, the breaking up of consolidated soil, the incorporation of organic material, the use of mulches and the provision of a maintained balanced supply of plant foods – in fact the good soil preparation and management which we will look at later.

As we cover other gardening techniques we will see more and more how an understanding of the role and needs of the root hairs is the prime secret of gardening success or failure.

The movement of soil moisture, once it has passed from the root hair into the main root system that we can see, is made possible by osmotic pressure and capillary action, or in other words by pressure that builds up between the walls of the narrow tubes, forcing the moisture upwards into the stems and shoots. As more moisture enters through the root hairs, this also forces movement up through the system from below.

In the spring deciduous plants have no leaves and even evergreen leaves are in a state of semi-dormancy, so there is no production of new energy, or very little, and all living things require energy to grow. A plant's energy comes in the form of sugar. When the leaves cannot manufacture this in the spring, the plant needs to find it elsewhere and it does this by laying down a supply, over winter, in its main root system. A carrot is a good example of an enlarged energy-food storage supply. Sugar itself is not stored; it is changed to and held as starch. We will see in a moment when and how this is done, but first we will continue to follow the movement of the soil moisture through the plant.

The soil moisture entering through the root hairs is able to absorb the root-stored starch and turn it into energy-producing sugar, or as we call it, 'sap'. The sap is passed from the roots into buds below ground, as in perennial plants and bulbs, or into the stems and shoots of woody plants such as trees, shrubs, roses, climbers, etc.

Seeds use the same system, but here the starch is stored and used in the seed itself. Again it is the rise in temperature that allows soil moisture to enter the seed wall, which then turns the starch into sugar and thereby energy for growth.

Some of the sap is redirected back to the root system to encourage it to produce more root hairs, and in those first few days of its growth a plant must be able to develop its root system over a wide area if it is to find all the food it needs for later growth development. Sap is moved into the underground buds or bulbs or up into a stem or shoot of a woody plant until it reaches the buds.

Buds are like suitcases, prepared and packed in the previous late summer and autumn and containing all the embryo leaves, stems, future replacement buds and, if of the right age and type, the potential flowers. Once a bud is packed the contents are the maximum it can produce in its life, although it may not release all of its potential in one year and in many cases some potential buds will become naturally dormant, a point we will consider in Chapter 8, in connection with pruning.

Once the sap reaches the bud the sugar is converted to energy and the first pair of leaves opens.

Up to this point the plant has used very little, if any, of the plant foods provided by and obtained from the soil moisture, depending entirely on the starch stored in its root system or bulb, so if too little or too much soil moisture is present the reaction – the unfurling of the first leaves – may not take place.

If the sun does not raise the temperature of the soil moisture soon enough the plant cannot react and will be in danger. Likewise if the first new root hair that develops cannot grow and start to spread the chain of new spring growth will be broken.

All these factors must be guarded against if failure is to be avoided and the plant develop and produce its full potential, so good soil preparation and management is essential.

Assuming that all is well, once the first two leaves have opened they start to work, using sunlight and carbon dioxide from the air to manufacture more sugar and returning the oxygen to the atmosphere for us to use. Mixed into the cocktail are the main plant foods of nitrogen, phosphate and potash, and the many trace elements that plants use. The green colouring of the leaves which we call chlorophyll serves to absorb the light and this provides the energy and the catalyst for the process, which is known as photosynthesis.

The newly produced sugar induces the opening of more leaves from late spring through to midsummer; it also fuels the growth of stems, by inducing the terminal or side buds to grow. If a flower bud is present it opens and then forms a fruit, and this in turn builds the store of starch in the seed, to be used at germination in the following spring.

By mid to late summer the soil-moisture temperature starts to cool and when it reaches a specific temperature for each variety of plant the cells in the root hairs start to close slowly, letting in less and less moisture. This is a signal for the plant to start to store sugar in its main roots in the form of starch for the following spring's development.

As far as soil management is concerned, it is important that we make sure that the right balance of plant foods is available at the right time, and we will look at this in Chapter 4.

The cycle is now complete: the deciduous plant loses its leaves and goes to sleep, the evergreen slows down for the winter, ready for the process to start again in the following spring.

As you will have realized, there are many ways in which the plant can be at risk in the period after planting and throughout its active life; the rules of good soil management and preparation described in the next section are aimed at minimizing the risks.

In this section we will look at the procedures we must adopt to achieve good plant management and minimize damage to the soil structure.

The right time

Often the structure and therefore the fertility of the soil is damaged by poor soil management, damage that can be avoided.

The gardener may feel under pressure to prepare the ground for planting, either because he has the time available or simply because a new plant has been acquired and he feels it should be planted as soon as possible.

However, to attempt to cultivate the soil, particularly with a rotovator, when it is too wet will lead to disaster; it will drive out most of the air, allow more moisture to be trapped than the soil needs, and consolidate and glaze the bottom of the planting holes or prepared areas of soil. In these conditions, the beneficial soil animals, such as earthworms, will die. If any planting is done, the fragile roots and, more importantly, the root hairs will be restricted in their movement and may be killed completely; this is one of the principal reasons for plant death in the early months and years following planting.

It is therefore better to wait until conditions are right, which in the spring can be in a matter of days as the surplus rain drains away or is evaporated off by the wind.

Using the weather to improve your soil

The weather is often seen as a foe by gardeners, but in soil management it can be a real friend.

Later, when we look at digging – by hand or using a small mini-digger, but not a rotovator – we will learn that if the soil is prepared in the early autumn and winter, prior to spring planting, the action of frost, wind and rain will break down the soil, by movement, erosion and expansion and contraction, and can assist the gardener to produce an almost perfect seed bed or growing environment.

The effects of weather can also help with minor levelling, as hollows may be filled in or are identified as highs and lows to be dealt with in final preparation.

Drainage

Clay and silt and soils high in organic material may require some form of drainage, and I feel it is worth considering this at the outset, ideally before the garden is constructed, although laying drains in an established garden rarely causes any long-term disruption.

Whether the traditional 4–6 in (10–15 cm) diameter clay land drains are used, or the newer perforated plastic tubing, the results are the same. Even trenches filled with coarse gravel or stones and bricks collected from the site can be used and will go a long way towards improving soil drainage.

Before any systems can be installed, consideration must be given to the way the ground slopes and where the collected water is to be deposited. The area to be drained may be small and isolated, and the use of a single line of drainage may be enough to clear the surplus water. Alternatively, a more complex system may be required with a network of interconnecting and branch drains; in some larger areas, it may be better to have a drainage system installed by a professional.

For small systems the work of excavating the trenches is done by hand, taking care that the minimum size of the trench is 18 in (50 cm) deep with a width of about 12 in (30 cm); the trenches should follow the slope of the land. Before the drain itself is laid, a 3–4 in (8–10 cm) deep layer of gravel is placed at the bottom of the trench and the piping is then laid on top and covered with a further layer of gravel to a depth of about 4 in (10 cm). Next, the soil is infilled and the work is complete. It will take two to three months to become fully operational as time is needed for the surrounding soil to connect the natural soil drainage to the new main drains. Every three to four years the drain will need to be inspected to check that it is running freely and may need clearing with drain rods.

Preparing your soil

Two possibilities exist, hand or mechanical preparation, and until recently I would have favoured the hand method only, and still do for small numbers of individual plants or small areas.

Whenever using tools, hand or mechanical, all aspects of health and safety must be considered and acted upon. In particular, remember that anyone working with the soil should have a course of tetanus injections.

A rotovator is, in my opinion, one of the most dangerous of soil preparation tools and I will explain this later. But the possibility of using a mini-tractor or digger with its power and flexibility should be considered by the gardener, particularly if large areas are to be planted.

Throughout this section reference will be made to organic material, and more details of the various types available and their preparation will be given later in this chapter.

Whether we use manual or mechanical methods of preparation, one golden rule exists: at no time should the topsoil and subsoil positions be reversed. This should always be carefully observed if the benefits of the topsoil are not to be lost.

Attempting to prepare the soil when it is too wet or frosted is also to be avoided. Compaction and treading when manual or mechanical preparation is being undertaken is inevitable but can be reduced by working from a plank or board which is moved along the line of digging as work progresses.

If you can plan ahead, covering part or all of the area to be worked on, say a week or two in advance, with plastic sheeting will keep off the worst of the rain; sacking, old carpet or similar material can be used to keep out frost. Then, provided that weather conditions do not deteriorate, the work can proceed as planned.

Advance preparation on a planned basis is always preferable, and early autumn is often an ideal time to start, so that planting can begin in mid to late autumn or late winter for hardy plants and late spring for the less hardy ones. Planting can also be undertaken at other times so long as the weather is dry and mild and there is no drought. Where organic material is to be incorporated, moving it conveniently close to the site and making it ready for use will save time later.

Manual digging tools

The following suggested methods have been practised by gardeners for generations and are, if followed, the most beneficial to plant establishment. Assuming that the operator is medically sound, manual digging is often satisfying, the good exercise a bonus. Never attack the job head-on, however. Start off with a planned approach as explained, doing as much as and no more than you find comfortable; even if you do only a small amount each time, the task will be completed surprisingly quickly.

In order to save effort it is important to have the right serviceable tools to hand. Tools come in a range of prices and it is tempting to choose from the lower end of the scale, but in the long-term this will prove to be a false saving. At the top end of the scale there are tools made entirely of stainless steel, but they cost a great deal more and they do not greatly reduce the amount of effort required.

Unless tools are kept clean and free from dried-on soil, they will be less efficient and may not last as long. If cleaned and lightly oiled at the end of each use they can last a lifetime, so purchasing the best tools you can and keeping them clean will be an investment. Storage of tools in a suitable secure, safe, damp-proof shed or garage is important, and when hanging tools against walls, take time to ensure that they cannot fall and injure anybody.

Never use a tool for a purpose that it was not designed for, for this may damage the tool and it can be dangerous to the user.

Most digging tools have been in use and constantly refined over hundreds, if not thousands, of years and if the simple rules of load, balance and effort are followed, less effort will be required. For instance, both forks and spades are forced into the soil to start the process of digging. The soil they are to move is the load; the leverage and the lifting applied to the shaft and handle is the effort; between these points is the balance-point. If all the movements are centred on this point, the effort required will be less and the work will be carried out safely. If you balance the length of the tool on the palm of your hand it will be apparent exactly where the balance-point is.

Digging forks

Digging or garden forks are the principal tools used for most major soil preparation. They are used for all the primary and secondary digging in the garden, at all levels from opening up the surface to digging and breaking up the subsoil for drainage.

The standard model has four square-pointed prongs, 9–10 in (23–5 cm) long, forged from steel; they are spaced approximately 2 in (5 cm) apart in a straight line and are curved slightly forward. The top end of the prongs form a foot tread, into which the central wooden or steel-shafted handle is fitted.

With wooden handles, if possible, shop around and find a sheath that is split, rather than fitting square, because it is at this point that the fork is under the most strain and most often breaks when in use. Try to find the length of shaft that suits you best.

The choice between a wooden or metal handle is relatively unimportant if a good-quality tool is purchased; wood is slightly lighter and metal slightly stronger, but if you use greater force you may damage the prongs. The top of the shaft will be surmounted by a D-, Y- or T-shaped handle; choose whichever you prefer.

Other models of fork are also available, including the ladies' or border fork, which has four prongs 6–7 in (15–17 cm) long and $1\frac{1}{2}$ in (4 cm) apart, forming a fork approximately 5–6 in (12–15 cm) wide. In all other ways it is the same as the digging fork and can be used for digging where the user needs a lighter tool, although the work will take longer and the digging methods described later may have to be amended slightly.

Stainless steel models are available for both the standard

and border forks. Their faultless smooth, shiny surface may decrease the effort required slightly, but whether this is cost-effective is debatable, as they can cost three to five times as much as the non-stainless models. However, they are a joy to own and any gardener would be delighted to receive one as a present.

Potato or flat-pronged forks have a role to play when preparing very light sandy soils or, of course, as the name implies, for harvesting crops such as potatoes.

Heavy-duty digging forks have reinforced sheaths that stretch further up the shaft and are constructed of stronger steel, but all this reinforcement means more weight and therefore more effort in use.

Spades

The primary use of a spade in soil preparation is for clearing the loose soil broken up by the fork from the digging trench, and for cutting the edges of a given area. On light sandy and organic soil types, they may replace the fork to prevent the looser soil from falling between the prongs.

The standard spade has a forged blade, 6–7 in (15–17 cm) wide and 9–10 in (23–5 cm) long. The lower leading edge is tapered but not sharpened; this edge is normally maintained by use but it may need 'sharpening' to renew it from time to time.

The blade is slightly concave down its full length and a few may still be forged with foot or boot treads along their upper edge. Those with treads are preferable to those without, but are scarce and more expensive. The tread, when available, protects the underside of footwear during use and prevents the spade blade cutting in.

As with the fork, the shafted wooden or metal handle is attached to the blade with a central metal sheath; if possible, choose the split version rather than the butted type as the former is the strongest. D, T or Y hand grips will be found; choose the one you prefer.

Spades, like forks, may be available with different lengths of handle and it is an advantage to have the one that is the right length for you.

Border or ladies' spades have blades 5–6 in (12–15 cm) wide and 7–8 in (17–20 cm) long and are lighter in construction but can be used for the same work as standard spades, although the work will take longer.

Stainless-steel models of both standard and ladies' or border spades are available, but they are expensive.

Clay-buster spades have four or five V-shaped sharpened indentations 2 in (5 cm) deep along the cutting edge of the blade to allow them to cut through clay soils. Their handles are also reinforced and are normally of metal. They do the job well and are worth purchasing, but clay soils make heavy digging.

Heavy-duty reinforced spades may be found and have a role to play if the user has the strength to use them.

Self-digging spades and forks

On sandy and loam soils these ratchet-operated tools can be successful to help the less physically able gardener to cultivate the soil, but they cannot dig deeper than, at best, 7–8 in (17–20 cm). Under normal circumstances they are not a substitute for standard forks and spades when you take into account the added cost and the limitations on their use. They normally have interchangeable fork or spade blades so only one tool needs to be purchased.

Other tools that may be needed

There are a number of tools that may be needed, on certain soils and in specific conditions, but it might be best to borrow them, if possible, rather than purchase them, as they will only be used occasionally.

A *shovel* may be required on sandy or light-textured soils, as its broad blade is ideal for the clearing of soil from the bottom of a trench.

Pickaxes may be required to break up pans, and consolidated and very chalky soil.

Mattocks with their rough cutting blades may be needed to remove and cut roots. They are also used to break up pans and consolidated soil. Even *axes* and *saws* are sometimes required if there are large tree roots to be removed.

Support and special tools

Of course a *wheelbarrow* will be needed to transport soil, organic material and rubbish.

Flat scaffolding or other *boards* are useful to work from and, if the soil is of a clay type or wet, will act as protection against soil structure damage. They may also be needed to lay on the soil so that wheelbarrows can move easily and safely, and to prevent damage when travelling over lawns.

Garden lines will help to define the area to be dug and are sometimes used to ensure a straight line when digging large areas.

Finally every gardener should find themselves a gardener's friend – no, not a human friend but a small piece of wood or metal that is shaped and used to scrape off soil from the blades of forks and spades.

Manual digging

In the history of gardening there have been many methods of digging, but the two that are used today are single and double digging.

Single digging

As the name implies, in single digging the soil is only cultivated to a depth of 9 in (23 cm) or, in other words, to the depth of a fork or spade blade.

The first operation is to mark out the area to be dug and, if it is more or less rectangular, to excavate with a fork or spade a trench 18 in (50 cm) wide and 9 in (23 cm) deep across one end and transport the soil to the far end, storing it on a board just off the area to be dug, ready for infilling into the final trench later.

If the area is irregular in shape, the trench is dug across the widest part, and the soil again transported to one end and stored on a board off the area to be dug. Once the first area has been dug, a second trench is dug next to the first, and the remaining un-dug soil area dug in the opposite direction. As the narrower parts are reached, soil from the first trench is used to fill in the open trench as required.

To dig the subsequent trenches, the fork or spade is used to

2. Single digging

turn the soil forward into the previous trench 3–4 in (8–10 cm) at a time and 9 in (23 cm) deep, working along the line of the trench. The process is repeated until the end of the area to be prepared is complete. Then the soil that was removed from the first trench and transported to the board is used to infill the last remaining trench.

Throughout the operation organic material is added, and I prefer to spread this on the surface of the soil to be dug and dig it in as the digging progresses. The rate of application is approximately one wheelbarrow-load per square yard (metre). If the digging is done in the autumn for planting in the spring, the surface can be left rough so that the weather can break it down, but it will require more attention in the spring to produce a broken-down, level soil surface.

Single digging is normally used to prepare the soil for annual crops such as vegetables, summer and autumn bedding, bulbs, etc. Double digging, however, is recommended in the first year to improve drainage, break up any soil pans and allow for deep root penetration for the crops that require it.

Double digging
With double digging the procedure for covering the area to be prepared is basically the same as for single digging; the difference is that it goes deeper.

25

3. Double digging

A trench 18 in (50 cm) wide and 9 in (23 cm) deep is dug across the full width of the area, at the end for regular shapes and at the widest point for irregular. The soil is transported to the opposite end, or to the end in the direction of digging, and stored away from the area to be dug, preferably on a board to aid handling later.

A 2 in (5 cm) layer of organic material is laid in the bottom of the trench and the bottom of the trench is dug to the depth of a further 9 in (23 cm).

Approximately a wheelbarrow-load per square yard (metre) of organic material is then spread over the surface of the rest of the area to be dug and, working along the edge of the trench using a fork or spade, the soil is dug to a depth of 9 in (23 cm) in 3–4 in (8–10 cm) slices and turned forward into the first trench.

This is continued until the first trench is full, so opening up the second trench. Once the next 15–18 in (40–50 cm) width is open the lower level is dug and manured as before and the process is repeated until the area is completely dug.

At first sight this may appear laborious, but the benefits outweigh the effort and the long-term results in plant growth are the reward. Carrying out the work in sessions of a sensible length is the best way to approach it.

Double digging is normally only done at the outset of planting or preparing a new area and will not usually be needed again, except for later interplantings.

Preparing a single planting hole

If only a single tree, shrub, conifer etc., is to be planted, it is not necessary to dig a large area. Nevertheless a certain amount of preparation is required if successful establishment and further development of the new plant is to be achieved.

You may also need to interplant into an existing border and in this case the same rules apply, although the area prepared may not be round or square but any shape that can be accommodated between the existing plants. The minimum area in both cases is important as it will be the area covered by the new plant's root system in the first spring following planting; if an adequate area is not prepared, there is always the risk of creating stress on the plant, leading to poor results or failure.

For a single planting hole, any grass or turf is removed first and stored as suggested later in this chapter to make topsoil for later use. A square or round area, 3 ft (1 m) wide, is cleared, and the top 9 in (23 cm) of soil is then removed with fork and spade, and stored on a board alongside the planting hole ready for later return to the hole.

A 2 in (5 cm) deep layer of organic material is then spread over the bottom of the hole and forked into the lower 9 in (23 cm) of soil.

Approximately three quarters to a full wheelbarrow-load of organic material is then forked into the stored topsoil and this is then returned to the hole. The soil is now ready for planting – see Chapter 2.

Planting holes and areas such as this should never be left unfilled, because the sides and bottom of the planting holes can become glazed; if they then dry out in the spring or summer, and rain follows, they can form sumps that fill with water and kill the new plants. This does not mean that they cannot be dug in late summer or early autumn ready for winter and spring planting, only that the soil should be returned to the hole to prevent possible problems.

Mechanical digging

Mini-tractors and diggers

Until recently the use of mechanical diggers was, in the main, impractical as they were too heavy and could do more harm than good to the soil structure. However, with the recent introduction of smaller, lighter mini-diggers, deep mechanical soil preparation without causing any damage to the soil is now possible, and if the area to be prepared is large, it is also cost effective.

The machine is normally hired for a period of days and is delivered to site by the hirer, who will also give some elementary instruction on operation. Hire and transport charges vary, so shop around first for the best terms.

Before hiring, however, you should measure the width of the entrance to the garden, though most machines will fit and pass through quite small entrances. Next identify the line of any underground services such as electricity, drains, gas or water mains, and mark them clearly, as damage to them can be expensive, and possibly dangerous.

Whether you operate the machine yourself or pay a skilled operator is a personal choice – the time factor has to be weighed against the interest of doing it yourself – but whatever you decide be sure to follow the health and safety rules, ensuring in particular that children are kept well away.

The major drawback to the use of a machine is its power – it is a temptation to use the power of the machine without due consideration to good soil management. It is important to prepare the site in advance as the machine costs money even when it is not working, so everything that is not required must be removed from the area. Boards will be needed for the soil excavated during the digging operation and these should be arranged for. Organic material will be required for incorporation during the 'digging', and this should be stored close by and ready for use.

The machine may be delivered with a number of digging buckets and normally the smaller ones will work the best for soil preparation. If the area to be prepared is covered in grass or turf, as long as it is not infested with perennial weeds such as couch grass, the machine can be used to scrape off a thin layer and stack it within reach of the digger arm on a board, ready to be incorporated into the soil later. If it does contain perennial weed roots they will need to be forked out and removed from the soil.

Next the machine is used to excavate the topsoil directly in front of it and within the reach of its digging arm. This topsoil is then stacked on to the boards, normally to the side or rear of the machine, taking care to remove only the topsoil and none of the subsoil.

If working near to trees and shrubs that are to remain, take care not to excavate so close to them that you encounter the roots and damage them.

Once all the topsoil is removed the machine is then used to break up the subsoil as deeply as possible. The surface of the subsoil is then levelled with a fork or the machine and any large roots removed.

The removed topsoil is checked for any roots, in particular those of perennial weeds, which must be removed by forking through the soil. Using the machine, the topsoil is then returned to the hole and levelled, and one wheelbarrow-load of organic material added per square yard (metre), forking it in by hand and finishing off the levelling at the same time.

In some cases there may not be enough topsoil and you will then have to import new topsoil to make up the shortfall.

On clay or silt soils it is important to fork the edges of the dug area lightly to prevent glazing and potential drainage restriction.

As long as the machine is worked from the soil which is to be dug or from boards, no damage will be done to any other part of the garden and the growth of new plants of all types will be exceptional following this form of preparation.

Using a rotovator
Using a rotovator for soil preparation is also a possibility but great care must be taken, for the following reasons:

If used when the soil is very wet or it is raining, the action of the rotary movement of the blades traps excess moisture into the soil and almost always damages the soil structure, rendering it unworkable for some time after rotovating.

If there are roots of perennial weeds such as couch grass, ground elder or nettles in the soil, these are cut up by the blades and so are effectively 'propagated' and increased at least tenfold. Even annual weeds are increased when seeds that lie dormant in the soil are brought to the surface by the action of the rotovator.

Pans, in the form of consolidated soil some 6–7 in (15–17 cm) deep, may be produced and these are often very detrimental to the plants' long-term well-being.

Finally, on all but the best and lightest of soils rotovators rarely penetrate the soil deeply enough for good plant establishment and growth.

They can be used with some success as long as wet conditions are avoided, to finish off and level, in particular, soils that have been prepared over winter and for areas to be used for lawns or other grass areas.

ANNUAL SOIL MANAGEMENT

In addition to soil preparation, there is a need for a number of annual operations that keep the condition of the soil in the best state possible; to avoid or overlook them can only lead to a decrease in the productivity of the garden.

Forking over

Two important plant needs are satisfied by forking over the surface of the soil at least once a year: firstly, air can enter the top 3–4 in (8–10 cm) of the soil and becomes available to plant roots, preventing suffocation; secondly, moisture in the form of rain can enter the soil instead of running off and being lost to the plants. Indirectly weeds are removed and other accumulated rubbish, such as leaves, is cleared away and the area worked on generally cleaned up.

When plant foods are applied in the form of fertilizers, these are quickly brought into contact with the soil moisture and are diluted and absorbed so as to be available for the plants.

The work can be done at any time but for preference autumn, winter and early spring are normally chosen. Both full-size digging forks and smaller border forks can be used for the work.

Hoeing

The use of a hoe on a regular basis throughout the spring, summer and early autumn aerates the soil as well as suppressing weeds and, by providing an aerated layer, insulates the soil from further loss of moisture.

There are a number of different types of hoe and the choice of tool will be a personal one; I prefer Dutch and draw hoes.

It goes without saying that when using a hoe care must be taken to protect the base of the plants from damage. A small number of plants dislike having their surface roots cultivated by fork or hoe: Alstroemeria and Viburnums are classic examples.

Mulching

Of all gardening techniques, except possibly for correct pruning, this is one of the most poorly understood.

Few gardeners, either amateur or professional, are aware that the vast majority of plants, if given the opportunity, would prefer to root upwards rather than sideways or down. Those that grow naturally in woodland environments are typical examples: each autumn they are treated to a natural mulching by the annual autumn leaf fall. The leaves fall, rot and form a layer of decomposing leaf mould which contains moisture and plant foods, and is of a perfect texture for root development and exploration.

However, in our gardens we rake up the leaves, and we may even burn this important source of mulching material instead of returning it to the plants that require it. Mulching, as well as benefiting the roots, has the added bonus of weed suppression and frost protection. Garden compost, well-rotted farm manure, cocoa shell, mushroom compost and many of the increasing army of peat substitutes are all suitable; I would avoid bark and straw, however, for the reasons given later.

The mulch should be at least 2 in (5 cm) deep if it is to be effective for the task; any less will not work fully and will therefore be unprofitable from all points of view.

With alpines, grit or fine gravel is often used instead of organic material; the word 'scree' is used to describe this type of mulch. The aims are almost the same except that the roots do not root into it but are kept cool, moist, weed-free and protected from frost.

It is important to implement feeding programmes, for organic material from whatever source contains little or no plant food and needs supplementing with fertilizer. The subject is more fully covered in Chapter 4.

Preparing garden compost

The preparation of your own garden compost has to be one of the most cost-effective operations in the garden. Almost any organic-based waste material can be composted, including the following:

Lawn mowings But not from lawns that have been treated with a hormone weed killer. Lawn mowings should be mixed with other composted material, and should comprise no more than 25 per cent of the bulk at any one time.

Leaves But not Sweet Chestnut, which can turn toxic, and Holly, Laurel and Beech, which due to their texture do not rot down quickly. However Beech can be composted on its own and will, after two years, produce a very useful leaf mould.

Garden waste Including all discarded bedding and vegetable plants.

Sweepings From paths and drives, except those treated with a weed-killer or contaminated with oil.

Annual weeds As long as they are deposited in the centre of the compost heap, where there should be adequate heat to sterilize them.

Paper Except glossy magazines, which repel water and do not rot; all other paper can be used but should be torn into thin strips.

Kitchen waste   As long as it is composted as suggested it will not cause a health hazard by encouraging rats and other rodents.

Woollen and other natural-fibre-based materials   Cut these up small.

Tea and coffee bags and dregs

Contents of the vacuum-cleaner

Discarded potting compost and grow-bags of all types unless contamination is suspected

Small domestic animals' droppings and used cat litter

Small amounts of sawdusts used as bedding for animals

All types of farmyard manure

In fact almost any natural, soft, easy-rotting material can be used, with only straw, wood and bark chips and material from shredders being unsuitable. (The reason for this will be explained later under 'Bark and Straw'.)

Before we discuss the construction of the compost heap we must understand how it works. All organic material is decomposed by microscopic soil animals and plants in the form of nematodes, bacteria and fungi. These animals and plants feed on nitrogen from the soil, which gives them energy to digest and decompose organic material. As they also require warmth, air and moisture to accelerate the rotting action, the compost heap must be built to provide all of these needs in the best possible way.

There are a number of proprietary compost bins and so on available and all in their way, if used as recommended, can form a useful basis for good composting, but they have the main drawback of maybe having too small a capacity for most gardens. The home-built version is often the best and if constructed correctly in the first instance can provide a long-term, easy-to-manage environment for successful composting.

The following method has been used by gardeners for many years and I have found it very reliable. It can be adjusted to suit your own garden.

The size and shape of the heap is one of the main aids to success, so some careful thought should be given to this. For a garden of less than, say, 400 square yards (metres) a compost heap of 4 ft (1.2 m) square and high is required for one year's composting, and, as composting takes up to two years, two containers will be required.

The container can be made of wire netting simply supported by strong posts at the corners, or of planks of timber, bricks or concrete blocks, but if these more solid materials are used provision for the free passage of air through the sides must be provided. One side of the container should be detachable to allow easy access to the finished compost. However, when I was an apprentice we built compost heaps 10 × 10 ft (3 × 3 m) and up to 8 ft (2.5 m) high without surrounds, and it may not be necessary to provide any container, particularly where there are large amounts of material to be composted.

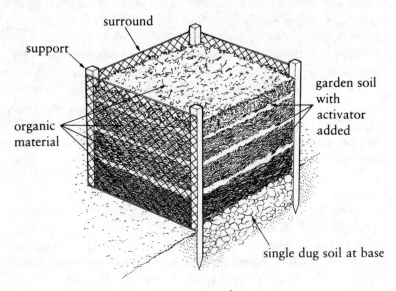

4. *Compost making*

Free drainage of the heap is important and to achieve this the soil on which the heap is to stand should be single dug. This also ensures that the soil organisms that will aid decomposition can gain entry to the base of the stack and work their way up through the lower layer of the material to be composted.

As material becomes available it should be placed in an even layer on the dug soil within the containing frame. Once the layer has reached 12 in (30 cm) a 1 in (3 cm) layer of garden soil is placed over the composting material. The soil can come from any area of the garden and is used to ensure that the soil organisms needed for decomposition are transported from the soil to this higher level of the compost heap. To ensure that these organisms have adequate food in the form of nitrogen, a small sprinkling of composting activator such as Garotta is added, as recommended on the packaging.

This layering of composting material, soil and activator is continued until the container is full or the winter arrives and active composting ceases.

As the heap is built up it will sink and heat up, good signs that it is working as planned. Because the soil organisms need moisture the heap should not be covered.

For the best weed-free compost the heap should be turned in the winter following its formation. For this a second container should be built into which the first year's compost is turned and restacked. The moving aerates the compost and ensures even decomposition. There is a temptation to use the compost at the end of the first year as decomposition is often well advanced by then. However, the compost may contain large amounts of unsterilized weed seeds that, if spread over or dug into the soil, will germinate and cause real problems. It is not necessary to introduce more soil in this restacking but feeding every 12 in (30 cm) with a sprinkling of Garotta will promote decomposition.

By the end of the second autumn a useful renewable supply of organic material will be available. Just one more precaution is needed before the compost is finally used, to ensure that the weed seeds do not cause a problem: the top 6–8 in (15–20 cm) and a 4–6 in (10–15 cm) slice from the outer edges is removed and placed on next year's heap, as it may not have been fully sterilized.

In larger gardens or in those with limited space it may be worth considering composting below ground. Suitable sites are at the back of shrub borders and other hidden but accessible places. Pits are dug 4 ft (1.2 m) wide and 4 ft (1.2 m) deep and the bottoms of the pits dug over to ensure good drainage. The pits are then filled in layers as for the standard compost heap until full, or until the winter comes and active composting ends. Compost produced in this way normally does not require turning and if the siting of the pits is chosen with care the compost can be made near where it will finally be needed. The only extra precaution that is required is to provide a strong cover to prevent anyone falling in by accident, but see that the cover allows rain to enter the composting material from above.

Preparing farmyard manure

Preparing farmyard manure for use may at first seem a wasted effort, but if we remember that when farmyard manure is decomposing it takes nitrogen from the soil, it is obviously better that this should happen before the material is used on the garden soil, otherwise deficiencies could be caused.

You may be lucky enough to find a farmer with manure that has been left stacked in his farmyard for a number of years; if so persuade him to supply this rather than the younger, fresher material. Unprepared manure also contains high amounts of weed seeds, and these will germinate if the manure is used too soon.

Stacking in a high square stack for one year is recommended; if the manure is tipped over a wide area it becomes less valuable. Whether it is horse, cow or elephant makes no difference, as long as it is stacked correctly.

Although farmyard manures and garden composts contain a little plant food, it is always necessary to supplement them; this is covered in Chapter 4.

If the gardener cannot stack and prepare his own manure there are many suppliers who can supply composted farmyard manure by the bag, but check its quality, cost and weight or bulk; shopping around in garden centres and other sources is advised.

Mushroom compost

Mushroom compost is one of the best soil improvers after garden compost and well-prepared farmyard manure.

As its name implies it is a by-product of the mushroom industry; it consists of a small amount of moss peat with specially composted horse manure. It has a higher plant food content than other soil improvers for plant foods are added to it during the growing of the commercial crop of mushrooms. There is always the possibility that you might get a crop of mushrooms, too, but this is not guaranteed!

It can be used in slightly smaller quantities than garden compost or farmyard manure, and shopping around for the best-priced supply is advised; some suppliers will deliver it in bulk, which is cheaper than compost sold in bags.

In the process of growing mushrooms small amounts of lime are added and this can raise the question as to whether mushroom compost should be used on acid-loving plants. My own opinion is that the amounts are so minute and the risk of changing the balance so small that it is not a problem.

Peat
The use of peat has become controversial from a conservation point of view. The need for either dry moss or wet sedge peats as soil conditioners is arguable, as there is a wide range of alternatives available, though I would defend the use of peat in potting compost, for reasons given in Chapter 10.

Bark and straw and material produced by shredding
Here I wish to express a personal opinion for which I can offer no scientific proof, only a conviction based on educated obser-vation. I feel strongly that the use of all grades of bark, if used as a dug-in or surface mulch, can lead to moderate or severe nitrogen deficiencies in all soil types, and this in turn leads to reduced plant productivity. There are no physical indicators such as leaf discoloration or deformity, but just a lack of growth over a number of years, which can only be detected by those with long experience.

Most soil improvers contain quite low levels of cellulose, and the amounts of nitrogen extracted from the soil by the various soil organisms to decompose them are quite small. This is not the case with straw and bark and shredded material, where the amount of nitrogen required is far higher, and much more effort is needed for the organisms to decompose the straw and bark. There is therefore a danger of nitrogen deficiency when these are used.

I also believe that the use of bark and shredded material is responsible for the spread of the parasite fungus armillaria, the honey or boot-lace fungus; increasing attacks are being reported in areas where they are not normally expected, causing levels of plant death not experienced previously.

Therefore my own view is that these materials are not good soil conditioners, even if the excessive use of nitrogen is supplemented by additional applications of nitrogen-based fertilizers. My own work with the material in the early 1970s bears out this statement.

Regarding straw, a number of processes are being developed to deal with the cellulose and there may be worthwhile advances that will make its use more acceptable.

Sewerage sludge
The problem of heavy metals and excessive salts in sewerage sludge is being eliminated, so over the next few years this may well become a very useful organic material.

Chicken, rabbit and other fringe animal waste manures
Many small livestock units, whether commercial or private, produce manure. There is a risk of root scorch with these products and I therefore feel it is wise to neutralize the possible effects by composting the material for one or two years before use.

Cocoa shell
Cocoa shell is a by-product of the chocolate industry. Judging by the speed at which it breaks down when used as a soil mulch, it appears to have low cellulose levels. My own method is to use it as a mulch first and compost it on the surface of the soil, and a year or two later dig it in as a conditioner.

When the product is first applied to the surface it smells of chocolate, and some ten days later a more undesirable smell is emitted under certain weather conditions, but this is short-lived and no more than would be expected from farmyard manure.

The white fungus that threads its way through the product is a natural decomposing agent and is in no way harmful. All in all I feel that this product has a good role to play in soil management.

Coir, composted paper and glass floss

There is an increasing number of materials becoming available to the gardener as the search for peat substitutes continues. My own view is that care is required when considering their use, as they are often not fully tested and evaluated under a wide range of gardening conditions before being offered for sale. Until I have tested and observed their performance over a wide range of geographical and weather conditions I cannot comment on them.

CHAPTER TWO

Plant Storage and Planting

The relationship between the soil and the plant, discussed in Chapter 1, is a fragile one due to the complex and minute components which can easily be damaged or abused, with potentially dire results, leading, at worst, to the death of the plant.

The correct soil preparation and treatment of the soil have been explained in Chapter 1. We must now consider the methods we use in planting, and in caring for plants prior to planting. Consideration must also be given to the plants' overall size, soil requirements, aspect and hardiness before purchasing and planting starts.

Selecting plants from garden centres and nurseries

Most garden centres and nurseries will offer advice as to the best planting times for specific groups of plants, and this advice should always be sought, not only because you want to plant at the most suitable time, but also because certain plants, such as bulbs and summer bedding, may not be available until the correct planting season, and you will need to include these plants in the overall planting scheme when you plan the work in advance.

Hardiness of a specific plant in relation to your own geographical location or to the stage of its production cycle or to the environment will also be important factors you must consider. Sadly this may not always be clearly explained at the point of sale, and advice should be sought.

Purchasing plants when they are in flower is a possibility and normally presents no problems, but it is not the only possibility or even the best.

It is difficult to give hard and fast rules for selecting the best plant, as all species and varieties differ, but for preference plants with a bushy growth formation are the ones to choose. A lot has been written about the amount of roots a plant should have and with plants sold 'bare-rooted', or in other words without soil around their roots, in the autumn, winter and early spring, a fibrous moist root system is the thing to look for.

Container-grown or containerized plants should have a root system that fills the whole soil area within the container but not to the extent of being so consolidated as to be pot-bound.

Ideal planting seasons

The following listings indicate the accepted best planting seasons for a range of groups of plants, although they may vary according to the geographical location and changing production processes within the horticultural supply system. Container-grown plants can be planted at other times, but the following planting periods give the best results.

Mid autumn to mid spring

BARE-ROOTED
Hardy trees, shrubs, Roses, fruit trees and bushes, hedging plants
(e.g. Beech, Thorn, Privet, Hornbeam), young forestry conifers.

ROOT-BALLED SHRUBS
Hardy Rhododendrons, Azaleas and many other acid-loving shrubs.

CONTAINER-GROWN
Hardy trees, shrubs, Roses, conifers, fruit trees and bushes, climbing plants (except Clematis), some hardy perennials.

SEED
Tender flower and vegetable seeds for sowing under frost-free protection in the greenhouse.

Mid to late spring to early summer

All the above except bare-rooted plants; also alpines, herbs, summer-flowering bulbs and corms, summer bedding and vegetable plants, containerized Roses, Clematis, tender shrubs and perennials, hardy flower seeds. Root-balled plants can also be planted with safety until late spring.

Lifting and carrying container-grown plants

Always lift and carry container-grown or containerized plants by the base of the pot and never by the stems, as this can damage not only the stems, but also the roots growing in the container.

Storing plants prior to planting

Even with pre-planning, plants may arrive when the soil conditions are too wet or cold, or the plant may not, as yet, be hardy enough to plant out and will have to be stored until such time as conditions are right. Often incorrect storage can place the plant at risk and the following tips may prevent damage.

Hardy container or containerized plants which have been grown or stored outside in the nursery or garden centre should continue to be stored in the same conditions; the temptation to protect them should be resisted, as this can lead to premature growth and the using up of energy that the plants will require later. Protected storage can also make the plant temporarily tender when finally planted out.

If there is a doubt regarding a plant's hardiness, non-woven, chemical-free, polypropylene-fibre frost protection (floating cloche) can be used without any of the side-effects that more permanent protection may present.

The plants should be prevented from falling over, as damage to the stems by rodents such as mice and rats are common when plants are not stored upright.

If a number of different species or varieties of plants are purchased, care should be taken not to mix them up or lose the labels.

Plants should not be stored touching each other, in particular conifers and other evergreens, as irreparable damage may be caused if they are in contact for any length of time.

With tender container or containerized plants, protection to the same degree as that provided at the place of sale should be given. This applies particularly to spring bedding and tender summer plants.

Bare-rooted plants should be kept moist at all times and whenever out of the soil for even short periods before heeling in they should be covered to prevent drying out. Should they arrive dry, report this to the supplier in case they fail later, and water at once to stop further dehydration.

Should bare-rooted plants arrive when planting conditions are unfavourable they should be stored outside. Try always to select a storage area that is not required for planting later because the working of the soil may, particularly if wet, make it unsuitable for planting for some time, often after planting should have been completed.

The plants should be 'heeled in', or in other words their roots temporarily covered with a good depth of soil. Single holes or trenches may be used, depending on the quantity of plants to be stored. Always heel in upright or at a very slight angle and firm lightly but, most importantly, allow for space between the plants so air can circulate, making sure that all labels are held away from the soil to prevent deterioration.

One danger is that the weather and soil conditions may stay unsuitable for some time and the planting time be shortened. Waiting as long as possible before planting is advised as soils can dry very quickly in mid spring, but if by late spring the soil is still unsuitable, and the new foliage of the plant is beginning to show, it will be necessary to plant it in its permanent home. Perennial plants can be given a little more time before planting and will establish with much more leaf development when soil conditions are right.

Preparing the planting site

In Chapter 1 we discussed the preparation that should be done in advance of the plants' arrival so that, if the soil and weather conditions are correct, the planting can then be carried out as quickly as possible.

Try not to walk directly on the prepared soil, working from the edge of the dug area whenever possible or off a short board, so preventing soil compaction or damage to its structure.

When more than one plant is to be planted they can be laid

out on the prepared soil in their planting positions, making any final adjustments to the positioning before actual planting starts.

If no prepared planting plan is to hand then making rough notes of the plants and positions and the dates they were planted will help with identification later and ensure that the plants can receive the correct aftercare.

Planting

Apart from specific planting techniques that we will cover later, the following guidelines apply to all plants.

If the plants are bare-rooted, prepared soil should be added or removed as required from under the roots to raise or lower the plant until it is at the right depth. The nursery soil mark is normally clearly visible and the plant is adjusted until this is just 1 in (3 cm) lower than the surrounding soil level. Soil should be worked in around the roots and the planting hole filled; then, using a foot, the soil is lightly firmed and the resulting depression filled again with prepared soil.

The same operation is carried out with plants that are root-balled or grown in containers, first raising or lowering the plant until the surface of the soil in the container is 1 in (3 cm) below the level of the surrounding soil.

Once a root-balled plant has been adjusted to the correct planting level, the sacking or other material covering the roots should be very carefully removed as it can cause drying out and prevent root development later if it is left on.

One important point to remember with grafted trees and shrubs is to ensure that the graft union is kept at least 3 in (8 cm) above the final soil level. This is particularly important with Apples and other grafted or budded fruit trees where the rootstock is chosen to influence the ultimate size of the tree. If the grafted variety itself roots, the size-controlling influence of the rootstock can be lost.

A suitable fertilizer for the time of year is applied at the appropriate rate for the plant; fertilizers are more fully explained in Chapter 4.

If planting when the soil is dry, a large watering-can of

water can be poured into the planting hole after firming has been done and before the planting hole is finally filled. This 'puddling' or 'coving' of soil traps water in the soil, just where the plant requires it in the coming spring, and prevents the water evaporating and being lost.

Further watering will be required and this is covered in Chapter 4. Staking and support may also be needed and this is covered in Chapter 3.

Balancing the shape of a plant
A plant may have grown one-sided in its early stages. If, when planting, the slower-growing side is planted facing the south, the plant will grow more strongly on that side; however, with or without such positioning the plant will eventually grow evenly on all sides.

Interplanting in existing borders

Planting additional or replacement plants into existing planted borders creates particular problems of preparation and establishment. We learnt in Chapter 1 that for the majority of plants, the prepared soil planting area should be no less than one square yard (square metre) and at first sight this amount of space may not seem to be available for interplanting. However, closer inspection of the proposed planting area will show that the planting hole can be dug in the irregular spaces between the surrounding plants; although it may not be round or square, the recommended area can be prepared and the roots of the new planting will quickly gain access to it.

In some cases there may be a need to cut back the root systems of some of the surrounding perennial plants to achieve the required soil area, but this should be resisted with more woody plants such as trees and shrubs.

Replanting or infilling Rose borders

The replanting or infilling of existing Rose borders can lead to problems with 'rose sickness'. This is often said to be due to the build-up of soil pests and diseases, and to some extent this is true, but my own opinion is that over the years the existing

Roses have extracted most, if not all, of the main plant foods and in particular the trace elements boron and magnesium from the soil and when new plantings are attempted the Roses are unable to find the important balance of plant foods they require in the early stages, and therefore deteriorate and may even die. (A further description of these plant foods and the specific feeding that Roses require is given in Chapter 4.)

If these problems are to be avoided, the soil must be removed to a depth of 18 in (50 cm) over an area of at least a square yard (square metre) for each new Rose to be planted, replacing it with new topsoil from elsewhere in the garden. As with all soil preparation, the incorporation of good amounts of organic material is very important, as is the provision of a suitable fertilizer.

Infilling gaps in hedges

The infilling of gaps in hedgerows offers the same problems as with 'rose sickness'; in addition, competition from the established plants at either end of the gap may lead to the failure of the new planting.

With Privet (*Ligustrum ovalifolium*), Beech (*Fagus sylvatica*), Holly (*Ilex aquifolium*), Western Red Cedar (*Thuja plicata*) and other generally used hedging plants, there may be a build-up of honey fungus. If this is the case, it is almost impossible to eradicate and the use of woven hazel hurdles or other fencing materials may be the best solution to replace the hedge and fill the gap.

Assuming there is no sign of honey fungus, the old plants and their roots are removed, in particular any plants at the ends of the gap that are in any way weak.

To ensure that the infilling is successful the soil preparation must be thorough and a trench at least 3 ft (1 m) wide and 9 in (23 cm) deep should be dug out, storing the topsoil on one side along the length of the gap, removing any remaining roots and adding generous amounts of organic material to both the top 9 in (23 cm) of the soil and the same depth of subsoil below.

In the spring following planting, very careful attention

should be given to watering, to compensate for the moisture used up by the remaining original plants in the hedge.

Planting wall shrubs and climbers

After preparing a planting hole 3 ft (1 m) square and 9 in (23 cm) deep, and adding organic material to a further 9 in (23 cm) of depth and to the soil removed, the plant should be planted 15–18 in (40–50 cm) away from the wall or fence and leant back towards it. This is done to ensure that the plants are not starved of moisture as is often the case when they are planted closer to a wall.

The foundations of walls absorb moisture and, like fences, deflect rain away from their bases; the 12 in (30 cm) of soil surface directly below the wall or fence can become very dry at any time but particularly in the spring and early summer, both critical times in plant establishment and growth.

We want, and expect, climbers and wall shrubs to reach

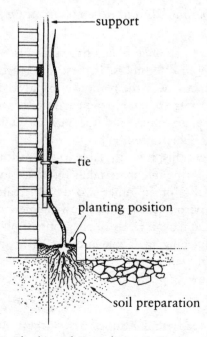

5. *Climbing plant tied to support*

substantial heights, but without constant moisture this is not possible. As the plant grows it will also gain stem girth at the base and if planted too close to the wall or fence this may be restricted or damaged.

In some cases it may not be possible to prepare a round or square hole because of paths or other obstructions in close proximity to the proposed planting position. In these cases the hole can be dug lengthways along the wall or fence until the recommended square yard (square metre) per plant is prepared. In some cases it may be possible to remove a paving slab or cut away the obstruction; even realigning the path might be worth consideration.

Should none of these alternatives be possible, then excavating under the obstruction and infilling with prepared soil may be possible but care should be taken not to cause subsidence.

Supports and feeding and watering are covered fully in Chapters 3, 4 and 5 respectively.

Planting perennials and other plants with fleshy root systems

A number of perennial plants have root systems that consist of fleshy roots or else tubers. If these specialist root systems are restricted in any way the plants almost always fail. The reason is that the roots are unable to penetrate the surrounding soil in search of plant foods and the new plant simply dies from hunger and dehydration.

To prevent this, it is advisable to add at least 50–60 per cent by volume of organic material as discussed in Chapter 1 to the planting area, or in other words to create a 'feather-bed' planting environment and so allow the new roots to penetrate the surrounding soil freely. This group of plants also responds well to mulching in late winter or early spring, again with organic material.

The following plants specifically require this soil treatment.

PERENNIALS
Aconitum, Agapanthus, Alstroemeria, Anchusa, *Arum italicum*, Caltha, Camassia, Ceratostigma, Cimicifuga, Clematis (perennial

forms), *Convallaria majalis*, Crambe, Dicentra, Dictamnus, Echinops, Eremurus, Eryngium, Galtonia, Gunnera, Gypsophila, Helleborus, Hosta, Incarvillea, Lathyrus (perennial forms), Ligularia, Limonium, *Lupinus arboreus*, Lysichiton, Meconopsis, Oenothera, *Osmunda regalis*, Paeonia, Peltiphyllum, Platycodon, Primula, Rheum, Rodgersia, Scabiosa, Smilacina, Tovara, Trillium, Tropaeolum, Verbascum, Zantedeschia.

SHRUBS
Acer palmatum and *A. japonicum* varieties, Azaleas, Camellias, *Cornus canadensis, C. florida, C. kousa, C. nuttallii*, Cortaderia, Crinodendron, Daboecia, Daphne, Drimys, Embothrium, Enkianthus, Erica, Eucryphia, Hibiscus, Hoheria, Hydrangea, Kalmia, Leptospermum, Leucothoë, Magnolia, Nandina, Paeonia (tree forms), Pernettya, Phormium, Pieris, Pseudosasa, Rhododendron, Sambucus, Staphylea, Trachycarpus, Vaccinium, Yucca, Zenobia.

TREES
Liquidambar, Liriodendron, Morus, Nyssa, Paulownia, Stuartia, Styrax.

Planting extra-large trees and shrubs

Due to their size, extra-large trees and shrubs are under extreme pressure at planting time and if they are to develop and establish without damage or total failure additional care needs to be taken with planting.

If the plants have been grown in containers in a nursery they will have been regularly watered and fed, and will have grown to their present size over a number of years, and they are at less risk than those that have been grown in the garden or even in a nursery in the soil and not moved for a number of years. In the move, however carefully they are dug up, they must lose a large proportion of their roots, which will put a great strain on the remaining ones and demands will be made on them by the plant in the spring which they may not be able to supply. Pruning at the time of planting will help, and this technique is covered in Chapter 8.

As well as pruning, additional care at planting time can reduce the risk. First, the planting hole should be prepared in advance of moving or delivery of the plant; this hole will need to be at least 4 ft (1.2 m) wide and perhaps as much as 6 ft (2 m). As a general rule the prepared planting area should be at least 2 ft (60 cm) wider than the plant's root ball.

The addition of generous amounts of organic material to the planting soil is important and once the plant is positioned with its root ball an inch or so below the surrounding soil surface, the roots should be carefully and thoroughly watered. Care must be taken not to wash off soil but the roots must be wet, because once the hole is filled it becomes more difficult to ensure that they are.

Next, at least a full wheelbarrow-load or more of very well rotted organic material or potting compost is built up around and over the root ball. It is into this material that the first vital roots will grow and establish before spreading further into the surrounding soil in the search for moisture and plant foods.

The planting hole is then filled to the surrounding soil level, the soil lightly firmed and the hole finally filled.

Staking and tying may be necessary, and this is covered in Chapter 3; Chapters 4 and 5 deal with feeding and watering.

Planting on permanently wet soils

One of the most difficult areas to plant is permanently wet soil because very few plants can tolerate these conditions and roots are damaged by suffocation in such soils.

Not all plants will respond to the treatment I suggest, but those that do respond well and, once established, grow on to dry out the surrounding soil and increase their growing area, with the benefit of a constant supply of moisture always in close proximity. The planting area is prepared as described in Chapter 1 for individual 3 ft (1 m) wide planting holes, but instead of finishing level with the surrounding soil the surface is raised 2 in (5 cm) overall.

On some occasions the soil is too wet or the plant is likely to require a greater area of soil. In these cases, for every 2 in (5 cm) of built-up soil height the hole should be 12 in (30 cm) wider.

Once planting is complete a V-shaped trench, 2–3 in (5–

8 cm) deep and wide is dug around the outer edge of the prepared hole to help drain away excess water from rain or melting snow.

The following plants respond well to this treatment and benefit from the continuous supply of water.

TREES

Acer platanoides varieties, *A. pseudoplatanus* varieties, *Ailanthus altissima*, Alnus, Catalpa, Fraxinus, Populus, Salix.

SHRUBS

Buddleja, *Cornus alba* varieties, *C. stolonifera* 'Flaviramea', *Cortaderia argentea*, *Fatsia japonica*, Hippophaë, Hydrangea (large shrub-forming varieties), Lavatera, Ligustrum, Pseudosasa, Rubus, Salix, Sambucus, Sorbaria.

PERENNIALS

Acanthus, Angelica, Aruncus, Asplenium, Astilbe, Caltha, Cimicifuga, Crambe, Eupatorium, Filipendula, Gunnera, Hakonechloa, Helictotrichon, Hemerocallis, Hosta, *Iris pseudacorus*, Ligularia, Lysichiton, Meconopsis, *Osmunda regalis*, Peltiphyllum, *Polygonum bistorta* 'Superbum', Primula, Rheum, Rodgersia, Smilacina, Symphytum, Thalictrum, Tovara, Tradescantia, Zantedeschia.

Building up planting areas over roots and hard surfaces

Often there is an inadequate depth of soil to achieve the recommended minimum planting depth of 18 in (50 cm), and building up the soil has to be considered.

If the build-up is over hard, consolidated ground or, worse still, concrete or similar base materials, some effort must be made to break the compaction up, or at the very least allow for drainage by some other route.

Building up over large areas infested by roots is even more difficult, because the roots of the existing planting will very quickly grow up into the new soil and defeat the object of building up in the first place. Until recently there was little that could be done to prevent this but now, with the advent of black, finely perforated, woven polythene matting, obtainable from most garden centres by the yard in a number of widths, this problem can be overcome.

Try to purchase the material in the greatest width possible because the danger point for infiltration by the roots from below is where the sheets overlap. The material will allow water to pass through, while at the same time deterring root penetration upwards.

In the main the problem should be overcome by this method, though of course the addition of organic material to the planting soil is also important.

Changing alkaline soil to acid

I have included this note as a warning, because I strongly believe that over, say, a five-year period you cannot change an alkaline soil to an acid one.

As we saw in Chapter 1, the acidity or alkalinity of soil is carried in the soil water, and if you simply add acid materials such as peat to the soil, even if a physical barrier is provided, some infiltration from the surrounding soil is inevitable over a period of time. Once the acidity lowers, the acid-loving plants planted in it start to die.

As there are so many beautiful plants that do not need an acid soil, why go to the effort and expense of trying to provide an artificial short-term change in the soil?

CHAPTER THREE

Staking, Tying
and Supporting Plants

Correct staking, tying and supporting of plants is important for successful establishment and for prevention of physical damage from wind, rain and snow – and also the secondary damage which occurs when pest and disease attacks enter the plant through damaged tissue.

Movement of a plant at ground level is also to be avoided because, if the stem is not secured where it comes into contact with the soil, a glazing process can take place which causes a build-up of moisture leading to rotting at ground level and ultimate death. In addition, when the glazed area dries out it can form a concrete-like wall, which may lead to further rubbing and chafing of stems, and this again can leave the plant open to fungus attack and rotting.

Sadly, in these days of mindless destruction, staking does not prevent damage to trees in public places by vandals.

Staking materials

There is a wide range of stakes from the proprietary to the DIY; the final choice will be dictated by the type and size of the plant being staked.

Split green canes

These are available in lengths between 12 in (30 cm) and 30 in (80 cm) and are used for supporting bulbs when in flower, taller-growing annuals, biennials and perennial plants.

Bamboo canes

These can normally be purchased from 2 ft (60 cm) tall up to 8 ft (2.5 cm), and sometimes even up to 10 ft (3 m).

They are sold in different thicknesses and I would choose the medium to thick because as well as being stronger they often last longer. No one garden centre or nursery will offer the full range and it is a case of shopping around to find the height and thickness required. From time to time they may be out of stock on a national basis, as they are grown in the Middle and Far East and they may be out of season or the crop may not have performed well. One good point about bamboo canes is that when the bottom of the cane, which is in contact with the soil, rots, the damaged section can be cut away and the cane, although shorter, can be reused.

Always be very careful, when inserting new or reused canes, that they do not break and cause physical injury. A cane cap should be fitted to the top of canes used in the garden to avoid potentially serious eye injury to the unwary gardener.

Bamboo canes are primarily used for supporting perennial plants, some newly planted shrubs and small trees, or for special plant training such as fan-training fruit and other climbing plants on walls. They are also commonly used to support runner beans, both in rows and arranged as tripods.

Bean poles
Hazel poles 8 ft (2.5 m) tall and ½–1½ in (1–4 cm) thick are cut in the late winter from hazel coppices and sold in bundles containing twenty to twenty-five poles; they are generally used as supports for Runner Beans and other annual climbing plants either in rows or arranged as tripods.

Plastic-coated wire and metal poles
Whether in the form of imitation stakes or canes, in a range of lengths from 3 ft (1 m) to 8 ft (2.5 m) and normally coloured a sickly green, or proprietary interlinking systems or special Y-shaped stakes, these offer good support for perennial plants and small shrubs, but even though metal they do need care when handling to avoid accidents.

Wooden tree stakes
All garden centres and nurseries offer wooden tree stakes in a range of different lengths from 3 ft (1 m) to 8 ft (2.5 m), as

well as a choice of thicknesses from 1 in (3 cm) for Dahlias and standard Roses up to 3 in (8 cm) for trees.

Normally for an average-sized tree I would recommend a thickness of not less than 1½ in (4 cm) and have no preference as to square or round, or whether they are peeled or still have the bark attached, or whether they are hard or softwood, although the hardwood often lasts longer.

Always check for knots in the wood as this is the main potential weakness – strangely many retailers do not do this when receiving deliveries. I always avoid creosoted stakes because of the risk of soil contamination, but find those that are green tannalized acceptable.

Tying materials

It seems that whenever industry produces a new or waste product that might be used as a tying material, particularly if it is coloured green, it is offered to gardeners without any tests being done or consideration being given to the damage it may do to a plant by strangulation.

With the possible exception of perennials, all plants require ties that can expand, can be adjusted or will rot within a year to prevent damage.

Recommended soft tying materials

Three-ply fillis string (untreated)
Raffia, although this is more expensive than fillis string
Small and large adjustable rubber or flexible straps, ensuring the size is adequate for the tree and that all are supplied and fitted with a buffer to avoid rubbing between the tree and stake; whenever possible, purchase the straps loose rather than pre-packed, as they are often cheaper

Tying materials to avoid at all costs

Polypropylene string
Binder twine
Wire
Plastic tying material that does not stretch as the plant grows
Rubber and plastic ties of the interlocking chain type

6. Figure-of-eight knot

Fillis and other soft strings and twines that are treated with creosote
 or green tannalized to prevent rotting
Modern tights and stockings produced from material that does not rot

Figure-of-eight knot

Over the years I have tried a number of different knots and
ways of attaching plants, other than trees, to their supports,
but the safest and most effective way has always proved to be
the figure-of-eight knot where the fillis string is looped around
the cane, support wire or individual anchorage point, crossed
over itself, looped around the front of the plant and secured
and tied with a reef knot, allowing just enough slack to
prevent restriction and strangulation.

If the plant is being attached to horizontal or vertical wires
or to canes, slipping will be reduced by making a second loop
around the wire or cane.

These ties are intended to rot and need replacing from time
to time, so regular checks should be made to ensure that the
plant is secure and is not being damaged by movement caused
by the weather.

Tree staking

Tree staking – for at least the first five to ten years – is one of
the most important aspects of plant support. Whatever the size

of the newly planted tree, support should always be given at planting time; it should never be left until later.

There is much controversy over whether stakes should be short or the full length of the tree stem being staked, and the subject needs to be clarified. In my opinion the research that was publicized in the gardening press did not take into account the full diversity of tree growth and speed of root establishment in ornamental species.

Certainly there may be a case for using the short-length staking method on fast-growing indigenous species such as Fraxinus (Ash), *Acer platanoides* (Norway Maple), *Acer pseudoplatanus* (Sycamore) and possibly the slower-growing Quercus (Oak) but most ornamental species are much slower to establish and they need secure staking to avoid damage. Also, in many cases the cellular structure of the stems is less resilient to bending, and breaking can occur in high winds.

Many trees are grafted either at ground level or as top-worked trees, and in both cases the graft union can be a weak point, often breaking or being damaged in such a way as to let moisture into the graft union, and this leads to rotting and possibly to death. Therefore I advocate full-length staking in all but a few species.

The first step is to purchase a suitably sized stake plus two plastic or rubber adjustable tree straps of an appropriate length for the tree being staked, not forgetting the buffers that will fit between the stake and the tree to prevent damage by rubbing.

For trees with a clear stem, the stake should be tall enough to be driven 15–18 in (40–50 cm) into the ground and, when driven in, to reach to just below the lowest side branch; where the branches are 'feathered' from or near ground level upwards, the stake should be at least three quarters of the full height, plus 15–18 in (40–50 cm) for driving in.

Whenever possible the stake should be driven in on the west or prevailing-wind side, so that the tree blows away from the stake for the majority of the time, thus helping to reduce the risk of rubbing. With those trees that have a clear stem, extra care should be taken to ensure that the top of the stake is just below the first branch and not in any way touching it. To achieve this the stake may need reducing in height with a saw after it has been driven in. Failure to do this is one of the major errors made by today's professional and amateur gardeners, giving rise to unnecessary damage to young trees.

If the tree is bare-rooted it should be turned so that the stake can be positioned safely between the roots.

With container-grown trees the stake is pushed carefully into the pot's soil ball; if a root obstruction is encountered it is withdrawn, the pot turned and the process repeated until the stake can pass down through the root ball before being driven in.

Damage to the top of the stake can be prevented by placing an odd flat piece of wood over the top of the stake before driving it into the ground with a sledgehammer.

The two tree straps are now fitted, the first just below the top of the stake and the second halfway between the first and ground level. The straps are pulled tight, with the buffers in place between the tree and the stake. A nail is driven into each stake through the strap just behind the buckle to prevent the strap from slipping down as the tree moves in the wind. The straps will require adjusting at least once a year and it is a good idea to nominate a specific date or anniversary to do the work so that it is not forgotten.

If a tree has been planted for some time without staking, the stake can be gently driven into the soil on the windward side, but if the roots obstruct the passage of the stake it should be repositioned and the process repeated until a clear passage is achieved. Always try to position the stake as close to the tree as possible. Once in position two tree straps should be fitted as described.

Staking large trees

The staking of trees when planted as large specimens or at extra-heavy sizes presents a different problem, as it is difficult to drive a stake through the consolidated root ball without causing damage. Also, the stake, once in place, is rarely strong or firm enough, and as trees of this size are substantially more

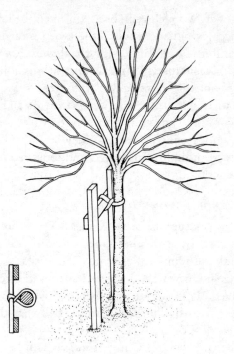

7. *Staking a large tree*

expensive, getting it right is important. Without suitable staking, the rate at which trees of this size become established can
be slowed down.

Unfortunately, due to the increased strength required, the
arrangement of the supports can often appear unsightly, but
they must be used. There are a number of methods used
incorporating wires and stakes driven in at angles in a number
of configurations. My own preference is to stake the trees for
five years or more as follows. Two 6 ft (2 m) long round or
square stakes with at least 2 in (5 cm) diameter tops are
positioned at least 18–24 in (50–60 cm) away from the tree on
either side and, if possible, on the windward side.

They are then driven in at a slight angle, sloping into the
prevailing wind, to a depth of 15–18 in (40–50 cm). The angle
acts as a lever or balancing action against the weight of the
tree and the force of the prevailing wind.

A strong, flat, wooden crossbar, ¾ in (2 cm) thick and 2–3 in (5–8 cm) deep is nailed between the two stakes as high as is possible without interfering with the lower branches. Using plastic or rubber adjustable tree straps, or possibly two joined together by one of the buckles, the tree is secured to the crossbar, with a buffer placed between the tree and the crossbar to prevent rubbing. The strap is then secured at the buckle end to the bar with a nail to prevent sideways slip. From time to time the straps should be inspected and loosened if required to prevent restriction.

Staking trees blown over by the wind

Sometimes, in severe weather conditions, quite substantial trees are blown over by the wind and all too often a tree, which has taken so long to reach its current size, is condemned. By using the staking method for specimen and large trees, they may be saved. It is important that the work is carried out within a few days of the first damage and that the following additional work is done.

Before the tree can be righted, thought will be needed as to how, once the new support stakes are in place, the tree is to be brought to the upright position. Manpower, winches and possibly a tractor may have to be used and care must be taken to prevent accidents to both the tree and those working on it; it is best to have skilled assistance.

To aid the uprighting, soil should be removed from under the roots on the side away from the direction of the fall. This will release the root and reduce soil resistance, and the tree will be more easily brought to the upright position.

Once the tree has been uprighted, the soil is replaced, but first any stray roots are cleanly cut off to prevent rotting.

Due to the loss of roots broken or damaged by the fall, the tree will be at a disadvantage when the leaves open in the following spring, and the roots may not be able to provide all the moisture required. For this reason, it is best to remove all grass and weeds in a circle of not less than 4–5 ft (1.2–1.5 m) diameter around the base of the tree. This circle needs to be very lightly forked over; in mid to late spring a dressing of

Growmore fertilizer should be applied as recommended on the packet.

In addition, as the canopy of leaves in spring opens and prevents rain from reaching the soil circle, it may be necessary to give water. Further spring feeding and additional watering may be required for a number of years after the initial damage.

It is also beneficial to consider reducing some of the side shoots to cut down the demands of the foliage. To do this the side shoots – not the main branches – should be removed or shortened, to reduce the overall total growth by one third, so balancing the root/foliage ratio. I would not advise reducing the length of the main branches as the tree may be slow to produce a new main framework and will appear stunted for many years.

Normally the supports will be required for more than five years and it is often better to wait until the stakes rot before removing them.

Staking perennial plants

Finding a cost-effective and labour-saving way of supporting medium- and tall-growing perennial plants needs thought if their displays are to be enjoyed to the full. The softer, less rigid shrubs will also benefit from appropriate staking. In all cases the supports must be effective without being visible and there are three methods I like. Whichever method you use, it is important to provide the staking in the spring, when the plants are young, allowing them to grow through the support to disguise it.

Pea sticks

These would always be my first choice, with three to five pushed into the ground in a circle around the outer edges of each plant, trimmed and cut off just below the expected ultimate height.

The only drawback to this natural-looking support is that at the end of the year the pea sticks have to be discarded as they do not keep from year to year. Sometimes they may be difficult to obtain and a number of garden centres or nurseries may have to be contacted before supplies are found. Alternatively a local forester or sometimes a coal merchant may be able to supply them.

Wire-formed grids
Round, wire-formed grids can be reused. Although not so easy to raise as the plant grows, they do hold and present plants in the most attractive way. They are normally 24–30 in (60–80 cm) wide and are available in galvanized or green, plastic-covered wire. Plastic types are available but to me these look unsightly and they may be weaker.

Linked sticks
Linked sticks are reusable and, with an interlocking system, are very adaptable for all sizes of perennial plants. Almost any configuration of sticks can be used and they can also be raised as the plants' growth matures. Other, similar, Y-shaped support sticks are available and these are also useful.

Supporting plants on walls
Supporting plants on walls is important, as only a very small number of climbers and wall shrubs are self-clinging and even those that are may need help occasionally. In addition, the aim in growing a plant against a wall is to form a fan-shape to cover as wide an area as possible. In a moment we will look at the range of supports available but first we should consider a number of basic points.

Selecting the right support and ensuring it covers the area required for a specific plant is important; so often a plant is provided with trellis where a wire system or individual anchorage points would be more suitable. Worse still, no support at all is given or a hotch-potch of nails and oddments of wire and string are used. This rarely presents the plant well, and it may lead to structural damage to the plant, allowing diseases to enter through the lesions.

The support and its fixings must be strong enough to carry not only the weight of the plant itself, but also the extra weight caused by rain and snow.

The environment created behind the support and the plant will be dry, sheltered and often warm, making it an ideal breeding ground for pests and diseases. This can be prevented by ensuring that the supports are always secured with an air space of at least 2 in (5 cm) between the wall or fence and the support. The trellis-type of support is best attached by securing upright, 2 in (5 cm) thick wooden battens to the wall, not less than 5 ft (1.5 m) apart, using screws and Rawlplug fixings as required. The trellis can be fixed to them and an air space is thereby provided behind.

In some cases it may be necessary to provide access to the wall or fence for maintenance and the choice of support should take this into account.

Finally it should look attractive or, better still, not be readily visible when covered by the plant it is supporting.

Trellis

The range of trellis and the materials from which they are manufactured is almost endless. Wire, either galvanized or plastic-covered, and natural, preservative-treated or painted timber, either flat, round or square, are the most common. Some are ridged, others concertina-ed in square, diamond or oblong trellis patterns; others are artistically designed, which is pointless because if the plant is planted and looked after correctly it very soon covers the trellis completely.

If a trellis is to be used, the DIY approach might be better. Battens 1 × 1 in (3 × 3 cm) thick purchased from the local timber supplier will make a strong support for a plant.

Some of the strong, off-the-peg trellis, and certainly the DIY types, can be provided with hinges along the lower edge and fixings at the top, so that in the event of access being required to the wall, it is a simple matter to undo the fixings and allow the trellis to fall forward with the plant still attached to it. Once the maintenance is finished the trellis and plant are simply reinstated in the upright position.

Wires

Horizontal wires, and sometimes vertical wires as well for Clematis, are my personal choice for the support of most climbers and wall shrubs. They are cost-effective, strong, can be added to as required, need little or no maintenance, last for many years and if fixed and arranged correctly can do little damage to the plant. Above all they present the plant in the very best growth formation, showing it off to the full advantage.

Use PVC-covered or galvanized straining wire of 2.5 mm thickness for horizontal and vertical wires. Secure horizontal wires to the wall using 4 in (10 cm) screwed vine-eyes, screwed into size 10 Rawlplugs, using a size 8 masonry drill bit to make the hole.

On wooden fences 3 in (8 cm) screwed vine-eyes can be screwed directly into the fence posts. The vine-eyes should be not more than 6 ft (2 m) apart in a straight line. Over long distances it may be necessary to use straining bolts at one end to tighten the wires.

Fix the first wire 18 in (50 cm) above ground level and subsequent ones every 18 in (50 cm) up the face of the wall. It may be necessary to adjust the distance between the lines of wires to fill the total height of the wall. Where there is a mortar course between bricks, this can be used as a guide to the horizontal line of the wires.

This arrangement is ideal for all climbing plants except Clematis; for these, vertical wires should be attached in addition every 12 in (30 cm) along the horizontal wire, making a network arrangement which will aid climbing and encourage a spreading habit.

If a cane is not supplied with the young plant, provide one to lead it to the first wire. Tie the plant to the wire using the figure-of-eight knot (p. 56), with an extra turn around the wire to prevent sideways slipping.

Individual anchorage points

Many plants, particularly wall shrubs, when grown against walls or fences, do not require trellis or wire supports and individual anchorage points can be considered.

There are two methods I like to use, depending on the size of the plant being secured. With both methods, young plants will require the initial use of bamboo canes as supports until they are tall or strong enough to be secured to the individual anchorage point. These canes are best fitted to an anchorage point to prevent movement.

The simplest and most secure method is to use screwed vine-eyes.

Careful consideration should be given to positioning the fixing before the hole is made; holding the plant to the wall first to mark the best position is advisable, making sure that the strongest part of the plant is chosen for the fixing point.

Once the vine-eye is in place it is a simple matter to tie the plant to it using the fillis string figure-of-eight knot.

A size 10 masonry drill bit and Rawlplug will be required to fix the screwed vine-eyes to the mortar course of the brickwork. With wooden fences the vine-eyes can normally be screwed straight into the posts. If the vine-eye is being fixed to a post, a large nail can be hammered in an inch or so and then withdrawn and the vine-eye screwed in.

For larger, heavier plants, stronger individual anchorage points will be required and for this I recommend the use of adjustable rubber or plastic tree straps, fixed as follows. First identify a suitable fixing point or points, depending on the size of the plant, trying to secure the plant by a strong main branch. Using a power drill with a size 10 masonry drill bit for brick walls insert a size 10 Rawlplug, ready to receive a size 10 $1\frac{1}{2}$ in (4 cm) long screw. For wooden fences it may be necessary to make a starting hole with a nail or old screwdriver into the post.

Carefully pierce a hole just behind the buckle in the tree strap; before passing the screw through the hole, pass it through a $\frac{1}{2}$–$\frac{3}{4}$ in (1–2 cm) wide metal washer, which is positioned between the head of the screw and the tree strap to prevent the screw head from being pulled through. Fix the screw and secure the plant with the tree strap in the normal way, remembering to position the buffer between the plant and the wall or fence to prevent damage by rubbing.

Should the plant's stem girth be more than the length of one tie, two can be joined together. This method only needs occasional checking to prevent strangulation and will support the plant in the roughest of weather.

Training supports for special purposes

Rows of free-standing ornamental and fruiting plants

Posts can be wooden or metal and are driven in, or better still, concreted in place, 6–8 ft (2–2.5 m) apart. The height of the posts will depend on the plants to be supported but as a guide a fan-trained Apple, Pear or Plum will need 10–12 ft (3–3.5 m) high supports, whereas horizontal trained trees will cover a height of up to 6–8 ft (2–2.5 m).

Most cane and vine fruits require 6–8 ft (2–2.5 m) supports. The height of supports for ornamental trees will depend on the species.

Fencing-gauge wire is stretched between the posts and fixed securely at 18 in (50 cm) intervals from the ground until the required height is reached. Some bracing of the posts and stretching of the wires may also be required on long distances.

Fan-trained plants

When plants are fan-trained on walls and fences, outdoors or under protection, the following additional support is necessary.

First horizontal wires are fixed to the wall or fence as suggested previously to act as supports for 6–8 ft (2–2.5 m) canes. The length of the cane will depend on the plant being trained and on the size of the wall, but as a rule the longer the better. The number of canes used will depend on the number of fan-trained shoots required or expected; each cane is attached to the support wire using fillis string and the figure-of-eight knot with the extra twist to stop slipping, in a fan shape.

The plant is then tied to the canes using the fillis string, tied with the figure-of-eight knot with the additional turn around the cane to prevent the knot slipping. Normally these cane supports are required for most, if not all, of the plant's productive life.

Supports for pleached trees

Pleaching or horizontal-training of selected trees requires purpose-built supports to aid their early and subsequent training. (See also Chapter 8.)

Often a 'bodge-up' of canes or timber battens is provided; although the following, more secure, supports will cost more, it should be remembered that they will be required for at least ten years and that the plant screen will form more quickly.

Dull olive-green or black painted angle-irons, as used for fencing and tennis court surrounds, positioned 8–10 ft (2.5–3 m) apart in a straight line, braced at the ends and corners and at least 8 ft (2.5 m) tall, are ideal and may only need some additional holes 18 in (50 cm) apart through which the support wires will be passed and secured. As always, fillis string and the figure-of-eight knot are used to attach the branches of the trees to the wires and the individual trees, positioned at the centres between the angle-iron posts, will also require staking. These stakes should be attached to the horizontal wires.

Supports for walkways

A number of proprietary manufactured products are available for this purpose and in the main they are all suitable. Having your own produced by the local blacksmith is also a possibility. The tunnel framework should be constructed from metal strong enough to act as a training support; it should also be able to carry the weight of the fully grown plants, with the additional weight of rain and snow, and this is not always the case.

The walkway will differ in every garden, as will the shape of the support itself, so to lay down hard and fast rules is difficult, but the following points should be considered.

Adequate headroom should be provided; often no allowance is made for the downward growth of the plants covering the walkway and this growth, at the height of the season, can be in excess of 24 in (60 cm).

As the plants that are to cover the framework will require fixing points at regular intervals it is important to ensure that these are provided either on the main structure or as additional wires stretched between.

Although the framework will eventually be covered with growth, for some time it will be a very visible object in the garden, so the colour it is painted is important – my own choice would be matt olive-green. The size and architectural appearance of the support should be considered; some very bad errors can be made.

Every design will be different but the following specification may be of value:

- Metalwork should not be less than $\frac{1}{2}$–$\frac{3}{4}$ in (1–2 cm) in diameter.
- The main supports in the line of the walkway should be no more than 8–10 ft (2.5–3 m) apart.
- The main supports spanning the pathway should be at least 8–10 ft (2.5–3 m) apart.
- The height of the centre of the main supports should be no less than 9–10 ft (2.7–3 m).
- The distance between supports and additional training wires should be 15–18 in (40–50 cm).
- The main supports should be concreted into the ground to a depth of at least 15–18 in (40–50 cm).

See also Chapter 8.

Tripods and archways

Many plants can be grown up tripods and over archways but care must be taken when producing your own or purchasing off-the-shelf products that they are strong enough; many models are not. Also, there is often a lack of securing points for the climber and additional wires may have to be added to ensure that good plant coverage is achieved.

Wiring in conifers

As the wiring of conifers is principally for support, I feel it is right to place it here, rather than in the chapter on pruning.

Many conifers as they mature start to spread, particularly after heavy snow, and wiring is required to bring them back into an upright shape.

There is no particular time that this should be done, but as the damage is caused in the winter, this is the time usually chosen, often as a first-aid operation.

First, gather together the branches of the damaged conifer by encircling the tree, approximately 6 ft (2 m) from ground level, with a strong rope which has a loop in one end, through which the other end can be passed to form a noose. Pull the rope tight, but not overtight, bringing the branches of the conifer together to approximately the same diameter as they were before they spread.

Take a discarded piece of hose-pipe, preferably dark coloured, long enough to surround the tree, and pass plastic-coated 2.5–3 mm wire through the middle, leaving enough spare wire at either end to secure it once it is in position. Carefully place hose and wire approximately 4 ft (1.2 m) from ground level around the conifer, tucking it in as much as possible behind the outer foliage to conceal it; once it is in position secure the ends of the wires.

Additional wires and hose will be required every 4 ft (1.2 m) up the conifer until it is fully tied in and secured. Depending on the height, it may be necessary, after the lower two wires are in position, to reposition the rope higher up until the conifer is completely secured and brought back to its former shape.

Occasionally there will be an odd side shoot that cannot be pulled in; if it is not of a major size, it should be removed.

This method works well with the following species:

Chamaecyparis lawsoniana varieties (Lawson Cypress), *Libocedrus decurrens* (False Cedar), *Thuja plicata* varieties (Western Red Cedar) and *Taxus baccata* 'Fastigiata' varieties (Irish Yew). It can also be used on the upright-growing *Prunus* 'Amanogawa' (Lombardy Poplar Cherry, Flag-pole Cherry) to good effect.

CHAPTER FOUR

Feeding Plants

The merits of feeding plants are obvious, but it is important to give the right feeding at the right time. This chapter sets out to guide the gardener to an understanding of what is not only beneficial to the plant but is cost effective, and makes the best use of time and effort.

How a plant uses food

Before we look at plant feeding and the fertilizers used we should take a moment to understand how the plant absorbs food from the soil.

In Chapter 1 the relationship between the soil and soil moisture was explained; the soil moisture contains the plant foods in a liquid form, and therefore the fertilizers that we apply to the soil must be integrated into the soil moisture before the plant can benefit from them. They must also, of course, be available at the time the plant requires them and can use them to the full advantage; if we give food at the wrong time we may cause damage to the plant.

Most garden plants use plant foods in May and June for growth and in July for storage for the following year. After July the plant begins to slow down its growth rate so that the growth can ripen to withstand winter cold. It is therefore important to ensure all fertilizers are in place in the soil as liquids by May and last until July if they are to be used to the best advantage.

Different plants use different combinations of plant foods and specific fertilizers will supply these needs and also rectify the deficiencies that individual soils or areas may present.

We discussed in Chapter 1 the use of organic material in preparing the soil for planting or in the application of a mulch. However, although these organic materials contain small amounts of plant foods they rarely supply the plants' full requirements. Also, if we want to grow a wide range of plants, we can use fertilizers to ensure that all their individual needs are being met.

Plant foods and fertilizers, and their effect on plant health

When the correct balance of plant foods has been absorbed by the plant it improves the plant's ability to protect itself against attacks of pests and diseases. In the event of an attack, applying the relevant fertilizers can speedily bring the plant back to full health, and, in some cases, enables the plant to produce enzymes that may kill the attacker or at least curtail its activities.

Deficiencies

Deficiencies of plant foods occur from time to time and are caused by a number of factors.

Geographical

Individual geographical areas are naturally deficient in certain plant foods.

Soil types

Lime or chalk (alkaline) soils in particular lock up the trace element iron; very alkaline soils also lock up magnesium. Clay soils and soils high in organic material hold plant foods well, but light sandy or chalk soils do not.

Specific plant food requirements

Many plant groups require a particular balance of plant foods, and if these are not present in the soil, it can lead to deficiency.

Effects of weather

Drought can result in plant foods not being dissolved in the soil moisture, leading to a temporary shortage. Excessive rain or snow can have the same effect, by leaching out the plant foods as the water drains away.

Effects of surrounding plants

Trees, large shrubs, conifers and hedges can cause deficiencies because their roots draw out the moisture and plant foods from the soil in close proximity to their bases.

The main plant foods

Three main plant foods are required by plants, nitrogen, phosphate and potash. They are often referred to by the chemical symbols, N, P and K, both in gardening books and on fertilizer products.

N = nitrogen

Nitrogen encourages stem and foliage growth in plants, ensures the green colour of the leaves and keeps them in full productivity.

In addition to feeding plants, it is the principal source of food in the soil for bacteria and other soil animals that help in

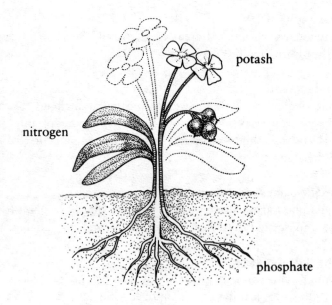

8. *Use of fertilizers: nitrogen for the foliage, phosphates for the roots and potash for flowers and fruit production*

the decomposition of organic material in the soil, releasing the plant foods they contain.

Therefore, if there is a shortage of nitrogen, plant growth is curtailed and a downward spiral begins.

Nitrogen can be added to the soil by using one of a number of organic and inorganic fertilizers, but only half of the nitrogen they contain will be released and very little is held for any time in the soil; application times and rates are therefore important if good results are to be achieved.

P = phosphates

Phosphates counteract the effects of nitrogen and control growth rates, so preventing the plant becoming over-extended and leggy. They also encourage root growth and buds to produce flowers and finally fruit.

Most of the phosphates in organic or inorganic fertilizers become available to the plant and good amounts are retained and stored both in the plant, in particular its roots over winter, and in the soil for future use.

K = potash

Potash principally affects the formation of fruit and its development, improving the size, flavour and colour. Both organic and inorganic fertilizers offer potash, but the inorganic ones are possibly the most effective.

Good amounts are retained in the soil and in the fruit and seeds of the plant, but many soils are naturally deficient in potash.

Trace elements

Many trace elements, although present in the soil in very small amounts, are very important to sustain plant growth, health and general well-being. Their absence is often dramatically signalled by leaf discoloration – chlorosis.

In all there are over thirty different trace elements but only a few are of interest to the gardener.

CALCIUM   Calcium occurs in the soil in the form of chalk or lime. Most garden plants require it in various degrees, as it acts primarily as a catalyst for chemical changes carried out by the growth-forming green chlorophyll cells in the leaves. Some plants require more than average amounts of calcium, but the group of plants referred to as 'lime-hating' or 'ericaceous', such as Rhododendrons and Azaleas, may react strongly against it if it is present in large amounts. Its role and effects make it a very important trace element and some would go so far as to describe it as a main plant food.

IRON   Iron also plays a major role in plant growth, again in the production of growth and as a balancing agent. All plants use it to some extent, but those in the lime-hating or ericaceous groups appear to need higher levels than most. If high degrees of calcium are present, the iron is locked up in the soil and the lime-hating plants cannot access it freely. Deficiencies of iron are identified by chlorosis in the younger leaves, later the older ones also turn from green to yellow or off-white between the veins. In severe conditions the plant may die.

MAGNESIUM   Heavy rain depletes the amount of magnesium available, and light sandy soils are most likely to suffer from a shortage of magnesium. The symptoms closely resemble those of iron deficiency, with yellowing between the leaf veins. Leaves of all ages are affected, but later in the summer than is the case with iron deficiency. In addition to the yellowing, a marbling effect of the central parts of the leaf may be seen. Whereas iron shortages may affect a wide range of plants, magnesium is more selective and Roses, Apples, root, pod and leaf vegetables, and annual plants are the most susceptible, not normally in yield of flowers or fruit, but in overall appearance. If magnesium is deficient, calcium is often absent too, and both must be supplied.

MANGANESE   Chlorotic yellowing of the leaves also occurs with manganese deficiency and, in addition, brown areas of rot may be seen on the leaf surface. Vegetables are usually most affected but the symptoms may be seen on a wide range of plants.

BORON Less of a problem than the others, but deficiency occurs more today than in the past, possibly due to the smaller amounts of organic material used now. Boron is released during decomposition and is held in the soil for some time. If it is absent, roots, stems and leaves become deformed and are reduced in quantity, leading to a downgrading of the plant's growth.

OTHER TRACE ELEMENTS Copper, sulphur and molybdenum, if in short supply, also have an adverse effect on plant growth, but the changes are less marked. General use of compound inorganic fertilizers is normally enough to maintain the correct balance.

Harmful trace elements such as aluminium, zinc, mercury, lead and other heavy metals, or excesses of the beneficial trace elements mentioned above, can produce toxic symptoms and may be fatal.

Fertilizers – their uses and timing of application

To ensure that the plants in our gardens are provided with the correct balance of foods we apply fertilizers, organic or inorganic, to the soil. Organic fertilizers are derived from plant and animal material that was once alive; inorganic fertilizers are manufactured by a chemical process. These fertilizers may be available as 'straights' or as compounds of more than one plant food.

There are important rules that must be taken into account before purchasing or using fertilizers.

1. Always store all fertilizers along with other garden and domestic chemicals under lock and key and out of the reach of children and animals. When used correctly, for the purpose intended, they are safe, but in the wrong hands they may cause problems.

2. Read the instructions on the product. Application at the wrong time and in the wrong amounts may cause problems and is a waste of time and money.

3. Attempt to calculate the amount of fertilizer needed and buy the size closest to what you require – to save storage space and money, and to avoid waste.

4. Always keep fertilizers dry in storage; wet fertilizers are useless because they have lost most, if not all, of their plant food content.

5. Never decant or separate any garden chemical, including fertilizers, from its packaging – the directions on the packet will be required at a later date for rates of application.

6. Never be tempted to use non-recommended inorganic fertilizers such as those used in farming, as the proportion of plant foods is far too high and can cause damage in the garden and to the environment.

7. Do not apply fertilizers except at the recommended times – if they are applied too early, the benefits may be leached from the soil before they can be used; if too late, the fertilizer may not be used and so will be lost or, in the case of liquid fertilizers, may produce late plant growth that will not have time to ripen before the winter, and may subsequently be damaged.

8. As the main feeding roots of plants are positioned in the soil at a point close to the outer edges of the stems and leaves of a plant, it is important to apply the fertilizer in this area.

9. Should very dry weather follow fertilizer application, the soil should be watered to ensure the food supply enters the soil moisture.

10. Always handle all fertilizers with gloved hands to avoid any contact with hands, skin or blood, since they can cause irritation or lead to diseases such as tetanus or anthrax (when using bonemeal).

11. As a rule, fertilizers with lesser-known brand names will be less expensive and will achieve the same results.

12. Always ensure that no fertilizer is accidentally deposited on the leaves of plants, as this can cause scorching and long-term damage.

When to apply particular fertilizers

Fertilizers take time to enter the soil moisture and become available to the plant, and this time delay must be taken into account when deciding when to apply them.

A good example is the well-known organic fertilizer, bone-meal. Bonemeal has been used for many years as a fertilizer for establishing and feeding a wide range of plants, in particular trees and shrubs. Before the advent of container-grown plants, most woody plants such as trees, shrubs and Roses were planted from mid October to Christmas, and it was recommended that bonemeal should be used at planting time, as it takes at least six months for it to decompose and dissolve into the soil moisture as plant food. Now container-grown shrubs may be planted at any season, but bonemeal should still be applied only in the traditional autumn planting season. Otherwise most of the benefit will not reach the plant at the right time; it will be leached out of the soil by the rain and so wasted.

Thus, if planting is carried out at other times, other fertilizers – not bonemeal – should be used that do act at the right time. In the listing of fertilizers on pp. 78–84 these lead-in times are given. The following is an outline guide.

BONEMEAL AND OTHER ORGANIC FERTILIZERS CONTAIN-ING BONEMEAL Bonemeal and the bone element in other organic composts take six months to enter the soil moisture and become available to the plant, so to be of benefit must be applied from October to December.

COMPOUND INORGANIC FERTILIZERS; FISH ELEMENT OF COMPOUND ORGANIC FERTILIZERS Most compound inorganic fertilizers, such as National Growmore, and the fish element of compound organic fertilizers take six weeks to enter the soil moisture, so they should be applied in March and April.

LIQUID FERTILIZERS AND FAST-ACTING ORGANIC FERTILIZ-ERS Liquid fertilizers and organic fertilizers such as woodash and dried blood take six days or less to enter the soil moisture but are quickly leached out if not used at once by the plant. Therefore they are normally applied in June or July; as most are liquid they are quickly available to the plant even in drought conditions.

Fertilizer types

No rates of application are suggested in this section as they will be given in the instructions on the packet. Always read the instructions before purchasing or applying a fertilizer.

Compound fertilizers

Compound fertilizers are today the mainstay of plant feeding. Many are of a general nature, others are more specific in the plants they cater for. They are, in fact, a comparatively recent introduction, born out of the need for inexpensive, fully beneficial fertilizers to boost production in the Second World War.

As with all garden chemicals it is important to follow the instructions. Fertilizers supplied in granular form or as powders are applied in March and early April and those in liquid form in late May through to July. As we will see from the following, some provide food in the late spring, others are more slow-acting. Most of the main suppliers of garden chemicals offer a range of products all doing roughly the same jobs, but at different prices, so shopping around to find the best value always pays.

NATIONAL GROWMORE This is the father of today's compound fertilizers, and still by far the best from the plants' point of view, as well as being good value for money.

It was formulated to benefit the widest range of plants possible, and it is hard to find a plant that does not benefit from its use. Taking some four to six weeks to become available to the plant, it is applied in March or April for the best results.

SLOW-RELEASE FERTILIZERS A number of fertilizers, supplied either in powder or granular form, contain a substance called Osmocote, which makes them release their plant foods over a longer period than other fertilizers, but they are more expensive.

Application is normally made in April for best results but it should also be remembered that in dry summers they will be rendered less effective by the lack of moisture to dissolve them.

LIQUID COMPOUND FERTILIZERS   As with the other fertilizers there are a number of different liquid types, including both general and specific formulations to feed different groups of plants.

Also, as before, each manufacturer will produce their own and, once a suitable type for the job in hand has been chosen, price can be the governing factor.

They are also fast-acting, as they are liquid in the first place, normally only taking six days to enter the food supply. Application is therefore made in the growing time, from late May to late July. With most plants, the rule is little and often.

COMPOUND FERTILIZERS TO CORRECT TRACE-ELEMENT SHORTAGES   For some reason these specialist fertilizers, which in their way are as important as the fertilizers that provide the main plant foods, are little known or used. They are stocked by the more informed garden shops and centres and it is worth searching them out as they work well for correcting particular deficiencies.

FERTILIZER SPIKES   For some time now fertilizer spikes containing specific plant foods for certain groups of plants have been available, particularly for house-plants. They are a good idea and work well as long as the plants do not dry out; they release plant foods to the plant when inserted in the spring and continue to provide them throughout the growing season.

SPECIAL COMPOUND FERTILIZERS FOR SPECIFIC PLANT GROUPS   Chemists and horticulturists have devised a range of special compound fertilizers, in dry or liquid form, for plants which require a slightly different combination of foods from the normal. Most are applied in the spring but a few in the summer or autumn, so checking with the instructions on the packet is important.

There are specific fertilizers for:

Cacti
Chrysanthemums
Conifers
Flowering plants
Foliage plants
Hanging baskets and tubs
    and containers
House-plants

Lawns, both for autumn and for spring	Shrubs
	Tomatoes
Rhododendrons and Azaleas	Trees
Roses	Vegetables

FOLIAR FEEDING   In summer plants can be fed by means of a foliar feed applied directly on to the leaves. It is often claimed that foliar feeding can assist a plant which is not performing as well as it should. My own view is that although a short-term improvement may be detected, it will not be long-term, as the cause of the problem has not been dealt with. Almost always it is the root system that is at fault and this must be improved. Also, foliar feeds are more expensive than other standard fertilizers for the benefits achieved.

Inorganic straight fertilizers

A number of inorganic fertilizers are applied 'straight'; they provide one or sometimes two specific plant foods and are often used to enhance the plant foods given by organic material. In the main they are available from garden shops and centres and are applied as dry powders and raked or forked into the soil surface.

SULPHATE OF AMMONIA   Sulphate of ammonia is a dry powder; it is the principal fast-acting provider of nitrogen. It is available on its own and it is also used to supply nitrogen in compound fertilizers.

It is used to enhance growth and improve the colour of leaves, and takes four to six weeks to enter the soil moisture and be available to the plant. In addition to being applied directly, it can be used to prevent nitrogen starvation when using bark or chippings as a soil mulch, for it will feed the soil bacteria that use nitrogen to break down the bark or chippings. When used for this purpose it is important to apply it annually. Likewise it can be added to the compost heap, again to feed the bacteria and other soil animals that help decompose the organic material.

SUPERPHOSPHATE   Superphosphate, as its name suggests, is

the principal supplier of phosphate; as a dry powder it is used to encourage the formation of fruit buds and also the long-term storage of plant food by the plant in its roots. It is needed by the plant in late June and as it takes six weeks to enter the food supply, it is applied in late April.

SULPHATE OF POTASH   This dry powder fertilizer is used to increase the yield of flowers and fruit in vegetables and fruit crops, and can also be used to encourage and improve perform-ance in ornamental plants. It takes four to six weeks to enter the food chain, so is applied in mid to late April.

NITRO-CHALK   This is supplied as a powder; it is used princi-pally on acid soils that require both nitrogen and calcium. Normally it takes six to eight weeks to enter the soil moisture, so is applied in March.

NITRATE OF SODA   Nitrate of soda is a fast-acting dry powder source of nitrogen for fruit and vegetable crops, and as it only takes four to five weeks to become available it is applied in April or early May.

MAGNESIUM SULPHATE (EPSOM SALTS)   The dry, powdered magnesium sulphate, or Epsom salts, is not given to the plant to cure indigestion! In fact, it is used to correct deficiencies in magnesium and, being fast-acting, taking only five to six weeks to be available to the plant, it is applied in April or May. If symptoms are seen later, application until the end of July may be useful. Later than this it is best to wait until the following spring; this will cause no ill-effect to the plant.

SULPHATE OF IRON   As its name would imply, this fertilizer is a way of correcting an iron deficiency. It is inexpensive and, as it is quick-acting, it is applied in late April or early May.

SEQUESTERED IRON   Obtainable either as a powder or in granular form, it can also be made into a liquid to apply to those plants that require acid soil conditions and that are showing signs of chlorosis or iron deficiency. The results are short-term, however.

Organic fertilizers

Organic fertilizers are derived from material that was once alive in the form of animal or vegetable matter and has been prepared so as to give up its plant food content as it decays. Many have been used by generations of gardeners and are tried and true. In fact, at one time or another, almost every organic waste product has been tried; the following are those that we still use today.

BONEMEAL Possibly the best-known of all garden organic fertilizers and rightly so. It is used as an autumn application to establish all woody plants, trees, shrubs and Roses. It is also used for spring-flowering bulbs planted in autumn; it provides a store of plant food in the soil with which the bulb will replenish itself, make new bulblets and set the flower for the following spring's display.

It is high in phosphates, with just enough nitrogen to start plants into growth in the spring without overtaxing their resources. It is applied in the autumn and early winter and takes at least six months to be broken down and become available to the plant through the soil moisture.

HOOF AND HORN Hoof and horn releases to the plant, over a long period, both nitrogen and phosphates in good amounts.

It was traditionally and still is used as a fertilizer for long-term potted plants and plants in patio tubs and containers. Outdoors it is best applied in the autumn and winter; indoors, where growth rarely stops, there is no particular season and it is normally added when plants are potted up.

FISH, BLOOD AND BONE For some reason this organic fertilizer has gained more popularity than possibly it deserves. Its triple-release time – first the nitrogen in the blood, followed by the phosphates from the fish component and finally the remaining phosphates and nitrogen from the bone – is well suited to Chrysanthemums. In general, however, it is difficult to see how this multiple release time can operate without being wasteful, releasing food at the wrong time and not when the plant requires it.

DRIED BLOOD   Not the cheapest of fertilizers, but possibly the best for feeding and improving the foliage colour and growth of conifers used either as hedging or as specimens. In particular, when used on newly planted Yew (*Taxus baccata*) hedges it substantially increases the growth rate.

Most conifers start their main growth at the end of May or early June; as the nitrogen in the dried blood is very quickly made available, but soon loses its effect, it is important to apply it at the right time – the end of April is ideal.

Dried blood can also be used as a 'pick-me-up' for plants that are not doing as well as expected; an application at the recommended time will go a long way towards improving their growth, but investigation into the plants' root development must also be made.

SEAWEED MANURES   Seaweed manures in their liquid form are unique, in that they primarily act as a root stimulant, activating the root systems into growth so that they can take full advantage of the plant foods in the soil.

The fertilizer in its dry, powdered form also supplies nitrogen and phosphate, and small amounts of trace elements.

All are quick-acting, so for the dry powdered form April application is recommended, and for the liquid form late May, June and July.

WOOD ASH   This is normally home-produced, as a by-product of garden management. It is high in nitrogen and also phosphates but the drawback is that it loses its food value very quickly and therefore must be stored dry and applied in mid to late April to achieve the full benefits.

GARDEN LIME   Garden lime is ground-up chalk that has been heat-treated; it is used mainly on acid soils for plants such as strawberries and potatoes which require high amounts of calcium. However, care must be taken to ensure that it does not upset the balance of acidity and alkalinity, since other plants growing in close proximity may not require the higher amounts of calcium.

It takes time to do its work and is therefore applied in January and February as a normal part of the winter digging.

HOME-MADE LIQUID FERTILIZERS   For those who have access
to a supply of fresh farmyard manure, such as cattle or horse,
the opportunity arises to produce home-made liquid fertilizer.

About a wheelbarrow full of fresh farmyard manure is
placed in a hessian sack; this is then lowered into a rainwater
butt or similar watertight receptacle. The butt is filled with
water and left for ten days or so; the resulting liquid will be a
very useful organic fertilizer, high in nitrogen, with some
phosphates and potash. It is quick-acting and can be applied in
May, June and July, but it does need diluting first with water
until the liquid is of a medium coffee colour. It can then be
used as a substitute for one of the routine waterings of the
plants grown in containers and can also be applied liberally in
May and June to plants growing in the garden.

Feeding tips

Bulbs

Autumn-planted, spring-flowering bulbs   Use bonemeal when
planting.

Spring-planted, summer-flowering bulbs   Use Growmore
when planting.

All bulbs   Just as the flowers are dying, feed with any liquid
fertilizer to ensure that adequate plant foods are present to
form next year's flowers. This should be repeated annually
and will prevent flower blindness in all bulbs.

Conifers

Feed with dried blood in April to improve foliage colour and
speed up the establishment of newly planted Yew (*Taxus
baccata*) hedges.

Wisteria

Feed Wisteria in April with superphosphate to speed up and
improve flowering.

Roses

Feed Roses with a specific rose fertilizer in April – these
contain extra potash as well as the trace elements Roses
require to grow well.

Just as the first flowers die, feed again with any liquid fertilizer and they may produce a second and, in many cases, a third crop of flowers.

Poorly growing and woody plants with root problems
Many shrubs, trees and other woody plants may not be growing as well as might be expected and if this is the case, carry out the following procedure. In March, scrape out all the surface soil under the canopy of the plant in question, excavating down until the surface roots are just exposed. Infill the hole, using a good-quality potting compost to which Growmore has been added. Mulch on top of the compost to a depth of 3–4 in (8–10 cm) with a well-rotted organic material. New roots and, more importantly, root hairs will grow into the compost and take up the food from the fertilizer and the condition of the shrub will improve over the following two years. Repeat the mulching and feeding each spring.

Lawns
In early spring, four weeks before sowing seed or laying new turf, apply a dressing of Growmore to give the new grass a boost as it starts to grow.

Always apply an autumn lawn feed in October or November to established lawns, to build up a store of plant food for the following spring.

Do not use a lawn fertilizer and weed-killer on a newly sown or turfed lawn; wait until the spring of the second year.

Lawn mowings that come from lawns that have been treated with a weed-killer should not be used on the compost heap.

Newly planted large trees and shrubs
In the first year following planting, feed plants once a week with a general liquid fertilizer in May, June and July to speed up establishment of the root system.

Containers and hanging baskets
Feed with a general liquid fertilizer from the end of May once

a fortnight throughout the summer to keep the plants growing and flowering.

House-plants
Use a specific house-plant liquid fertilizer on a regular basis in spring, summer and early autumn – or use house-plant fertilizer spikes – but stop feeding in late autumn and winter.

CHAPTER FIVE

Watering

Few gardening publications allocate a chapter to watering but in my understanding watering is as important as any other gardening technique.

Correct watering improves the whole well-being of the plant and plays a major role in propagation, establishment after planting, absorption of plant food, growth production and even resistance to pest and disease attack.

Many plant problems can be directly or indirectly referred back to inadequate watering or the over-supply of water.

Water and the soil

In Chapter 1 we explored the role of soil moisture; we saw how this microscopic film of moisture controlled the plants' clock and how the rise and fall of the temperature triggered the start of growth in the spring, flowering in summer and finally the autumn close down and storage of food for the following spring.

The water-table, sometimes referred to as groundwater, is as important as direct rainfall, for it is this underground water reservoir that releases a continuous supply of water to the upper levels of the soil. Water, or more correctly moisture, is forced up through the lower levels of the soil through the gaps between the soil particles. This movement is called the capillary action of the soil; the depth and range of water movement can be extensive.

Should the water-table fall, due to drought, water extraction or, in some cases, disturbance due to building excavations, the flow can be interrupted and the plants will react unfavourably and become root damaged, although the results may not be seen for months or even years.

Alternatively poor drainage or excessive water from winter

rain or snow may lead to a build-up of too much groundwater; the water-table will rise, the plants' roots will suffocate due to lack of oxygen and the plants will slowly die.

Apart from not physically damaging the water-table and, to some extent, controlling it by good planting practices and providing drainage, there is little else the gardener can do to control the movement of the water-table, as it depends on factors beyond our control.

Soil water and its effect on acidity and alkalinity

As we also learnt in Chapter 1, the soil moisture controls the acidity and alkalinity; since there is such a vast amount of water in the soil, it is almost impossible to change or control for any length of time the acidity and alkalinity of a given soil – that which exists in a particular locality will always be the norm.

The effect of water on the plant

It is worth spending a moment to look at the various roles water plays in the growth and overall structure of a plant.

We have seen already how the soil moisture and the water-table contain and carry plant foods, and that they enter the plant through its root hairs. Once inside the plant, water takes on other roles:

1. Water acts as a transport system, moving plant food to where it is required through numerous interlocking plant cells which make up a series of 'tubes'.

2. Water filling the individual cells of the roots, stems, leaves and flowers during transportation keeps the plant rigid, enabling each part to perform its individual role. Botanically this action is said to be keeping the plant 'turgid'. Once turgidity is lost the plant cannot function and may die unless the supply of water is restored.

3. Water in the leaf and green stems of plants supports the green cells called chlorophyll; by using sunlight, plant foods and carbon dioxide from the air, these produce the energy in the form of sugar that allows the plant to grow and develop. In the process, plants release into the atmosphere the oxygen which we breathe.

4. The water in the plant cells helps produce and carry the various natural enzymes that act to combat attacks from pests and diseases; if the plant is deprived of part of its water supply, this natural defence is reduced or lost and infestation levels of attack are experienced. Water is thus the first defence against attack.

5. The amount of water in a plant controls its internal temperature. By controlling the flow through pores in the leaves and stem − called stomata and lenticels respectively − the plant responds to temperature changes, and also wind changes, releasing water when it has too much and conserving it when it has not.

If, due to the action of direct sunlight, the temperature rises too high in the leaves of certain plants such as golden or variegated shrubs or, say, *Acer palmatum* (Japanese Maple), the water in the leaf cells will boil and the cells are destroyed, causing brown leaf scorch. To a certain extent we can prevent this by choosing for hot spots plants which have leaves with thick, heat-resistant skins. Those that cannot withstand the heat should be planted in the shade or semi-shade to protect them and keep them out of direct sunlight.

6. Water swells the roots of vegetable plants, providing us with foods such as potatoes, carrots and other root crops, and also the leaves of leaf crops such as lettuce and cabbage. Without water, plant fruits would not swell and fruit such as Apples and Pears would not exist.

All in all, water is of paramount importance to the plant and it is essential that we should manage it well. Too much water can flood the cells and make them inactive by suffocation or the drawing-out of oxygen from the plant cells − many a house-plant has been killed by overwatering. Poor soil preparation can lead to a build-up of excess water and so is often the cause of plant failure.

Humidity
Humidity produces a cool, moist environment or atmosphere, and many plants require such growing conditions to help them

to control their temperature and the loss of water from their leaves and stems. Control or provision of humidity can, with many plants, be very important to their well-being; Cacti, which require low humidity, and Orchids which require high humidity, are good examples.

Plants that need high humidity in the environment surrounding them do so for a number of reasons:

1. To act as an external leaf- or stem-cooling agent.

2. In some plants, such as large-leaved water-associated plants like Hostas, to act as a secondary supply of water; in a few, such as succulents and Orchids, the primary source.

3. A few plants are able to extract plant food from the humidity in the air – Bromeliads and Orchids are prime examples.

4. Many plants use the humidity to wash their leaves and keep their leaf- and stem-breathing pores open so that they can control temperature and moisture levels.

5. In propagation, humidity is the principal element that keeps cuttings alive until they can produce their own roots; if the humidity is lost the cuttings will dehydrate and die.

6. On the other hand, excessive, prolonged high humidity can kill seedlings and newly rooted cuttings by suffocation.

7. High humidity and temperature are the ideal environment for some fungus diseases such as damping-off, botrytis and a whole range of moulds and rots which may attack and kill plants. On the other hand, other fungus diseases will be killed in such conditions.

8. With plants growing indoors or in greenhouses or conservatories, one of the main problems is low humidity, and attempts must be made to rectify this.

9. Damping the floor of the greenhouse or conservatory every few hours in hot weather is a very good practice. Even having a full watering-can stored within the greenhouse at all times can help raise the humidity level.

10. Greenhouses and conservatories can have internal water storage tanks under the benching which will increase the humidity.

11. The installation of a humidifier can also be considered in a conservatory where other forms of damping down might be difficult.

12. Small fountains in the more ornamental sun-rooms and conservatories are an attractive and useful aid in increasing humidity.

13. Creating sufficient humidity indoors can sometimes be difficult but a container of water in close proximity to house-plants can often provide the level required. Growing them or occasionally giving them a rest in a humid bathroom can help the plant to clean its breathing pores and take advantage of the high humidity levels found there.

Occasionally, too, it is necessary to control humidity carefully because some plants are particularly sensitive to humidity at certain times in their growing cycle.

Drought

That drought weather conditions can have an effect on the water content in the soil is obvious, but one point that is not generally understood is that certain plants react to drought more dramatically than others, and it is wise to keep a careful watch on those worst affected and supplement their water when necessary.

Many shrubs such as Viburnums, Deutzias and Buddlejas, and even some trees like Beech (Fagus) and many large-leaved perennial plants have, in the main, surface root systems that react quickly to dry conditions, sometimes dramatically and to the detriment of the overall health of the plant. It is good garden management to supplement their water supply and provide them with an organic mulch that will act as a store of water in times of scarcity.

Wind

Wind can also deplete the soil and deprive plants of water. In nature, many plants growing in dry, windy areas have small, thin or leathery leaves that are able to withstand the wind; in others the leaf surface is covered with a layer of hairs to protect the breathing cells or stomata from direct exposure to the wind.

The wind affects the water content in the soil and in plants as follows:

1. The wind passes across the soil surface and as it does it draws off and evaporates the soil moisture. Although this is detrimental, it can also be an advantage to the gardener, drying out wet soils prior to winter and spring cultivation.

2. The wind passing over the surface of leaves can also draw out moisture; if the water content is too much reduced, the plant's turgidity may be lost.

3. If the wind is interrupted by a solid object such as a wall, the wind hitting the windward side of the obstruction is accelerated up the side of the wall and is joined by wind passing over the top, and the combined force is then directed downwards on to the lee side at up to twice its original speed, causing physical damage to plants and increasing the potential for water loss.

All these effects can be reduced by providing or planting wind breaks that filter the wind but do not block it, so reducing the flow of wind over soil and leaf surfaces.

Shade

Shade reduces the loss of water from the soil by reducing the amount of direct sun hitting it and thereby lowering the temperature. So plants that do not like strong sunlight – such as golden, variegated or large-leaved plants, which can suffer from leaf scorch – are much happier in part or full shade, depending on their individual needs.

Particular problems can arise if shade is provided by a tree, rather than by a fence or building, as its roots may well deprive other plants of water and induce false drought conditions by drawing off water for itself. In addition, its canopy of foliage can lead to rain being directed away from the soil directly under its branches.

Many plants associated with water, such as Hostas and Astilbes, prefer light shade as long as the soil has a continuous supply of water and is high in organic material. This is a situation not easy to produce artificially, but if it exists or can be created, it is one of the best of all planting positions.

In such conditions foliage and flowers are large, bold and interesting due to the constant supply of water, whereas in dry, sunny conditions the reverse is often found.

Watering and pollination

There are some plants that are aided in their pollination by rain – *Phaseolus coccineus* (Runner Beans) and Pyracanthas (Firethorn) are good examples – and it has long been garden practice to spray the flowers with water in the evenings when they are fully open to ensure that pollination takes place. The pollen grains that make fertilization possible are floated in the water and so are able to reach the female element of the flower.

Rules of good watering

To supply water to the plant in the most beneficial way without causing damage we need to remember the following rules:

1. Never water plants in strong sunlight as this can set up a magnifying-glass situation, where the sun passing through the droplets of water on the surface of the leaves can scorch or burn. In these conditions, the water will in any case be evaporated before it can be absorbed by the soil. This is not to say the area around the plants should not be kept humid; this is best achieved with a 2–3 in (5–8 cm) deep organic mulch applied in winter or early spring.

2. Whenever possible, use stored rainwater rather than mains water as the former is normally free of calcium, which may affect acid-loving plants. Tap water also contains chlorine, which can cause problems with some plants.

3. Always attempt to water with a watering-can fitted with a long spout as this slows down the water flow and prevents soil erosion or physical leaf damage. The use of a watering-can rose to give a fine spray of water is also beneficial. If watering with a hose, then a fine spray adaptor should be used rather than an open end or jet.

4. Never water directly on to the centre of plants such as

Begonias which grow from a corm root system, as water on the corm could rot it.

5. In winter water pot-grown plants as little as possible, if at all. This does not mean that the plants should be allowed to dry out completely, but they should be just moist enough to keep them alive.

If this is done, many more container plants, both indoors and out, will survive the winter. Soil water freezes in cold weather, denying water to the plant and freezing out oxygen; less water will mean less solid freezing and will keep the potting compost more loose and open in structure.

6. When watering containers both indoors and out in summer, water little and often rather than allowing them to dry out and then watering them excessively.

7. Before potting up plants or sowing seeds, ensure that the water in the potting compost is at room temperature, as cold water may damage plant roots and kill seeds and seedlings.

8. Always water house-plants from the bottom by placing water in a saucer and leaving the plant in it for say twenty minutes; if all the water has been taken up by the soil, put more water in the saucer and wait for an additional ten minutes. If after the first or second watering any water is left, tip it away; do not allow plants to stand in water for any length of time.

9. When spring approaches, water every other day. Once summer has arrived, watering once a day may be necessary, reducing the frequency to every other day in the autumn.

10. With seeds and cuttings, water as little as possible and always use a watering-can with a fine rose.

11. When watering newly planted plants – either in the garden or in containers – that have been grown in a pot or root ball, direct the water on to the soil where it will soak the pot root or root ball, as well as on to the general area. The reason for this is that for a week or two, particularly in the spring, the plant's roots may not grow out beyond the original root area and watering around the general area can leave the plant itself dry, even to the point where it may die.

Hand-watering versus sprinklers

Certainly using a sprinkler at times of drought – assuming there is not a hose-pipe ban – over large areas has its advantages, but there is little control of the application of water to an individual plant. With water metering the use of sprinklers, with their high wastage, becomes less attractive from a financial point of view.

If sprinklers are used then care must be taken not only to avoid overwatering but to avoid using them at times of the day when leaf scorching might occur. Care is also needed to ensure that areas or individual plants are not missed by the sprinklers.

On the other hand, piped self-watering drip or trickle watering – where water is supplied automatically from the mains water supply or from a pump – has real merit, and the purchase and setting-up of a permanent system for containers or hanging-basket plantings, or a temporary system for newly planted areas, is worth careful consideration.

Hand watering of individual plants with can or hose is time consuming, but gives the best control.

Testing for dryness

Knowing when to water has always been a problem. Gardeners must use their instincts and careful observation to decide when watering is needed.

With small pot-grown plants, the weight of the pot is often the indicator used. Larger pots are more difficult, but with terracotta pots the colour of the pot itself can be a useful pointer: the darker the pot, the wetter it is. With other pots visual inspection of the plant itself is needed, to observe how it presents itself just before becoming dry and drooping or losing its turgidity.

To complicate the situation further, today's potting composts dry out at different speeds, some extremely rapidly.

There are a number of electronic moisture meters available; these are expensive, but they can be useful. Small paper or card indicators, purchased from garden centres, show the water content of the potting soil in a pot; these could be used to help you build up your knowledge of how your plants look when they are in need of water.

Placing a small, say 1 in (3 cm), square of newspaper on the soil surface is also a good indicator. If it fails to become wet, watering is normally required.

Conserving water

Many of the ways in which we can reduce the need for watering have been practised by gardeners for decades, and many are

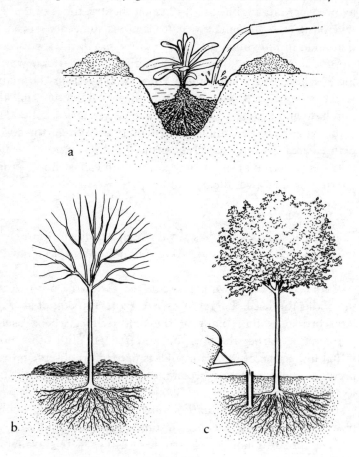

9. Watering
(a) Water added at planting time before final infilling of soil
(b) Mulching   (c) Pipe to direct water to root supply

covered in other chapters, but it is worth reminding ourselves of these techniques in the context of water conservation.

1. Adding good amounts of organic material to the soil at planting time is one of the best ways; as well as encouraging root development it gives rechargeable water storage below the surface where evaporation by wind and sun is reduced.

2. Also, with spring planting, use the technique of water 'puddling': before the planting hole is finally refilled, water is poured into the planting hole and then covered with soil to protect it from evaporation.

3. Mulching with organic material has always been used by gardeners to conserve moisture and has the added bonus of providing the perfect environment for root development. It produces a root system that is strong and able to make the best use of moisture and plant foods.

4. Shading areas either permanently or temporarily cuts down water loss. Non-woven, chemical-free, polypropylene fibre, which in gardening is primarily used for frost protection, can provide good temporary shading when used on newly sown grass seed; it keeps the moisture in while letting rain through, and has the added advantage of preventing bird damage.

5. When planting indoor and outdoor containers or hanging baskets, mix in water-retaining polymer granules as recommended by the manufacturer. These will retain large amounts of water and, when required, make it available to the plant.

6. Use broken-up polystyrene packaging as drainage, for it not only gives good drainage, but acts as a reservoir of moisture from which the roots can draw later water and plant food as required.

7. Sink a 9–10 in (23–5 cm) long, 1–2 in (3–5 cm) diameter tube vertically into the ground, 12–15 in (30–40 cm) away from a newly planted tree, shrub or conifer; water can be poured into it straight to where the new roots are likely to grow. A plastic lemonade bottle with the bottom cut away and the cap removed, inserted upside down into the soil alongside the newly planted plant, is excellent for this.

8. Many proprietary storage systems and reservoir products are becoming available for watering newly planted trees, shrubs

and conifers, and for installing in tubs and containers. Many tubs and hanging baskets now have these built in.

9. Try to purchase a watering-can with a long spout as this is designed to slow down the flow of water and use less, as well as preventing damage to the plant and the potting compost. The use of a watering-can rose will reduce wastage.

10. If using a sprinkler or a self-watering system, purchase a good-quality, non-kink hose and fit it with good fittings so that no leaks occur.

11. Consider using a trickle hose rather than sprinklers, as this directs water closer to the plants and therefore is more economical with water and less likely to miss a plant.

12. With large-scale watering, consider installing underground piping and computer-controlled sprinklers and other self-watering devices.

In some areas a licence is needed to use water in the garden, for which a fee is charged; most water companies now insist on a non-return valve being fitted to taps where hose-pipes are used to prevent return flow and possible contamination of the mains water supply. These are available from garden centres and shops.

CHAPTER SIX

Weeds and Weeding

Weeds mostly arrive in the spring when gardeners have more than enough to do, and then persist in staying through the summer and autumn when we would rather sit back and enjoy the fruits of our labours. By cultivating the soil we provide them with the ideal growing conditions – after all, what is a weed, other than a plant growing in the wrong place?

Some weeds have been around since the time of the dinosaurs – such as Mare's Tail (*Hippuris vulgaris*), which grew as giant trees, many hundreds of feet tall. If they have survived so long, we stand little chance of defeating them for good. We need every available technique to keep them under control.

Where do weeds come from?

It may seem, when we look at the weed-free surface of our soil in winter, that there are no weeds present, but of course there are. Many survive over winter as perennial roots growing below the soil surface, or as seed, lying on or just below the soil's surface, ready to germinate when triggered by the rising soil temperature in the spring.

The seeds may have been dropped from last year's crop or blown in by the wind from the surrounding area and there is little that can be done to stop this. Other seeds may have been brought to the surface by cultivation, after being dormant for many years; as the seed is brought closer to the soil surface it germinates under the influence of the higher temperature and light levels. Perennial weeds have roots that can grow and travel many yards underground with no respect for boundaries.

Garden plants, too, can be a problem; self-sown hardy annuals and invasive perennial plants will multiply, often to nuisance level, and may have to be treated as weeds.

The importance of controlling weeds when young

Of course, trying to prevent infestation in the first place is the best policy, and dealing with weeds when young, whether manually or with chemical weed-killers, is important. The control is always faster and more effective at the early stages of growth than when the weeds are well established. The principle of weeding is to starve the weed or to cut it off from its water or light source, and all weeding techniques set out to do this; the younger the plant, the sooner it will die. When chemical control is adopted, far better results are achieved when the weed is young because the chemical used can be more quickly absorbed through the young, active leaves, stems and roots.

Weed types

Before we attempt to eliminate the weeds in our gardens we should understand a little more about them. They can be divided into three groups, and each group requires a different approach as far as weeding is concerned.

Annual weeds

Annual weeds germinate from seed, mainly in the spring, but some continue to germinate in the summer and autumn, so a watch needs to be kept throughout the growing season and efforts made to control them.

Some weeds can grow, flower, seed and germinate more than once in the same year. Many can be cut off from their roots and still continue to grow, flower and seed, so they must be removed completely to prevent this.

There is a very large number of annual species; the following are the most common in gardens:

Annual Meadow-grass (*Poa annua*)
Bittercress (*Cardamine flexuosa*)
Chickweed (*Stellaria media*)
Dead Nettle (*Lamium*)
Groundsel (*Senecio vulgaris*)
Mayweed (*Tripleurospermum inodorum*)
Shepherd's Purse (*Capsella bursa-pastoris*)
Speedwell (*Veronica persica*)

The control of these weeds will be dealt with in the sections on manual and chemical control.

Perennial weeds
Although annual weeds are a nuisance, certain perennial weeds can be even more difficult to control. They have a network of very deep single tap roots or underground shoots with growth buds that can very rapidly form a new plant if even the smallest section is broken off the parent plant. These root systems grow very deep and are often out of the reach of manual cultivation; if just a small part is left in the ground at any reasonable depth, it will form roots and shoots, and grow. This ability has sustained these plants for thousands of years, so the problem faced by the gardener is by no means a small one. Methods of control will be dealt with shortly; if there is an overriding rule, it is that of perseverance and repeating of treatment until they are eliminated, or at least kept under control.

If you have these weeds in your garden, it is unwise to use a rotovator, as the rotating action of the blades chops perennial weed roots and underground shoots into very small pieces, so propagating them and *increasing* the infestation.

The most important perennial weeds are:

Bracken (*Pteridium aquilinum*)
Broad-leaved Dock (*Rumex obtusifolius*)
Clover (*Trifolium* spp.)
Couch Grass or Twitch (*Elymus repens*)
Creeping Buttercup (*Ranunculus repens*)
Creeping Thistle (*Cirsium arvense*)
Lawn Daisy (*Bellis perennis*)
Dandelion (*Taraxacum* spp.)
Ground Elder (*Aegopodium podagraria*)
Japanese Knotweed (*Polygonum cuspidatum*)
Large-leaved Convolvulus (*Calystegia sepium*)
Lesser Celandine (*Ranunculus ficaria*)
Mare's Tail or Horsetail (*Equisetum* and *Hippuris* spp.)
Perennial Nettle (*Urtica dioica*)
Rosebay Willowherb or Fireweed (*Epilobium angustifolium*) – also grows from windblown seeds
Small-leaved Convolvulus (*Convolvulus arvensis*)
Spear Thistle (*Cirsium vulgare*)

101

Problem woody plants

There are a number of woody plants, both native and introduced, that freely invade our gardens, given the chance.

By their very nature, being woody and having strong penetrating roots, they are difficult to eliminate, particularly if given time to become established.

In the main they are distributed by seed, either by the wind or by animals or birds eating them and depositing the seed in new locations in their droppings; hence they often grow along fences and hedgerows, or among other shrubs and trees where birds perch.

Because they are woody in nature and quick-growing they soon become established, so constant watch must be kept to stop them gaining a foothold and to avoid the greater effort which will be required later to dig them out.

The most important are:

Ash (*Fraxinus excelsior*)   Holly (*Ilex aquifolium*)
Bramble (*Rubus fruticosus*)   Ivy (*Hedera helix*)
Dog Rose (*Rosa canina*)   Sycamore (*Acer pseudoplatanus*)
Elder (*Sambucus nigra*)   Wild Cherry (*Prunus avium*)

MANUAL CONTROLS

If it is at all possible to avoid the use of chemicals – and I cannot remember when I last spent money on chemical weed control in my own garden – we should certainly do so, in order to protect the environment. In addition, manual weed control has many useful advantages for the plants we grow.

Hand weeding

This, at first sight, may seem self-explanatory and simple to do, but the following tips may prove useful.

I try to do the weeding just after rain – but when the foliage is dry – as the soil is looser then, and the roots are more easily separated from the soil. With annual and young perennial weeds, take hold of the weed as close to ground level as possible and feel with your fingers for the centre of the weed.

Once you have gained a grip, pull upwards. Normally it will come out in one go: if not, then re-grip and try again. In some cases loosening with a hand fork will be of assistance. Insert the fork centrally and as close to the weed as possible. Push it in to two thirds of its length and gently pull the handle back, away from the weed, while pulling the weed firmly upwards with your fingers. If this too fails to remove the weed, use a digging or border fork.

Whichever stage you reach, try not to separate the main or tap root of the weed from the top growth, as any root left in the soil may be able to regrow.

Always wear gloves when working with the soil. You should also have had a course of tetanus injections.

Weeds and the compost heap
Annual weeds are quite safe on compost heaps as long as the heap is constructed as suggested in Chapter 1. Even perennial weeds can be considered as long as the heap is large enough.

Hoeing
Hoeing is the mainstay of weed control in gardens, and no gardener should enter their garden without a hoe in their hands. By constant use of the hoe, all gardens can be kept almost weed-free. Hoeing works very well with annual weeds and if the job is done when the weeds are young, good long-term results can be achieved.

Hoeing mid-morning and allowing the afternoon sun to dry up the hoed-off weeds can often be enough to eliminate them. If, however, the soil or the weather is wet, the weeds should be raked up and removed, taking care not to remove too much of the topsoil with the weeds.

Hoeing off the leaves of perennial weeds so that they cannot function fully also works well. If repeated whenever the leaves show, the weeds will be slowly starved to death, but a number of hoeings will be required to achieve good long-term control.

Hoe types
There are two main types of hoe, the Dutch or push hoe and the draw or swan-necked hoe.

DUTCH OR PUSH HOE   The blade of the Dutch or push hoe is pushed forward just under the surface of the soil, cutting off the weeds as it does so. The advantage is that you work backwards so avoiding walking on the soil you have already worked. Of course, care must be taken not to damage the stems of the plants you wish to keep.

SWAN-NECKED OR DRAW HOE   This hoe is used with a light chopping action, slowly working forward over the area to be weeded. By using the hoe to one side of the body, depending on whether you are left- or right-handed, the problem of treading on the soil already cultivated is avoided. All weed groups can be dealt with using this tool, even, when young, those of a woody nature.

ONION HOE OR HAND HOE   This small hand-held hoe is ideal for working in confined spaces and is used in the same way as a swan-necked hoe. It is a tool I particularly like and have found most versatile.

Purchasing a hoe
Hoes come in a range of qualities and prices. It is important to choose one that will last for a long time. Never purchase a pressed tin type as these are of little use; look for a forged steel blade with a good strong, long, varnished handle. Stainless steel hoes are good, but they are much more expensive.

There are a number of adapted hoes on the market, but most are more costly than the basic type or work less efficiently in all but the best of soil conditions.

The advantages of hoeing
Hoeing has the added advantage of aerating the soil; by allowing air to enter the upper surface, it creates a layer of open aerated soil which acts as insulation, helps conserve soil moisture and keeps plant roots cool in summer.

Many soil pests that live just below the surface are exposed and duly dealt with by birds, and the appearance of the soil surface in general is improved, giving the garden a well-cared-for look.

Other weeding tools

There are two other useful weeding tools – the daisy grubber and the weed knife.

DAISY GRUBBER   This small hand tool has a handle, leverage point and two forked prongs; it is used for levering out individual weeds, particularly in lawns.

WEED KNIFE   This hand-held tool is L-shaped, with the upper arm being a handle and the lower one a sharpened blade. This blade can be inserted between paving and other restricted areas to remove the weeds that have established themselves.

Digging out

If hand weeding and hoeing fails, then forking over the infested area with a digging or border fork must be considered. Almost any weed can be dealt with in this way, but it is normally used for deep-rooted weeds such as Couch Grass and Ground Elder.

If this method is adopted it is important to make sure that the work is carried out thoroughly and all roots are removed, otherwise they will regrow. There is the added advantage that the soil is dug and aerated at the same time as the weeding.

Smothering

Smothering weed growth can be done in a number of ways; all entail covering the weeds to eliminate the light from the leaves of perennial weeds and to suppress the germination of seeds of all sorts, so starving them to death. The following methods can be used.

Mulching

Although mulching will not stop persistent perennial or problem weeds, it will suppress the growth of annual weeds, as well as setting up an ideal growing environment for plant roots and acting as a reservoir of plant food. Moisture and air is also retained and soils kept cool in hot summers. The layer of organic material must be at least 2–4 in (5–10 cm) deep and must cover the entire area to be effective.

Covering

Covering the area with an old carpet, carpet underlay or black polythene sheeting acts in the same way as a mulch and is equally good for both annual and perennial weeds. A great deal of work is now being carried out with both man-made and synthetic materials to produce breathing mulch materials that will allow rain to pass through, so ensuring replenishment of the moisture in the soil.

It is also possible with this method to grow plants through the material while the weeds are being controlled, but care must be taken to ensure that no weed gets a foothold at the base of any of the plants.

The cover normally needs to be in place for at least six spring or summer months if good control is to be achieved.

Plant growth

Planting crops of potatoes or large-flowering dahlias on newly cultivated soil can suppress the growth of annual weeds. The cultivation required to plant, grow and harvest the crop disturbs the roots of perennial weeds and prevents germination of seedlings.

Planning and planting

Planting to a detailed plan ensures that, after the first year, much of the area where weeds could establish is covered by the plants and no place is left for weeds to establish, so weed growth is suppressed.

Barriers

Perennial weeds that spread by producing an underground carpet of penetrating roots or shoots can be stopped by sinking a physical barrier into the ground. Until recently sheets of corrugated tin were used for this, but now black polythene sheeting has also become popular. It has the advantage of being flexible, so that it can be positioned around corners, and fewer joins are needed through which roots could grow and move beyond the barrier. Whichever is used, the minimum depth must be at least 30 in (80 cm) unless the weed is Ground Elder (*Aegopodium podagraria*) or Mare's Tail (*Hippuris vulgaris*), when a depth of 36 in (1 m) or more must be considered.

CHEMICAL CONTROL

First a word of caution. Chemical weed-killers are designed to destroy green plants, so if the powder, liquid or even the vapour of chemical weed-killers comes into contact with plants you want to keep, damage can be caused and is often terminal.

One other problem with chemical weed-killer is that many are introduced in the first instance for use in commercial horticulture or agriculture, and are then packaged for gardeners; because there is such a wide range of plants in our gardens, it is quite possible for damage to be caused to a specific group that has not been tested under the narrower monoculture of the commercial sectors.

A great deal of work is continually being carried out to make chemical weed-killers safer for the environment, but extreme care should always be taken in their use and storage – they should always be kept out of the reach of children and animals.

Legislation also states that no person not qualified or certified to apply weed-killers should apply them outside their own property, even if they are doing a good deed for the church or scouts' hut. There have been successful prosecutions under the law where this has occurred.

Also, anyone giving advice about the application of a specific chemical must be qualified and certified for the purpose, so I shall give no more than an outline of the types of chemical available and the ways in which they can be used, and will recommend no specific product or rate of application. This is legislation that I strongly agree with and abide by.

Always read the packet in advance of purchase, to ensure that the product is suitable for the intended purpose. Only take advice from those qualified to give it – the only sure source of information is the manufacturer's advice desk.

Kitting oneself out with protective clothing such as respiratory face-mask, eye goggles, rubber gloves and boots, and a set of waterproof leggings, jacket and hood, is advisable.

Used with the utmost care, chemical weed-killers do have a role to play in our fight against garden weeds.

Types of chemical weed-killers

Herbicides

These are intended to over-stimulate the growth activity of the leaf cells; when they are unable to produce more growth, the cells collapse, killing the weeds. To do this they use sunlight, so the stronger the sun, the quicker the effect.

They work well on annual weeds by killing the leaves, but the chemical is not passed down into the roots, so regrowth of perennials is not prevented. It can be argued that repeated applications will kill weeds in this group, but so does hoeing, which costs less.

Herbicidal weed-killers cannot be used on lawns as they kill all groups of plants, including grass.

Total weed-killers

SODIUM CHLORATE   This weed-killer has been used for many years; it remains active in the soil for months, if not years, and only becomes inactive when it is finally diluted into the soil moisture.

Thirty years ago sodium chlorate was treated with the greatest respect and only used as a last resort to weed large areas of driveways or to eliminate weeds from under the foundations of soon-to-be-constructed buildings.

The main problems are its longevity and the risk of damaging other areas and plants in close proximity.

In certain conditions it can be an oxygenating agent and fire-related accidents are reported annually, particularly in hot summers.

TOTAL WEED-KILLERS THAT WORK BY TRANSLICATION
Most of today's commercial weed-killers work by translication
of the chemical through the leaves and down into the roots,
where they kill and stop growth. Once they come into contact
with the soil they are said to become 'inactive' and 'safe'.

DEFOLIANTS   Tested in the Vietnam War, these weed-killers,
containing 24 D, kill by defoliating the weed, and killing the
stems and roots. They are very effective but may have side-
effects that we are not fully aware of; they should be used as a
last resort when manual control has failed.

PRE-EMERGENT WEED-KILLERS   These work by placing a
long-term barrier of weed-killing chemical just below the soil
surface – as seedlings germinate and come into contact with
the barrier they absorb it and are killed.

The range of plants not affected by these chemicals is
limited, so of the wide variety of plants in our gardens, many
may be at risk of damage if the directions are not closely
followed. The product is said to have some use in a mono-
planting of roses, but even here doubts may be raised.

WEED-KILLERS FOR PATHS   Path weed-killers are normally a
mixture of translicated and pre-emergent weed-killers, attack-
ing any foliage above ground and, in theory, forming a weed-
killer layer just below the surface. I cannot comment on them
as I use a hoe for the purpose and, between paving, a weed
knife.

LAWN WEED-KILLERS   Selective lawn weed-killers may have a
use for killing weeds and moss. Some are designed to kill specific
weeds, others are more general. However, there are some weeds,
such as chickweed, that require a specific lawn weed-killer, so
identification of the weed in the first place is important.

When weed-killer has been used, an area of bare soil is left,
in which weed seeds will fall, germinate and grow. To prevent
this, in April, once the lawn has been scarified, raked and all
dead material removed, sow the bare patches with good-quality
grass seed. This will grow and prevent further weed infestation,
as well as generally improving the texture of the turf.

Touch and spot weed-killers

There are 'touch' and 'spot' weed-killers that can be used to eradicate individual perennial weeds, but the use of the daisy grubber (p. 105) to lever out these weeds is often more effective.

Applying chemical weed-killers

After putting all the suggested precautions – see p. 198 – into effect, the following should also be considered:

1. Never spray in wind or even a very light breeze, as this may spread the weed-killer beyond the intended area.

2. Do not spray or apply weed-killers in hot sun as the liquid can evaporate; the ensuing vapour will spread upwards and if there is a breeze it will carry to surrounding plants, causing extensive damage in your own and neighbouring gardens.

3. Excessive rain after application may nullify the effects of the chemical and, in some cases, spread it beyond the treated area.

4. Spray open areas first, wait for results, and then spray closer to plants you do not want to damage.

5. Use a low-pressure sprayer or a watering-can with a weeding bar.

6. Consider whether you need a spray-guard for your sprayer to prevent drift and damage to surrounding plants.

7. Never leave made-up weed-killer in sprayers or watering-cans; dispose of it in line with the directions on the packet.

8. Have separate marked sprayers and watering-cans for applying weed-killers.

9. Have separate marked sprayers and watering-cans for applying lawn weed-killers.

10. Never walk from the sprayed area on to the lawn or other possibly susceptible areas, or trail used spraying equipment across them, as damage can be caused by the smallest amounts of residual weed-killer.

11. Keep children and pets out of sprayed areas for the times recommended on the product, and possibly longer.

12. Do not smoke, eat, drink or go to the toilet while spraying or applying weed-killers.

13. Wash hands and any contaminated skin as soon as possible after use and before smoking, eating or drinking.

14. Never store weed-killers out of their packets, as in an emergency this may be the only source of information for medical help.

15. Never use a weed-killer other than for the purpose stated on the packaging.

16. Always keep unused and stored weed-killers under lock and key, and inaccessible to children and pets.

17. Never dispose of chemically killed weed remains or grass mowings on to other areas of soil or compost heaps, as the chemical may stay active within the treated plant for some time.

18. Consider the cost of the treatment in financial and environmental terms.

19. Consider using a manual method as an alternative to a chemical weed-killer.

CHAPTER SEVEN

Propagation

For over twenty years, I was responsible for the propagation of a very wide range of plants in a commercial nursery, and even today I find the urge to start new plants into life is irresistible. But the main benefit is of course that the gardener can increase his plants at very little cost.

To pass on the full range of techniques of propagation would take a whole book, possibly several books, for each species and variety requires its own minor adjustments in such things as timing, watering and growing on. The gardener must observe the differences in the seasons, year by year, and adjust his technique accordingly. But even with experience on their side, professionals do not always get it right. No one should be disheartened by failure to propagate a particular plant; record what may have gone wrong and then attempt to put it right the following year.

Successful rooting is only the first stage – the art of growing plants on to establishment must also be carefully considered. It takes time for plants to grow, so time, patience, observation and technique are all part of the process of producing new plants. In the past a complete garden would often be propagated by the head gardener. There are a number of drawbacks, however: you can only propagate plants from your own garden or those of friends and there is always the danger of propagating diseased material, particularly plants affected by virus diseases, such as Daphnes. When you are successful, there is the problem of looking after the young plants and dealing with the surplus which so often occurs.

Despite the drawbacks, propagation is certainly worth the effort, and in the following notes I will attempt to pass on as much information as possible.

There are two basic methods of propagation:

1. Sexual propagation, or the raising of new plants from seed.
2. Vegetative propagation, or the raising of plants by using sections of plant growth and encouraging them to produce roots, as with cuttings and layering; by providing rootstocks, as in grafting and budding; or, as in the case of perennial plants, by dividing the roots.

Equipment

Before we look more closely at these two methods we should consider some of the equipment required.

Propagators

Propagators provide a controllable environment that can be used to ensure that the embryo plant has the very best conditions. They range from a simple plastic bag up to an electrically heated, computerized, thermostatically controlled growing room.

CLEAR OR OPAQUE PLASTIC BAGS

These are simply ordinary plastic bags, which can be used in two ways:
- Filled approximately one third full with a rooting medium; cutting are inserted directly into the rooting medium and the bag sealed.
- Seeds are sown or cuttings inserted into pots containing rooting medium; the plastic bag is placed over the top and secured by a rubber band, so achieving a protected propagating space.

While the use of plastic bags can work well, to my mind they are just a little too basic and the controlling of humidity is difficult.

PLASTIC BOTTLES

A clear one- or two-litre plastic soft-drink bottle, cut in half, can produce two very useful 'propagators' that can be used to cover the top of a pot of the same diameter. Good numbers of plants can be raised under these home-made propagators and, if the cap is kept, one half of the bottle even has the advantage

113

of an adjustable ventilator. They cost nothing, assuming the family consumes the contents in the first place.

OTHER UNHEATED PROPAGATORS

These consist of manufactured transparent tops, tailored to the size of small pots or standard or half-size seed trays, or multiples of these. They may be rigid or flimsy and I would chose the former for longevity, even though they are more expensive at the outset. They may be purchased with or without the pot or tray. The size of propagator you purchase will be dictated by the amount of propagation you intend to do and the flexibility you require.

HEATED PROPAGATORS

Base heat is often required to encourage seed germination and, in a few cases, to help the formation of roots on cuttings. There are three types of heated propagators.

The simplest and possibly the most cost-effective is the *electrically heated base tray*. Manufactured in the standard seed-tray size or in multiples of this, they are normally not temperature-controlled but hold a constant soil temperature of 62–65°F (16.5–18°C). Unheated propagators are simply stood on the tray and gain the heat they require through the base.

There are also *seed trays with heating elements*. The heating element is encased in a standard single or double plastic seed tray with a clear ridged plastic top. They give a soil temperature of 62–65°F (16.5–18°C). These do not normally have any other temperature control.

Thermostatically controlled propagators are heated propagators with thermostats included; they can provide and maintain a particular level of soil temperature as required, and can be pre-set. They are normally in double seed-tray sizes, as the expense of fitting the controls to a single-size propagator is felt to be non-commercial. This type of propagator has the potential of a managed temperature that can be controlled, which makes them more flexible, but this degree of control may only be required for propagating a limited number of plants.

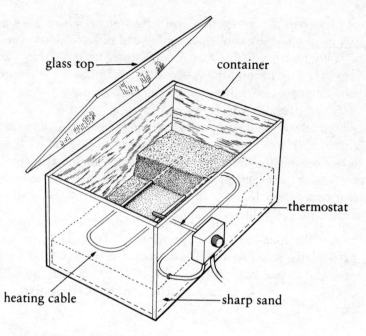

glass top
container
thermostat
heating cable
sharp sand

10. Home-made propagation case

BUILDING YOUR OWN THERMOSTATICALLY CONTROLLED PROPAGATOR

If serious numbers of plants are to be produced on a semi-commercial scale it may be worthwhile building a controlled unit in the greenhouse where the scope of size and control are endless. The construction could be as follows:

1. On the greenhouse bench, a box, normally of timber, is built with sides at least 12 in (30 cm) deep; it is designed to support a clear glass or plastic top cover.

2. The greenhouse staging bottom of the box is lined with a rot-proof material and a 3 in (8 cm) deep layer of sharp sand spread over it.

3. An electrically heated warming cable and thermostat are installed in the sand according to the manufacturer's instructions.

4. At this stage it is worth considering and installing, if

115

required, an automatic mist watering system. These units are plumbed into the main water supply and provide cuttings with a continuous very fine mist of moisture, never letting them dry out, so widening the range of species that can be propagated and possibly raising the overall success rate.

5. A further 3–4 in (8–10 cm) layer of sharp sand is then placed on top of the heating cables and the propagator is ready for use. It may be covered with clear plastic or glass, or opaque plastic; alternatively it may have no cover at all – the choice will depend on experience and the type of plants being propagated.

NB. The advice of a qualified electrician must be sought to ensure the long-term safe operation of electrical equipment, particularly when it is used in association with water; as the propagator will require electricity to run it, a fully qualified electrician should be employed to ensure the installation is safe.

Rooting medium
FOR CUTTINGS

Personally I prefer sharp or silver sand as the rooting medium for the majority of cuttings with the exception of leaf cuttings, where a peat-based potting compost appears to give better results. Sharp sand is the one I normally use, and silver sand when sharp sand is unavailable.

It might be asked where the plant obtains its food, as sand is an inert substance. In fact, the plant needs no feeding in the early stages of root development, and the presence of food may lead to rotting of the cutting, or die-back.

The main benefit of sharp sand is in its free-draining properties, which makes it ideal for propagation: it never becomes waterlogged and therefore cuttings are not subject to constant water at their bases before the roots are formed. Nor, when the first fragile roots appear, is there a fear of suffocation from waterlogging, again a principal cause of failure. The new roots are encouraged to grow well and form a strong network, putting the new plant in a strong position to grow away when potted on.

The temperature of the rooting medium stays almost constant and is normally cool but not cold, again a good rooting environment. Alternatively, where an individual species requires more heat, the sharp sand responds quickly to outside basal heat, as in a heated propagator.

Sharp sand is also very forgiving if watering mistakes are made, making it an ideal rooting medium for the beginner.

FOR SEED SOWING

There is a wide range of potting composts formulated for seed sowing.

John Innes Seed-sowing Compost gives a steady, uniform germination and growth rate. The seed formulation can be used for all seeds except possibly for Begonias and Primulas, where a peat-based compost might be more successful.

John Innes Seed and Potting Compost No. 1 is useful for sowing larger seeds such as Beans, Sweet Corn and Sweet Peas, as it contains more of the nutrients that the young seedlings require once they have formed their first true leaves. Always look for the John Innes Manufacturers' Association mark quality and possibly avoid the so-called John Innes Universal Composts for propagation purposes.

There is a very wide choice of *peat-based seed-sowing composts*, as almost every peat producer and packager offers their own formulation, which in many cases may simply be a bag of milled peat, with or without added plant foods.

Levington is possibly the best-known peat-based compost and is commonly used in commercial growing, but it may be difficult for the home propagator to manage, either drying out too quickly or easily becoming waterlogged. Germination and growth is fast and care must be taken to ensure that the plants do not 'bolt', or in other words become elongated and weak in their constitution.

Although peat-based, *J. Arthur Bower's Seed and Potting Compost*, with its added fine clay, seems to me to be ideal for raising all types of seedlings. Germination is fast but not to the extent of leading to weak growth. It is kind to those with little time as it dries out slowly and is easy to re-wet, and also helps propagation by being free-draining.

Peat and conservation

As a plant lover I, as much as any other, believe in conservation but I feel that at the present time it is still necessary to use peat in potting composts, as long as it is not harvested from sensitive conservation sites. The alternatives require a great deal more research before they can reach the success rates of potting and seed-sowing composts containing peat.

Using seed-sowing compost

Keep at room temperature for at least a fortnight before using, as cold compost can delay germination and may rot seeds before they can germinate.

Never alter the formula of the compost unless the product specifically suggests you should do so for a particular crop, as much research has gone into optimizing the formula.

Try to purchase no more than you need for one season as old compost loses its nutrients and can become sour and cause failure in germination if kept for longer than six to nine months. Always purchase compost in clean, freshly printed bags, as this normally indicates the new season's stock.

If possible always purchase from retailers who store and sell the compost from under cover; avoid those who do not.

Many retailers offer discounted prices for compost in early winter when they take in new stock in bulk and it may be worth purchasing at that time to save money.

Preparing the sowing or rooting medium

With both seeds and cuttings the overriding factor is correct moisture level. The compost should be wetted before use, ensuring that it is not over-wet or too dry.

When wetting the compost always use a fine watering-can with a rose to disperse the supply and prevent localized build-ups of water. Standing the filled watering-can at room temperature for a few hours before watering will also help with seed germination and root development.

Never recycle the propagating soil or sand as it may well carry within it spores of the damping-off fungus, which can play havoc with the next batch of plants being propagated.

VEGETATIVE PROPAGATION

Before we look at the various techniques of taking cuttings we should take a moment to understand how a cutting works. The whole object of taking a cutting – hardwood, semi-ripe, softwood, leaf or root cutting – is to create a new plant by vegetative propagation that is in every way identical to its parent, and to encourage roots to form where, at the time of preparing the cutting, none exist.

In every shoot, stem or branch there is a layer of tissue just below the skin or bark called the cambium layer. This cambium layer is the growth or cell-producing part of the plant; twice a year, once in the spring and again in the autumn, it generates the ring of new growth which we can observe as the annual growth rings in the trunk of a tree which has been cut down.

If we take a young shoot and lightly scratch the skin, we should be able to see the cambium layer just below the skin, showing as a thin, dark green layer of tissue.

When the cutting is taken from its parent and inserted into soil, it has no roots and therefore no long-term way of obtaining its own water supply from the surrounding soil. If the conditions are right, this shock stimulates the cells in the cambium layer to generate energy by using the starch stored within itself. The starch is turned into sugar or glucose, the cells in the cambium feed on this sugar and the cutting is encouraged to turn its growth potential to the formation of new roots. Of course, if the cutting has foliage this produces a certain amount of sugar by using sunlight and carbon dioxide from the air, further assisting rooting.

To balance the potential shortfall of starch and sugar in cuttings with no foliage, we make them longer and start them off in the early spring, just before growth starts, when they will have the best chance of developing a root system. An application of hormone rooting powder, as we will see in a moment, can also help stimulate the root development in both groups.

As roots grow from material that has a limited amount of

energy and time to produce roots, all our efforts are directed to providing the ideal conditions for rooting to take place.

Not all plants will produce roots on cuttings and for these other vegetative propagation methods, such as layering, division, grafting and budding, have to be used, and we will look at these later.

For all the different methods of taking cuttings you will need – in addition to rooting medium and propagators – rooting hormone, knives, pots and trays.

Rooting hormone

With some types of cuttings it is necessary to assist with the breaking down of the outer skin of the cutting so that the roots that form at the cambium layer can grow through; rooting hormone is a weak acid and this is the first role it plays.

Its second role is to feed the plant cells at the cambium layer, so helping them to produce more quickly the cells that will form the roots.

A number of cuttings do not require rooting hormone, but it is best to use it on all cuttings until more experience has been gained.

Personally I dislike the use of the liquid and gel types of rooting hormone as I feel the action of the hormone in breaking down the skin should be a steady process, which is better achieved with the powder types.

Many people use the powder directly from the container it is supplied in; I prefer not to do this, as it can lead to the contamination of the remaining powder by water, turning it solid and therefore making it useless for the future. Although there is no known risk in using rooting hormone, I always wear plastic gloves for safety's sake and decant a small amount of the hormone powder into a shallow saucer.

A second saucer is filled with tap water. The bottom $\frac{1}{2}$ in (1 cm) of the cutting is rolled in the water and any surplus water knocked off before rolling the cutting in the hormone powder contained in the other saucer. This ensures that the base of the cutting is moist and the hormone powder is spread evenly over its surface and adheres to it.

By using this method any chance of the rooting hormone not becoming moist when the cutting is inserted into the rooting medium is avoided. Moisture activates the acid and the cutting's skin is broken down for the roots to penetrate.

Secateurs and knives

Secateurs and knives are possibly the most important propagation tools. They must be sharp and in good order, because if the cuts made are not smooth and clean, the cuttings will be at a disadvantage when it comes to rooting. The plant cells at the cambium will have difficulty in closing the wound made when taking the cutting and will not be able to form a callous, slowing down the first stage of rooting.

Many gardeners keep a set of knives and secateurs specially for the job of taking cuttings, and others for grafting.

The knife is probably the best tool to take cuttings with but the inexperienced propagator may prefer secateurs; these cause no harm to most cuttings, as long as they are sharp.

The anvil (rollcut) type of secateurs is best, as the action of the cutting blade cutting down on to the anvil is ideal for taking cuttings.

Choose a knife with a good-quality steel blade; the blade can be either straight or curved.

The knife or secateurs need to be regularly sharpened as described in Chapter 8.

When using sharp tools great care must be taken, not only when working with them, but in the way they are stored. Many accidents are caused by knives and secateurs lurking unseen amongst the discarded plant material.

At the end of each individual batch of cuttings it is advisable to clean cutting tools with strong soapy water or household disinfectant to prevent possible cross-contamination of fungus diseases between different batches of cuttings.

Pots and trays

New plastic pots and trays and yoghurt and margarine tubs are equally suitable for propagation as long as the following rules are borne in mind:

1. All pots and trays must be clean to prevent contamination from fungus diseases; washing with warm soapy water or household disinfectant is advisable for used pots or trays.

2. The chosen container must be of a suitable depth to accommodate the length of the cutting comfortably and leave room for the roots to develop.

3. In the garden, small numbers of cuttings will be taken so the small and medium-sized pots and trays may well be the most useful.

4. Unused pots and trays should be stored out of the propagation area, again to prevent cross-contamination of fungus diseases.

Hardwood cuttings

Hardwood cuttings are possibly the easiest cuttings to take; sharp secateurs are usually chosen for this work.

From mid autumn to early spring, 10–12 in (25–30 cm) long cuttings are cut from deciduous shoots produced in the previous summer. Depending on the species a number of cuttings can be taken from each length of shoot. It is best to choose shoots that are about the diameter of a pencil and above, and discard any that are diseased or damaged in any way. The top 12 in (30 cm) of the shoot is avoided, as are any which may have started to branch and form side shoots.

The top of the cutting is cut just above a bud with a cut sloping away from the bud at an angle of 35°; the bottom end is cut square. As well as encouraging the rain to run off the top of the cutting, the sloping cut identifies it as the top.

Evergreens such as Aucuba (Spotted Laurel), *Euonymus japonica* (Japanese Euonymus), Griselinia, *Prunus laurocerasus* (Cherry Laurel) and *Prunus lusitanica* (Portugal Laurel) can be propagated by hardwood cuttings, where, because they are evergreen, the top two leaves are left on but are reduced in size to cut down moisture loss. Size, time of preparation and growing on are the same as for deciduous hardwood cuttings.

Gooseberries and Red and White Currants are also grown from hardwood cuttings, but are made not less than 12 in (30

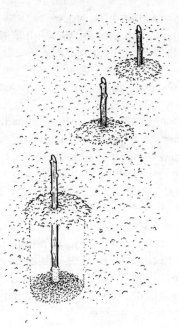

11. Hardwood cuttings

cm) long, with all but the top three buds on the cutting removed with a knife so that when the cutting grows it will form a clearly defined stem (or 'leg').

All hardwood cuttings prepared before early spring are tied in bundles of not more than twenty, keeping the bottom ends level and tying them tightly with string 7–9 in (17–23 cm) from the bottom and of course labelling them so they can be identified later. Early spring cuttings can be prepared and lined out in their rooting positions as soon as taken.

The bundles are then placed upright in trenches 5–6 in (12–15 cm) deep, dug in cultivated soil. Normally this is in the vegetable garden or in an area put to one side as a nursery or propagation bed. They are left there until March when the next stage of growing on is carried out.

In early spring the cuttings can be planted out to root, either in their final positions or in trenches.

IN THE FINAL GROWING POSITIONS

They can be planted *in situ* in their final growing positions, single or double digging the soil thoroughly first. A hole is then dug out with a trowel, 6–8 in (15–20 cm) deep and 3–4 in (8–10 cm) in diameter, in the bottom of which a handful of sharp sand is placed.

The bottom 1–2 in (3–5 cm) of each cutting is treated with rooting hormone and inserted upright with the sloping top end uppermost so that, when the hole is filled in, 3–5 in (8–12 cm) of the cutting is protruding above the soil surface. Normally three cuttings are inserted, 12–18 in (30–50 cm) apart, at any one location, to allow for some failures.

The cuttings are left until mid to late autumn, only being watered in very dry weather. They should also, of course, be kept weed-free. By this time there will be definite signs of new growth in the form of shoots and leaves; the strongest-growing rooted cutting is then chosen and the remaining ones dug up and used elsewhere if required.

IN TRENCHES

Cuttings are placed in rows into trenches in cultivated soil into which moderate amounts of organic material have been added. The trenches are made 7–9 in (17–23 cm) deep, and a 1–2 in (3–5 cm) layer of sharp sand placed in the bottom. The bottom 1 in (3 cm) of the cuttings is treated with rooting hormone and pushed, sloping end uppermost, upright into the sharp sand with about 3–4 in (8–10 cm) protruding above the soil surface. The trench is then filled in.

The cuttings are left in the rooting trench until the following mid to late autumn when they are dug up and planted into their final planting positions.

In both cases, the cuttings are watered in dry weather throughout the summer and kept weed-free. In the following year in early spring all the previous season's growth made by the cutting is cut back to within 2–3 in (5–8 cm) of its origin to form a bushy young plant. As the shrub grows it is pruned as recommended in Chapter 8.

Plants which can be propagated by hardwood cuttings

TREES

Populus, all varieties except *P. lasiocarpa* (Poplar)

Prunus cerasifera 'Nigra', and all varieties in the ornamental plum group except *P.* × *blireana* (Ornamental Purple Plum)

Salix varieties (Willow)

SHRUBS

Abelia varieties* (Abelia)

Artemisia varieties (Southernwood)

Aucuba varieties * (Spotted Laurel)

Berberis, strong-growing varieties * (Barberry)

Buddleja varieties (Butterfly Bush)

Caryopteris varieties (Blue Spiraea)

Ceanothus varieties, deciduous forms only (California Lilac)

Chaenomeles varieties (Ornamental Quince)

Cornus alba varieties (Red-barked Dogwood)

C. stolonifera varieties (Yellow-stemmed Dogwood)

Deutzia varieties (Deutzia)

Diervilla varieties (Bush Honeysuckle)

Escallonia varieties* (Escallonia)

Euonymus europaeus varieties (Spindle)

E. japonicus varieties* (Japanese Euonymus)

Griselinia varieties* (Broadleaf)

Hydrangea paniculata varieties (Panick Hydrangea)

Hypericum varieties (St John's Wort, Rose of Sharon)

Jasminum nudiflorum varieties (Shrubby Jasmine)

Kerria japonica varieties (Bachelor's Buttons)

Kolkwitzia amabilis varieties (Beauty Bush)

Lavatera varieties (Tree Mallow)

Ligustrum varieties* (Ornamental Privet)

Lonicera varieties (Shrubby Honeysuckle)

Neillia thibetica (Neillia)

Philadelphus varieties (Mock Orange)

Physocarpus varieties (Nine-bark)

Potentilla, strong-growing varieties (Shrubby Cinquefoil)

Prunus laurocerasus varieties* (Cherry Laurel)

P. lusitanica varieties* (Portugal Laurel)

Rhodotypos scandens (White Jew's Mallow)

Ribes varieties (Flowering Currant)

Rosmarinus varieties* (Rosemary)

Rubus, shrubby varieties (Flowering Bramble)

Salix varieties (Willow)

Spiraea varieties (Spiraea)

Stephanandra varieties (Stephanandra)

Tamarix varieties (Tamarisk)
Weigela varieties (Weigela)

CLIMBERS
Celastrus orbiculatus (Staff
   Vine)
Jasminum varieties (Jasmine)
Lonicera, climbing varieties
   (Honeysuckle)
Lycium varieties (Duke of
   Argyll's Tea Tree)
Polygonum baldschuanicum
   varieties (Russian Vine)
Solanum jasminoides varieties
   (Potato Vine)

ROSES
Shrub Rose varieties
Species Rose varieties
Climber varieties
Rambler varieties
Hybrid Tea, strong-growing
   varieties
Floribunda, strong-growing
   varieties

SOFT FRUIT
Gooseberry varieties
Red, White and Black Currants,
   and some hybrid berry
   varieties

* Indicates evergreen species where the hardwood cutting should be taken
with its top two or three leaves intact and the rest removed.

Softwood cuttings

Softwood cuttings are used primarily for the propagation
of soft-wooded plants such as Geraniums and Fuchsias or
for certain plants, such as Rosmarinus (Rosemary), Salvia
(Sage) and Lavandula (Lavender), at a soft stage in their
development.

It is an important method and is used for a very wide-
ranging selection of plants, grown both indoors and outdoors.
For this reason the timing of preparing the cuttings is widely
spread but the following can be used as a guide:

• Soft, woody-stemmed, tender plants such as Geranium, Fuchsia, Argyranthemum (Marguerite), Helichrysum (Curry
  Plant), and Felicia (Blue Marguerite); and house and conservatory plants with the same soft woody characteristics,
  can be successfully propagated from early spring onwards,
  and again in midsummer for a source of plants to overwinter
  under cover.

126

- Some hardy herbs and shrubs such as Salvia (Sage), Rosmarinus (Rosemary), Helichrysum (Curry Plant), Hebe (Veronica), Vinca (Periwinkle) and Lavatera (Tree Mallow) can be propagated from softwood cuttings from mid to late spring.
- Commercially, some plants, particularly Azaleas, are grown under protection to encourage them to make growth earlier in the spring and the resulting induced growth is used for softwood cuttings in mid to late spring.

In fact if the conditions are right, a wide range of plants can be propagated by softwood cuttings; however, as we look into other cutting methods we will discover that there may be more reliable ways.

Once suitable disease-free stock has been located, 3–6 in (8–15 cm) shoots of the current season's growth, produced in the late winter to early summer period, are removed once they have become reasonably firm in their constitution; they must then be kept moist throughout the preparation process.

The lowest point is cut cleanly directly below a leaf joint with a sharp knife or secateurs, at an angle of 35°.

There are two different leaf formations, opposite or alternate, depending on the species. The first pair of leaves (opposite) or single (alternate) leaf is removed in the second case, the next leaf is also removed. Remove the leaves as close to the shoot as possible without damaging the buds, which are situated at the point where the leaf stalk joins the shoot.

A cut, again at 35°, is made above the next pair of leaves or, in the single leaf formation, above the next two leaves. If the remaining leaves are more than 1 in (3 cm) long, they are cut in half, leaving the half closest to the shoot intact. This is done to keep the moisture loss from the leaf to a minimum and give the cutting every chance to root before dehydrating.

The finished cutting may appear to be much smaller than those normally taken by the amateur but the object is to reduce the trauma of propagation to a minimum and thereby reduce the possible losses. The total length of the cutting is controlled by the distance between each leaf formation on the stem, so a Lavandula (Lavender) cutting may only be 1 in

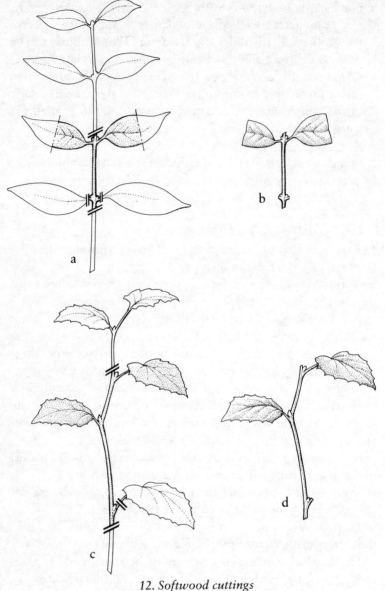

12. *Softwood cuttings*
(a) *The selected shoot prior to preparation* (leaves opposite)
(b) *The finished cutting* (leaves opposite)
(c) *The selected shoot prior to preparation* (leaves alternate)
(d) *The finished cutting* (leaves alternate)

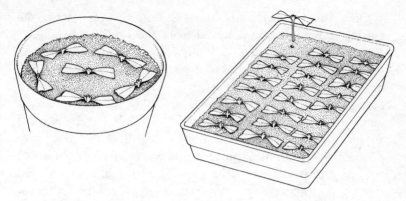

13. Softwood cuttings inserted into trays or pots

(3 cm) or so long, whereas a strong-growing Geranium can be as much as 4 in (10 cm).

The bottom $\frac{1}{2}$–1 in (1–3 cm) of the prepared cutting is rolled in water and then in rooting hormone powder before being inserted into pots or trays containing moist sharp sand.

The cuttings are inserted into the trays with their leaves all facing in one direction; alternatively five to six cuttings $\frac{1}{2}$ in (1 cm) long can be inserted around the edge of a 5 in (12 cm) diameter pot with one or two more in the centre. The base of the pair or first single leaf should touch the surface of the rooting medium.

Most softwood cuttings should now be placed under a propagator to help control their environment, labelled with their name, date of preparation and, possibly, origin.

The propagator is shaded with newspaper or other material for up to fourteen days and, if required, the cuttings are watered once or twice a day, using a watering-can with a very fine rose. This is important, to prevent waterlogging, and only the minimum of water required should be given.

Damping off can be a problem at this stage and, to prevent it, a systemic fungicide should be added to the first or second watering according to the manufacturer's instructions.

Any propagator vents should be kept closed for seven days and a watch must be kept for the first signs of rooting – new growths appearing from the buds at the joint where the remaining leaves join the cutting.

129

Once these growths are about $\frac{3}{4}$–1 in (2–3 cm) long, the cutting is ready to be removed from the rooting medium. It should be removed very carefully, doing as little damage as possible to the new, fragile root system. They are then potted on into 3–4 in (8–10 cm) pots; I would use J. Arthur Bower's Seed and Potting Compost for this, but other peat-based composts can be considered.

During the rooting period, some, if not all, of the leaves may drop off; this is not a problem, indeed it is often a sign of rooting and is caused by the swelling of the growth buds on the cutting forcing off the old leaves. Any leaves that fall must be removed as soon as possible to prevent the spread of fungus diseases, which could form on the decaying material.

After four to six weeks the new plants can be planted out in their final growing positions; if outdoors, only after all likelihood of frosts has passed.

House-plants propagated by this method will require potting on into larger pots as they develop to ensure their continued growth.

Semi-ripe cuttings

Semi-ripe cuttings are prepared and rooted in the same way as softwood cuttings, the only difference being that the growth used is more mature, or ripe; the bulk of these cuttings are taken in late spring to midsummer, after which time the growth used is normally too mature for rooting to take place easily, although it is not impossible.

The shoots chosen for propagation will have been produced from between late winter and early spring to the time of removal from the parent plant.

Many shrubs, climbing plants and a small number of trees are propagated by semi-ripe cuttings.

Rooting takes longer with some species, up to ten weeks or more, so more patience is required than with softwood cuttings.

Once the cuttings show signs of rooting, producing new shoots from the buds, the pots or trays can be removed from the propagator and stood in a cold frame or cold greenhouse until the following mid to late spring; during this time they do not require any fertilizer but they are kept watered as required. (All of the deciduous species will lose their leaves, as will some of the evergreens, but this is normally not a sign of a problem.) They are then carefully removed from the rooting medium and potted individually into 3–4 in (8–10 cm) pots, using J. Arthur Bower's Seed and Potting Compost or an alternative peat-based potting compost.

They can then be stood outside in a sheltered corner of the garden and grown on until the following spring, when any growth is pruned hard back to within 2 in (5 cm) of its origin, before finally being planted out into their permanent growing position.

The following plants can be propagated from semi-ripe cuttings.

TREES

Acacia varieties (Wattle)
Acer negundo varieties (Box Maple)
Amelanchier varieties (Snowy Mespilus)
Arbutus varieties (Strawberry Tree)
Magnolia varieties (Magnolia)
Morus nigra (Common or Black Mulberry)
Nyssa sylvatica (Black Gum)
Oxydendrum arboreum (Sorrel Tree)
Parrotia persica (Persian Parrotia)
Populus varieties except *P. lasiocarpa* (Poplar)
Prunus, plum varieties except *P. × blireana* (Purple Plum)
Salix varieties (Willow)
Stuartia varieties (Stuartia)
Styrax varieties (Japanese Snowbell)

SHRUBS

Abelia varieties (Abelia)
Abeliophyllum distichum (Korean Abelia-leaf)
Abutilon varieties (Trailing Abutilon)
Acanthopanax varieties (Five-leaf Aralia)
Amorpha varieties (False Indigo)
Andromeda varieties (Bog Rosemary)
Arctostaphylos varieties (Red Bearberry)
Aronia varieties (Red Chokeberry)
Atriplex varieties (Tree Purslane, Salt Bush)
Aucuba varieties (Spotted Laurel)
Azalea, see Rhododendron
Azara varieties (Azara)
Berberis varieties (Barberry)
Buddleja varieties (Butterfly Bush)

Bupleurum varieties (Bupleurum)

Buxus varieties (Common Box)

Callicarpa varieties (Beauty Berry)

Callistemon varieties (Australian Bottle Brush)

Camellia varieties (Camellia)

Carpenteria californica (Carpenteria)

Caryopteris varieties (Blue Spiraea)

Cassinia varieties (Golden Heather)

Ceanothus, both evergreen and deciduous varieties (California Lilac)

Ceratostigma varieties (Shrubby Plumbago)

Chaenomeles varieties (Ornamental Quince)

Chimonanthus varieties (Fragrant Wintersweet)

Cistus varieties (Rock Rose)

Clethra varieties (Summersweet Clethra)

Colletia varieties (Anchor Plant)

Colutea varieties (Bladder Senna)

Cornus alba varieties (Red-barked Dogwood)

C. *kousa* varieties (Chinese Dogwood)

C. *mas* varieties (Cornelian Cherry)

C. *stolonifera* varieties (Yellow-stemmed Dogwood)

Corokia varieties (Wire-netting Bush)

Coronilla varieties (Coronilla)

Corynabutilon varieties (Flowering Maple)

Cotoneaster varieties (Cotoneaster)

Crinodendron varieties (Lantern Tree)

Cytisus varieties (Broom)

Daphne varieties (Daphne)

Desfontainia varieties (Desfontainia)

Deutzia varieties (Deutzia)

Diervilla varieties (Diervilla)

Dipelta varieties (Dipelta)

Elaeagnus, both evergreen and deciduous varieties (Elaeagnus)

Elsholtzia stauntonii (Mint Bush)

Embothrium varieties (Chilean Fire Bush)

Escallonia varieties (Escallonia)

Eucryphia varieties (Brush Bush)

Euonymus, both evergreen and deciduous varieties (Spindle)

Exochorda varieties (Pearl Bush)

Fabiana varieties (False Heath)

× Fatshedera varieties (Aralia Ivy)

Fatsia varieties (Castor Oil Plant)

Feijoa varieties (Guava)

Forsythia varieties (Golden Ball)

Fothergilla varieties (Fothergilla)

Fremontodendron varieties (Fremontia)

Fuchsia, hardy forms (Hardy Fuchsia)

Garrya varieties (Tassel Bush)

Genista varieties (Spanish Gorse)

Griselinia varieties (Broadleaf)

Halesia varieties (Mountain Silverbell)

× Halimiocistus varieties
(Halimiocistus)

Halimium varities (Halimium)

Hebe varieties (Veronica)

Hedera varieties (Ivy)

Helianthemum varieties (Rock
Rose)

Hydrangea arborescens varieties
(Smooth Hydrangea)

H. aspera varieties (Rough-
leaved Hydrangea)

H. macrophylla, Hortensia
varieties (Big-leaf or Mop-
headed Hydrangea)

H. macrophylla, Lacecap
varieties (Lacecap Hydrangea)

H. paniculata varieties (Panick
Hydrangea)

H. quercifolia varieties (Oak-leaf
Hydrangea)

H. sargentiana varieties (Sargent's
Hydrangea)

H. serrata varieties

H. villosa varieties

Hypericum varieties (Rose of
Sharon, St John's Wort)

Ilex × altaclarensis varieties
(Altaclar Holly)

I. aquifolium varieties (Common
Holly)

I. crenata varieties (Box-leaved
Holly)

I. verticillata varieties
(Winterberry)

Indigofera varieties (Indigo
Bush)

Itea ilicifolia (Holly-leaf
Sweetspire)

I. virginica (Virginia Sweetspire)

Jasminum, shrubby forms
(Shrubby Jasmine)

Kalmia latifolia (Calico Bush)

Kerria varieties (Jew's Mallow)

Kolkwitzia varieties (Beauty
Bush)

Lavandula varieties (Lavender)

Leptospermum varieties
(Manuka)

Lespedeza varieties (Thunberg
Lespedeza)

Leucothoë varieties (Drooping
Leucothoë)

Ligustrum, both evergreen and
deciduous varieties (Privet)

Lomatia varieties (Lomatia)

Lonicera, shrubby forms
(Shrubby Honeysuckle)

Lycium varieties (Duke of
Argyll's Tea Tree)

× *Mahoberberis aquisargentii*
(Mahoberberis)

Myrtus varieties (Myrtle)

Neillia thibetica (Neillia)

Olearia varieties (Daisy Bush)

Osmanthus varieties (Sweet
Olive)

Ozothamnus varieties
(Ozothamnus)

Palurius spina-christi (Christ's
Thorn)

Pernettya varieties (Pernettya)

Philadelphus varieties (Mock
Orange)

Phillyrea varieties (Jasmine Box)

Photinia varieties (Chinese
Hawthorn)

Phygelius varieties (Cape
Figwort)

Pieris varieties (Lily of the Valley
Shrub)

Pittosporum varieties
(Parchment Bark)

Potentilla varieties (Shrubby Cinquefoil)

Prunus, shrubby forms (Cherry)

Pyracantha varieties (Firethorn)

Rhamnus, both evergreen and deciduous varieties (Buckthorn)

Rhododendron, dwarf forms and tall-growing varieties (Azalea)

Rosmarinus varieties (Rosemary)

Rubus, shrubby varieties (Flowering Bramble)

Sarcococca varieties (Christmas Box)

Senecio varieties (Shrubby Ragwort)

Skimmia varieties (Skimmia)

Sophora, shrubby varieties (New Zealand Kowhai)

Spartium junceum varieties (Spanish Broom)

Spiraea varieties (Spiraea)

Stachyurus varieties (Stachyrus)

Staphylea varieties (Bladdernut)

Stephanandra varieties (Stephanandra)

Symphoricarpos varieties (Snowberry)

Tamarix varieties (Tamarisk)

Ulex varieties (Furze, Gorse)

Vaccinium varieties (Blueberry)

Viburnum, apart from those varieties that are grafted (see 'Grafting', p. 165) (Viburnum)

Weigela varieties (Weigela)

Zenobia varieties (Dusty Zenobia)

CLIMBERS

Akebia quinata (Chocolate Vine)

Ampelopsis varieties (Pepper Vine)

Aristolochia sipho (Dutchman's Pipe)

Billardiera longiflora (Apple Berry)

Campsis varieties (Trumpet Creeper)

Celastrus orbiculatus (Staff Vine)

Decumaria barbara (Decumaria)

Hydrangea petiolaris (Climbing Hydrangea)

Passiflora varieties (Passion Flower)

Pileostegia viburnoides (Climbing Viburnum)

Polygonum baldschuanicum (Russian Vine)

Schisandra varieties (Schisandra)

Schizophragma varieties (Japanese Hydrangea Vine)

Solanum jasminoides varieties (Potato Vine)

Sollya fusiformis (Australian Bluebell Creeper)

Stauntonia hexaphylla (Stauntonia)

Trachelospermum varieties (Chinese Jasmine)

ROSES

Strong-growing varieties of Climbing and Rambling Roses

Strong-growing varieties of Hybrid Tea and Floribunda Roses

Strong-growing varieties of Species and Old-fashioned Roses

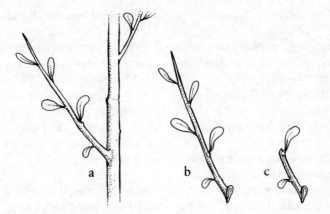

14. Semi-ripe cutting with a heel   (a) Shoot prior to preparation
(b) Removed selected shoot   (c) Finished cutting

Semi-ripe cuttings taken with a heel

Some evergreen shrubs can be slow and difficult to root as
standard semi-ripe cuttings so taking them with a 'heel' is
recommended – the heel is a small section of last year's shoot.
Whereas soft and semi-ripe cuttings are taken from current
season's wood, these cuttings are side shoots of the current
season's growth removed, with a heel, from the point where
they join the previous year's growth.

This heel is trimmed to only $\frac{1}{4}$–$\frac{1}{2}$ in (5–10 mm) or so long
and wide. The cutting is then prepared as for soft and semi-
ripe cuttings and treated the same way throughout its rooting
and growing process.

The following evergreen shrubs can be propagated from
semi-ripe cuttings taken with a heel:

Aucuba varieties (Spotted
   Laurel)
Azalea, see Rhododendron
Azara varieties (Azara)
Berberis varieties (Barberry)
Camellia varieties
   (Camellia)
Carpenteria varieties
   (Carpenteria)

Ceanothus varieties (California
   Lilac)
Cotoneaster varieties
   (Cotoneaster)
Crinodendron varieties (Lantern
   Tree)
Daphne varieties (Daphne)
Desfontainia spinosa
   (Desfontainia)

Drimys varieties (Winter's Bark)

Elaeagnus varieties (Elaeagnus)

Embothrium varieties (Chilean Fire Bush)

Eucryphia varieties (Brush Bush)

Garrya varieties (Tassel Bush)

Ilex varieties (Holly)

Kalmia varieties (Calico Bush)

Laurus nobilis varieties (Bay)

Leptospermum varieties (Manuka, Tea Tree)

Leucothoë varieties (Drooping Leucothoë)

Mahoberberis varieties (Mahoberberis)

Osmanthus varieties (Sweet Olive)

Phillyrea varieties (Jasmine Box)

Photinia varieties (Chinese Hawthorn)

Pieris varieties (Lily of the Valley Shrub)

Prunus varieties (Laurel)

Rhododendron, dwarf and tall-growing Azalea varieties

Skimmia varieties (Skimmia)

Ulex varieties (Furze, Gorse)

Viburnum, evergreen varieties (Viburnum)

Zenobia varieties (Dusty Zenobia)

Semi-ripe conifer cuttings

Conifer cuttings are prepared with the heel as described but in addition a narrow, very shallow 1 in (3 cm) long cut is made down one side of the bottom end of the cutting, slicing off the skin and exposing the cambium layer. This removes the layer of resin that is situated just below the surface of the conifer shoot, which may prevent roots being formed if it is not removed.

The only other difference in preparation is that instead of reducing the size of the leaf, the frond of the conifer growth is reduced by cutting square across the frond, removing the top third, again to reduce the moisture loss.

On the whole, conifer cuttings take longer to root, with some taking up to a year or more. For a long time they form a callous at the base of the cutting, but no roots. This callous covers the wound made by taking the cutting and can take in moisture before the true roots form.

Unlike other semi-ripe cuttings, conifer cuttings are not trimmed back before potting on or planting out but are left to grow away as they wish; however they can be helped to form better shapes by pruning as described in Chapter 8.

The following conifers can be propagated this way:

Calocedrus varieties (Incense Cedar)

Cephalotaxus varieties (Cow's-tail Pine)

Chamaecyparis varieties (False Cypress)

Cryptomeria varieties (Japanese Cedar)

× *Cupressocyparis leylandii* varieties (Leyland Cypress)

Cupressus varieties (Cypress)

Ginkgo biloba (Maidenhair Tree)

Juniperus varieties (Juniper)

Metasequoia glyptostroboides varieties (Dawn Redwood)

Microbiota varieties (Microbiota)

Podocarpus varieties (Alpine Totara)

Taxus baccata varieties (Common Yew)

Thuya varieties (Arbor Vitae)

Tsuga varieties, in particular dwarf forms (Hemlock)

Clematis internodal semi-ripe cuttings

With other cutting methods, the lower cut has been made just below a bud. With Clematis, in mid spring and through into midsummer, once the growth has become semi-ripe, and is rigid, a section of the current season's growth is removed, just above the point where it emerges from the main stem. A cut is then made at an angle of 35°, halfway between the lowest two pairs of leaves, and then a similar cut is made just above the first remaining pair of leaves, again at an angle of 35°, being careful not to damage the buds or the leaf stalks.

If the leaves are more than 1½ in (4 cm) long the leaf is halved to cut down any potential moisture loss.

Next a small amount of rooting hormone is applied, using a gloved finger, at and around the leaf joint, wetting the area with water first.

The prepared cutting is then inserted in rows 1–1½ in (3–4 cm) apart into deep seed trays or pots containing sharp sand, with their leaves facing left and right of a centre line in rows across the tray. Or six to eight cuttings may be inserted around the outer edge of a 5 in (12 cm) pot filled with sharp sand, 1–2 in (3–5 cm) apart and ½ in (1 cm) in from the edge of the pot. They are pushed into the sharp sand, using a pencil or thin stick, until the leaf joint is just touching or below the surface.

The cuttings are then treated as for semi-ripe cuttings until planted out into their final planting position.

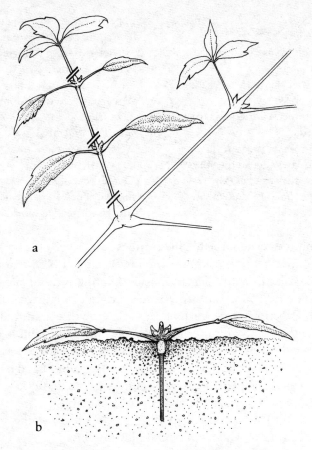

15. *Clematis cutting* (*a*) *Selected shoot cut into sections*
(*b*) *Cutting inserted into sharp sand rooting medium*

All varieties of Clematis can be rooted in this way.

Vine stem cuttings

Not all varieties of the Vine family can be propagated by the
following method – the others must be grafted. However, most
of the ornamental varieties and some wine or dessert grapes
are successful.

In early to mid spring, just before the leaves are formed,
sections of the previous season's shoots are removed from the
parent vine, as close as possible to the point of origin from the

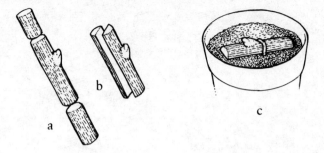

16. Vine cutting   (a) First cuts made in selected shoot
(b) Prepared section of shoot cut lengthways
(c) Prepared cutting pinned on to surface of rooting medium

main stem. Sections 1 in (3 cm) long, each with a bud in the centre, are cut from the selected shoot.

These sections are then cut lengthwise into two equal halves, taking care to ensure that all the bud area is included on one half; the other half is discarded. The retained half is then treated with rooting hormone on the cut side, moistening it first with water, and placed cut side down on to sharp sand in pots or trays. The prepared section of shoot is held in place with small hoops of wire, similar in size to paper clips and normally made from strong florists' wire.

They are then treated the same as semi-ripe cuttings in a propagator, the only difference being that they are not cut back once they grow away. Within eighteen months new plants will be ready for planting out in their growing positions.

The following Vines can be propagated by this method:

Vitis 'Brant', V. coignetiae (Crimson Glory Vine), V. vinifera 'Purpurea' (Purple-leaved Vine) and V. vinifera, fruiting and wine-making varieties (although some varieties may have to be grafted).

Leaf-stalk cuttings

Mahonia japonica and similar varieties, such as Mahonia 'Charity' and the well-known house-plant Ficus elastica (Rubber Plant) are propagated by leaf-stalk cuttings, with a few changes in the method for the individual species.

In all cases leaves produced in the previous year are removed

139

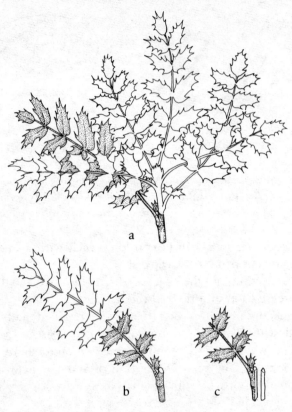

17. *Leaf-stalk cutting*
(*a*) *Before cutting is selected*   (*b*) *Selected section of shoot*
(*c*) *Shoot reduced in length; the stalk will be cut lengthwise
and the section with the leaf attached inserted into
the rooting material*

from the parent plant with a small section of stem attached.
This entails removing the entire leading shoot and dissecting it
accordingly. The shoot is cut into sections approximately ½ in
(1 cm) long with a full leaf attached by its leaf stalk to each.
The selected section of the stem is then cut lengthwise ensuring
that the leaf stalk and leaf are in the centre of one of the
halves. Only this section is retained; the other half is discarded.
The selected section is further trimmed and reduced to half its
size to form a shield of shoot with the leaf attached.

140

The multi-sectioned or pinnate leaf of Mahonia is now reduced in length, with only three of the pairs of leaflets being left intact at the shoot end, whereas the leaf of *Ficus elastica* is rolled up into a tube and held with a rubber band. Both are treated with rooting hormone, applying it to the remains of the shoot sections, before being inserted into pots or seed trays of sharp sand. Alternatively a peat-based potting compost can be used for *Ficus elastica*.

The cuttings are inserted into the pots or seed trays with the leaf blades all pointing in one direction, about $1\frac{1}{2}$ in (4 cm) apart.

Both types respond better if the propagator is heated to a temperature of not less than 65°F (18°C); the heat stimulates root development.

From here on the rooted cuttings of the Mahonia are treated and grown on as semi-ripe cuttings and those of the Ficus as softwood cuttings.

Leaf-blade cuttings

BEGONIAS

Up to now the propagation methods covered have seemed logical and it is obvious where the new roots are expected to originate from. Not so with this group of cuttings: in its simplest terms, a small piece of leaf is placed on a rooting medium, and it roots and grows to a new plant.

Primarily it is the foliage varieties in the Begonia Rex group that are propagated from leaf-blade cuttings, but many other varieties of Begonia also respond to this treatment, so it is always worth trying to propagate any fibrous-rooting variety by the method.

The cuttings can be taken at any time, although the spring tends to give the best results and ideal conditions after rooting for the plant to grow on to a usable size. A healthy leaf is chosen that is from six months to a year old, and it is completely removed from the parent plant. The selected leaf is then placed upside down on a firm, level, cutting surface.

The thick raised veins of the leaf that radiate out from the leaf stalk are identified – it is from these veins that the roots will develop. Using a sharp knife $\frac{1}{2}-\frac{3}{4}$ in (1–2 cm) squares are cut from the leaf, ensuring that a section of a vein passes through

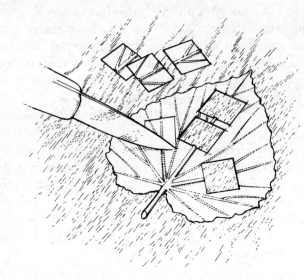

18. Preparation of leaf cuttings (Begonia)

the centre of each leaf square. The leaf squares are then placed 1 in (3 cm) apart, in rows 1½–2 in (4–5 cm) apart, underside down in seed trays or pots containing pre-moistened J. Arthur Bower's Seed and Potting Compost or other peat-based potting compost.

The filled seed trays or pots are then placed in a shaded, closed, heated propagator at a soil temperature of 60–65°F (15–18°C) for approximately fourteen days, watering as little as possible with a very fine rose and very lightly, possibly two or three times over a two-hour period. The biggest danger with this form of propagation is over-watering, leading to rotting of the delicate leaf sections.

Once the newly formed plantlets have developed to 1 in (3 cm) tall, the heat is turned off and the propagator slowly ventilated over the next fourteen days, after which the young plants can be removed from the rooting medium and potted off singly into 3 in (8 cm) pots filled with J. Arthur Bower's Seed and Potting Compost, to be grown on until they require to be potted on into larger pots. Of course, as house, conservatory or greenhouse plants, they require frost and temperature protection throughout their lives.

PROPAGATION

STREPTOCARPUS

Apart from the different preparation of the leaf-blade cuttings, the propagation of Streptocarpus is the same as for Begonia varieties. The cuttings are taken by removing completely from the parent plant a healthy leaf six months to one year old.

Inspection of this leaf will show it is lance-shaped and has a strong vein running up the centre which is more visible on the underside than from the top. Turning the chosen leaf upside down on a firm, level, cutting surface, the central vein is divided in two with a sharp knife along its entire length so that two equal portions of leaf and leaf vein are formed. Care should be taken to ensure that a proportion of vein is attached to each side of the divided leaf blade.

Next, the two halves of the leaf are cut lengthways into 2–2½ in (5–6 cm) long sections. These are then inserted lengthwise and upright ¼ in (5 mm) deep into seed trays containing J. Arthur Bower's Seed and Potting Compost or other peat-based potting compost.

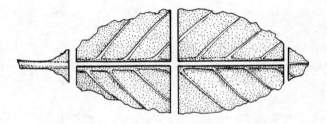

19. Preparation of leaf cuttings (Streptocarpus)

From here on the cuttings are treated the same as for the Begonia until the new plantlets are formed along the length of the leaf section. Once large enough to handle the new plantlets are divided from the leaf-blade section and potted individually into 3 in (8 cm) pots containing J. Arthur Bower's Seed and Potting Compost or an alternative peat-based compost. In two to three months, they will need to be potted on into larger pots to grow and flower.

Root cuttings

There are a small number of plants that can be propagated by root cuttings and they can be divided into three groups:

1. Alstroemeria, *Incarvillea delavavi* (Garden Gloxinia), *Romneya coulteri* (Californian Tree Poppy), Gypsophila (Baby's Breath), Macleaya (Plume Poppy), *Phlox paniculata, Tropaeolum speciosum* (Flame Vine) and Scabious.

Sections of root rather larger in diameter than a pencil are removed from the parent in early spring and cut into 1–1½ in (3–4 cm) lengths. These lengths are then laid horizontally in seed trays, half filled with moistened sharp sand. The lengths are then covered with a further layer of sharp sand until the seed tray is completely filled. The sharp sand is then compressed and the tray stood in a closed, shaded, unheated propagator for up to twenty-one days, being watered only if they appear dry; after this time the first shoots appearing from below ground level should be seen.

The trays are then removed from the propagator, stored in a garden frame or cold greenhouse, and kept watered until well-established or even until the following spring, at which time the new plants are removed from the sharp sand and potted individually into 3–4 in (8–10 cm) pots containing J. Arthur Bower's Seed and Potting Compost or other peat-based potting compost and grown on before being planted out in their final position in the following spring.

The propagation of *Phlox paniculata* (Perennial Phlox) by this method has the advantage of preventing the transfer of virus diseases, which are present in most varieties and are passed into the new plants if softwood cuttings are used as the propagation method.

2. *Crambe cordifolia, C. maritima* (Sea Kale) and perennial Verbascums are propagated by removing from the parent plant one or more of the strong vertical tap roots, but taking care not to put the parent plant at risk by removing excessive amounts of root.

These roots will be ¼–2 in (5 mm–5 cm) thick and are cut

into 2–3 in (5–8 cm) lengths, with the top cut being made square and the bottom at an angle of 35° so that it is possible to identify which way up they are. The cuttings are then inserted into 6 in (15 cm) deep pots containing J. Arthur Bower's Seed and Potting Compost or other peat-based potting compost and left in a closed garden frame to develop; in the following spring they can normally be planted out into their final growing position.

Alternatively the cuttings can be inserted directly into the final growing position, which of course has been well dug and has had up to 50 per cent by volume of sharp sand added to the dug soil.

3. Rheums, including both the culinary and ornamental varieties of Rhubarb, are best propagated by dividing or cutting up the woody root clump in early to mid spring.

The operation entails digging up the parent plant and dividing it into sections, best described as chunks, each of which should show signs of having a bud. These buds are normally bright red or green at this time of year, and are easily identifiable.

Each section can then be planted out in its new planting position or potted into 8 in (20 cm) pots containing J. Arthur Bower's Seed and Potting Compost or other peat-based potting compost, stood in the open and grown on for a year before being planted out into their final growing positions in the following spring.

Micropropagation

This is a method of propagation now widely practised by professionals, using laboratory conditions; it entails taking from a chosen parent plant a single tip shoot and propagating it on in a culture medium. Once it becomes a plantlet it is divided and grown on again and again until the required number have been propagated and are ready to grow on.

At this stage the young plants are called 'plugs', or 'liners', and they are taken by nurserymen and grown on to form saleable plants.

The laboratory propagators are not normally available to

the amateur but plugs are now being sold by garden centres as baby plants for growing on.

In a way micropropagation is reducing the skill of the propagator, as many of the plants that were difficult to propagate in the past are now becoming readily available.

Irishman's or self-rooting cuttings

Irishman's cuttings is a nursery term given to rooted plantlets produced in the garden by the parent plant; these can be removed, potted up and grown on, or can be planted out directly in a new planting position.

Many plants perform in this way and it is worth watching for self-rooted layers as an easy, small-scale form of propagation.

Alpines and ground-cover plants are among the most likely to produce their own rooted offsets and quite large numbers will be found.

Ground-layering

Layering is the inducing of roots on a selected shoot while it is still attached to the parent plant. Of the two main forms of layering, ground-layering is the most widely used. Many woody plants will ground-layer and many do it naturally. Commercially it is normally used for the choicer plants, which may root from cuttings but cannot be relied on to do so; in some cases, also, ground-layering is quicker than cuttings and easier than grafting.

Most professional nurseries grow specially prepared parent plants that offer an abundance of new, previous season's shoots, the most successful material for ground-layering.

In gardens this may be the first obstacle to carrying out ground-layering, as the most suitable shoots may not be present or – as often the parent plant is well-established – if the shoots are present they may be too high on the plant to be brought down to ground level for layering. If there are no suitable shoots, they must first be induced to grow. To do this, in early to mid spring, a few – or even just one – sizeable shoots of the parent plant are selected and pruned hard back. The new

20. Ground layering

resulting shoots from the pruning should be growing close enough to the ground to be bent down for ground-layering. To encourage these new shoots the plant should be fed with Growmore in the early spring according to the manufacturer's recommendations; one selected shoot can be cut to within a few inches of ground level and removed. Where possible, choose a shoot on the outside of the shrub. One other problem may be that when there are suitable shoots to work with, there may not be enough room at the base of the plant to actually carry out the ground-layering. Where space is limited, or where the soil is poor, it may be possible to add a soil-based potting compost such as John Innes No. 3.

When suitable shoots are present, the process of ground-layering can start: double digging, in winter or early spring, an area of soil close to the base of the plant where the induced shoot can be brought down to ground level. Adding 50 per cent by volume of sharp sand to the soil will also aid rooting. If it is not practical to do the work at this time, although it is best to do so, the soil can be prepared just in advance of layering.

In early to mid spring, before the leaves form with deciduous shrubs, the selected shoots are bent down on to the surface of the prepared soil and their positions plotted. They are then released while trenches 2–4 in (5–10 cm) deep and the length of the shoot are excavated. A layer of sharp sand is placed in the bottom of the trench to a depth of 1–2 in (3–5 cm). Next the selected shoots are again bent down, this time into the trench, and fixed in position using wire or wooden pegs. If the selected shoot has side shoots (spurs) the trench is widened to accommodate them and these are also pegged down.

The end 3–6 in (8–15 cm) of each main or spur shoot should protrude out of the soil and should be tied upright to a short bamboo cane; it is from this tip, both on the main growth and on the spur shoots, that the new rooted plants will form.

Before the shoots to be layered are pegged down they are wounded by cutting away a sliver of skin (bark) $\frac{1}{4}$ in (5 mm) wide and 1–1$\frac{1}{2}$ in (3–4 cm) long, about 2 in (5 cm) below the point where they emerge from the soil and if possible below a bud. The wound is moistened and rooting hormone applied to aid rooting. Any side shoots to be layered are treated in the same way. Any leaves that would be buried must be removed before pegging down.

Once pegged down, a further 1 in (3 cm) of sharp sand is placed in the trench to cover the layer and then the trench is filled in with soil. The layer is left attached to the parent, in most cases until late summer, when it is severed, but the new plant is left in the soil between mid autumn and early spring; then it can be dug up and planted out in its new home or potted up for planting out later.

With shrubs such as Cotinus (Smoke Tree) where there are a number of side shoots, it is possible, by waiting until late spring when it is in leaf, to bring the shoots down to allow each group of leaves along the shoot to emerge above the soil, when roots will be formed at each leaf joint. The wound in this case must be made under each leaf joint and the rooting hormone applied to it.

The trees and shrubs in the following list can be propagated by ground-layers:

TREES

Acer rubrum varieties (Red
  Maple)
A. saccharinum varieties (Silver
  Maple)
Arbutus varieties (Strawberry
  Tree)
Cercidiphyllum varieties
  (Katsura Tree)
Cercis siliquastrum (Judas Tree)
Davidia involucrata (Dove Tree)
Liriodendron varieties (Tulip Tree)
Nyssa sylvatica (Black Gum)
Parrotiopsis jacquemontiana
  (Persian Parrotia)
Sassafras albidum (Ague Tree)
Styrax varieties (Japanese
  Snowbell)

SHRUBS

Acanthopanax varieties (Five-
  leaf Aralia)
Acer ginnala (Ameur Maple)
Aesculus parviflora (Buckeye)
Amelanchier varieties (Snowy
  Mespilus, Service
  Bush)
Aralia elata, but not variegated
  varieties (Japanese Angelica
  Tree)
Azalea, see Rhododendron
Callistemon varieties (Australian
  Bottle Bush)
Camellia varieties (Camellia)
Cornus alternifolia varieties
  (Pagoda Dogwood)

C. controversa varieties
  (Wedding-cake Tree)
C. florida varieties (North
  American Flowering
  Dogwood)
C. kousa varieties (Chinese
  Dogwood)
C. nuttallii varieties (Pacific
  Dogwood)
Corylopsis varieties (Cowslip
  Bush)
Corylus varieties (Hazel, Filbert,
  Cobnut)
Cotinus varieties
Desfontainia spinosa
  (Desfontainia)
Disanthus cercidifolius
  (Disanthus)
Distylium racemosum
  (Distylium)
Drimys varieties (Winter's Bark)
Elsholtzia stauntonii (Mint
  Bush)
Embothrium varieties (Chilean
  Fire Bush)
Eucryphia varieties (Brush Bush)
Exochorda varieties (Pearl Bush)
Fothergilla varieties (Fothergilla)
Hamamelis varieties (Witch
  Hazel)
Kalmia varieties (Calico Bush)
Rhododendron varieties
  (Rhododendron and Azalea)
Rubus, creeping and ground-
  cover varieties (Brambles)
Stachyurus varieties (Stachyurus)

Air-layering

Air-layering can be used to propagate those plants that are
too special to risk pruning to produce suitable shoots for

ground-layering and are difficult to propagate by other techniques.

Shoots not more than two years old are selected, ensuring that when they finally root and have to be removed the overall shape of the parent plant will not be seriously damaged. They should be just thicker than a pencil at a point 12–15 in (30–40 cm) from the end of the chosen shoot.

In early spring a wound $\frac{1}{4}$ in (5 mm) wide and long is made at the back or at the side of a bud on the selected shoot and the wound treated with rooting hormone. Then a handful of moistened J. Arthur Bower's Seed and Potting Compost or other peat-based potting compost is made into a ball around the wound and held in place – a second pair of hands may be useful at this stage. The compost is then encased in damp, coarse moss, which in turn is enclosed in a black polythene cover, secured to make a large Easter-egg-shaped ball. Specially designed air-layering containers are available and although I have never used them I can see that they might be of value.

In about twelve months from the time of air-layering, roots should have formed inside the 'egg' to such a degree that the layered growth can be cut off just below the level of the layer joint. The black plastic is then removed and, if possible, any surplus moss that has not been rooted through.

The young rooted plant is then potted into a suitable pot and grown on to the autumn before being planted out into its final new home.

The following plants can be air-layered with success.

SHRUBS
Aesculus, Buckeye varieties
    (Buckeye, American
    Chestnuts)
Azalea, see Rhododendron
Camellia varieties (Camellia)
Fothergilla varieties
    (Fothergilla)
Magnolia varieties
    (Magnolia)

Pieris varieties (Lily of the Valley
    Shrub)
Rhododendron, particularly
    large-leaved varieties
    (Rhododendrons and Azaleas)

HOUSE-PLANTS
Ficus varieties (Rubber Plant)
Monstera deliciosa (Swiss-cheese
    Plant)

Stooling

This method of propagation is often overlooked, but there are many shrubs that may, with or without prior preparation, lend themselves to stooling, with very high success rates. A few trees are also propagated in this way, as are – commercially – the rootstocks of Apples and Pears. It is worth trying almost any shrub to see if it will stool.

The first criterion is that there should be a number of shoots larger in diameter than a pencil, produced by the plant the previous spring and summer, and growing from below or close to ground level.

In commercial propagation this is ensured by pruning the three-year-old established shrub to within a few inches of ground level in early spring with the resulting shoots being 'stooled' early in the following spring.

The first stage is to remove, in early to mid spring, any dead growth or other rubbish from the base of the shrub. The surrounding soil is then lightly forked in a circle equal to the spread of the shrub's main shoots. Into this soil a dressing of Growmore is applied, as recommended on the packet.

Equal parts of sharp sand and J. Arthur Bower's Seed and Potting Compost, or other peat-based potting compost, are mixed together to produce enough bulk to build a 6–8 in (15–20 cm) deep layer in and between the bases of all the shrub's shoots, whether they are being stooled or not. The mixture should be moist before use and needs to be thoroughly worked in between the shoots to ensure that there are no air pockets.

Through the summer the soil mixture is kept moist and weed-free until late autumn, when one of the selected shoots is carefully exposed and inspected, to see if a good number of roots have formed. Should the inspection prove negative, the mixture is returned and the plant left until the following autumn. Normally, however, roots will be found at the first inspection and it is a simple matter to cut the selected rooted shoots as low down below the roots as possible and remove them from the parent plant.

These are then pruned by being cut back to within 6–9 in

(15–23 cm) of the roots. They can then be potted into 5–6 in (12–15 cm) pots and grown on for one more year, or planted out into their final planting positions.

The following plants, if suitable propagating material exists low enough down, can be propagated by stooling.

TREES

Acer negundo varieties (Box
  Maple)
A. *rubrum* varieties (Red Maple)
A. *saccharinum* varieties
  (Silver Maple)
Aesculus varieties (Buckeye)
Alnus varieties (Alder)
Amelanchier varieties (Snowy
  Mespilus)
Castanea varieties (Spanish
  Chestnut)
Kalopanax varieties (Prickly
  Castor-oil Tree)
Koelreuteria varieties (Chinese

Rain Tree)
Prunus cerasifera varieties
  (Purple-leaved Plum)
Rhus varieties (Sumach)
Tilia varieties (Lime)
Ulmus varieties (Elm)

SHRUBS

Cornus alba varieties (Red-
  barked Dogwood)
C. *stolonifera* varieties (Yellow-
  stemmed Dogwood)
Cotinus varieties (Smoke Tree)
Osmaronia varieties (Oso
  Berry)

The above are the main species produced commercially by stooling but many more species can be attempted if suitable shoots are available.

Propagating from suckers

A number of shrubs and trees produce suckers that, if removed from the parent plant and replanted, will grow into new plants.

However, there is a very good chance that the sucker, although of the same species, will not be the same variety and will normally be inferior to the parent plant (see Grafting and Budding, p. 165), but if this is not a problem, then – ideally between mid autumn and early spring – these suckers can be removed with their roots and, before replanting, cut back to a height of 6–9 in (15–23 cm) to encourage them to branch.

Rather than listing those which can be propagated in this

way, the following lists those plants whose suckers may not be true and in fact should be removed in the interest of the plant's overall well-being (see Chapter 8). (A few of these – for example, Ameliancher – may be on their own roots, in which case the suckers can be used for propagation.)

Suckers not suitable for propagation

Amelanchier, grafted plants (Snowy Mespilus)

Crataegus, grafted plants (Thorn)

Gleditsia, grafted plants (Honey Locust)

Kolopanax, grafted plants

Caragana, grafted plants (Pea Tree)

(Prickly Castor-oil Tree)

Malus, grafted plants (Crab Apple)

Prunus, grafted plants (Flowering Plum/Peach/ Cherry)

Robinia, grafted plants (Acacia)

Rosa, budded or grafted plants

Plants which can be propagated from suckers

The following are in fact propagated by suckers in commercial production.

Acacia varieties (Wattle)

Amelanchier, except grafted plants (Snowy Mespilus)

Nyssa (Black Gum)

Paulownia (Foxglove Tree)

Phellodendron (Cork Tree)

Sassafras (Ague Tree)

The only other rooted suckers that might be kept but not directly grown on are those that can be used as stocks for budding or grafting, such as Roses. The preparation and use is explained in this chapter under Budding and Grafting (p. 165).

Division

Division is the principal method of propagating a wide range of perennial and alpine plants; some sub-shrubs, such as Astilbes, can also be propagated in this way.

Most perennial plants grow out from a central point and, as they age, die from that point, so propagation by lifting, dividing and replanting is necessary, not only to produce more plants but to eliminate dying off at the centre.

153

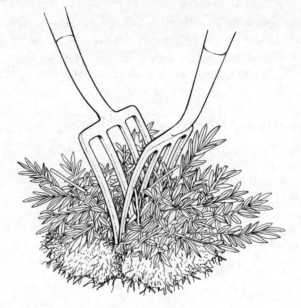

21. Division

It has the advantage over seed and cuttings of being faster to produce sizeable flowering plants; also, many perennial plants do not come true when raised from seed (see Seed, p. 156).

New plants to be used in a pre-planned planting can be bulked up by division, working to the formula of five plants from one after a year of growing on in the garden or nursery bed, making it possible to plant large areas at a very reduced cost.

Propagation of perennial plants grown in the garden for more than one year can normally be carried out in early to mid spring, preferably when not in leaf, but this is not imperative.

A few strong-growing species can be divided in the autumn, but care must be taken to select carefully, as many may not be able to withstand the winter cold and wet; it may be best to avoid this time and wait until the spring. Dividing the parent plant in autumn and potting the plantlets into 4–5 in (10–12 cm) pots is an alternative, and will give more time for planting out later.

In larger plantings, where the planting plan entails planting in odd numbers of more than three, the division can be phased on an ongoing replacement plan whereby the planting scheme is never totally destroyed by the need to divide.

In year one the perennials are planted in the spring and early summer and left to grow on until the spring of year three, when a third of the group are lifted and divided; a good-sized clump is then replanted in the original position, after the soil has been dug and liberal amounts of organic material added.

The operation is repeated in the following spring with another third of the total number being divided; in the next spring again, the plants hitherto untouched are worked on. Then the process starts all over again, thereby ensuring the plants are kept in the best growing conditions and give the best possible performance.

The alternative is to lift, after year three or four, in the spring, all of the plants, divide and replant them; however this can be laborious and reduces the flowering capacity of the plants in the year following division.

The division of the individual plants themselves can be done in a number of ways depending on the size and species of plant being divided, as follows.

The plant is dug up in the autumn or spring, whichever is appropriate for the species. It may be possible by using both hands, one each side of the clump, to force and pull it into a number of chunks, each about the size of a fist. Many of the perennial plants propagated by division fall into this group.

With many of the stronger-growing species, two digging, border or hand forks will be needed to divide it, depending on the size of the clump.

The forks are forced, back to back and touching, into the clump on the line where the division is to be made; then, by forcing the fork handles together, the prongs are forced outwards, thereby prising the clump apart. The process is repeated until the original clump has been divided into as many fist-sized pieces as possible.

It may be necessary to use an old knife to cut and prise the various sections apart, continuing until all of the clump is divided. Hostas and Astilbes are two species where this extra help may be required. A few very interwoven or woody plants may require either chopping with a small axe, or even sawing, to divide them into sections.

Care must be taken to ensure the section removed has at least one or, better still, a number of growth buds. These buds are normally visible in the spring or can be assumed to exist at the base, where part of last year's dead shoot will normally still be visible.

SEED

Raising plants from seed has been the foundation of plant propagation for as long as plants have been collected, grown and propagated; however, because it is a sexual method, it may be unreliable since not all plants can be raised true to type from seed.

The problem arises with those plants that are pollinated by insects, when the insect visits more than one of the parent plants. Wind-borne pollination may also, in our confined, multi-planted gardens, present similar problems.

The insect does not intend to do the pollination for us – it is searching for food in the form of nectar which is normally stored at the base of the flower. As it brushes against the stamens it collects small amounts of pollen on its body. It then flies on to the next flower and in its efforts to retrieve nectar deposits some of the male pollen on to the female stigma, pollination then takes place and the seed will be formed.

Problems arise if the first flower of a species visited is, say, white and the second red; pollen is transported between the two and the resulting new plants may be white, red or a mixture in between. So plants raised under these conditions may not be true to colour and will upset a planned planting. There is also the possibility that the size and growth potential will change and that the resulting plant will not grow as expected.

There is, of course, the very slim chance that the new plant will be an improvement, but this is very rare; those who grow seedlings for this purpose have to grow many thousands, if not tens of thousands, to achieve a new commercial variety.

In recent times we have seen the introduction of F 1 and F 2 hybrid seeds produced in laboratory conditions, where known plants are used for fertilization, under very controlled, isolated growing conditions, which are normally not possible in the garden environment. Should the seed be gathered from F 1 and F 2 hybrids grown in the garden, it will not come true; many will not germinate at all.

Home grown

There is, then, a real risk of disappointment with collecting your own seed, but the excitement of trying is often irresistible.

If you do decide to try, the procedure is as follows:

1. Wait until the seed is ripe, normally indicated by it being free-moving in its seed case, except where the seed has a fleshy coat and has to be stratified.

2. Store it dry in a sealed envelope in a dark, dry, frost- and rodent-free place.

3. Write on the envelope the name and when and where it was collected.

4. Recording its condition and when you feel you should sow it might be useful.

With your own saved seed, you will have to decide for yourself when to sow. Most seeds can be safely saved and sown in the spring, but just a few require stimulation by extremes of temperature. The only way to identify these seed types is to read reference books or other sources; my own hunting ground for information is on seed packets of similar varieties on display in garden centres.

Stratification

Some seeds have either a fleshy or a hard nut-like shell and in the wild this coat is removed naturally by decomposition, but the rate of loss is not controlled and the seed is also open to attack from rodents and other animals during this time. In cultivation we use stratification to control this decomposition and protect the seed.

To do this, in the autumn when the fruits are ripe, wooden or plastic trays, not less than 6 in (15 cm) deep, with drainage holes, are selected and prepared. A 2 in (5 cm) layer of moist sharp sand is spread over the bottom of the tray and the fleshy or hard-coated seeds are scattered evenly over the sand surface. A further layer of moist sand 2 in (5 cm) deep is then used to cover the seed evenly. Further layers can be built up if there is adequate depth.

Before the trays are stood outside they are surrounded with a small-mesh wire netting to prevent pilfering by rodents such as squirrels, rats and mice.

Normally all hardy species of small fruits can be treated in this way but should the subject be known to be tender, it must be stored under protection. Throughout the winter and spring the trays should be kept moist but not over-watered.

In early spring the seed, whose coat will by now have softened or gone completely, can be removed by tipping out the trays; it is then resown in seed trays, pots or a seed bed in the garden. In just a few cases seeds can be left to germinate in the tray they were stratified in and many Acers (Maple), Cotoneasters and Pyracanthas (Firethorn) can be raised this way.

Once sown, the seed will normally germinate and is treated according to its seedling requirements; however, some species, in particular Acers (Maples), may take up to three years to germinate fully, often with a few seedlings being produced each year.

Packed seed

Packed seeds purchased from garden centres and other retail outlets do not carry the problems associated with your own collected seed and the resulting new plants raised normally come true to type.

Most commercial seed companies offer similar ranges of species and varieties, and the main point to consider before purchasing is the price and amount of seed in the packet. All the information you will need to know is given on the seed packet and, if these instructions are followed, few problems in growing should be experienced.

The instructions may offer a band of sowing times from say late winter to mid spring and if this is the case then sowing later rather than earlier is the best advice to ensure that the seedlings can be protected and grown on at a speed and size not likely to damage them. Geographical location will also play a part in the ideal sowing time: the further south the earlier the seeds can be sown.

The instructions may give information on work that will be required at a later stage, so it is useful to keep the packets for future reference.

Sowing in seed trays under protection

This method of sowing is possibly the most usual method adopted by the home gardener and the following notes outline the procedures that should be followed. A few individual plant species may require more detailed practices and these are normally shown on the packet or can be discovered from reference books.

It may be thought, when sowing seed, that a full-size seed tray is required, but often this is not so and the rule of using the smallest tray or pot for the number of plants to be produced should be followed whenever possible. Not only does this stop wasteful overproduction but it ensures that the smallest amount of space in the propagator is used and that the seedling crops you grow are as flexible as possible, allowing for moving on within a production programme.

If not new, the trays or pots should be washed in soapy water or mild household disinfectant to ensure that no diseases are transferred to the newly sown crop.

When not in use all trays and pots should be stored away from the growing area, ideally in a separate building, again to stop disease cross-contamination. In fact the growing area should not be used to store any items other than those in use, as all carry the potential for spreading disease.

Sowing

1. The selected container is filled to the top with moistened J. Arthur Bower's Seed and Potting Compost, or alternatively John Innes Seed Compost or another peat-based seed-sowing compost.

2. Lightly firm the compost using a home-made firming board that just fits the inner diameter of the container and will, when gently pressed down, consolidate the potting compost without compressing it too much.

3. Use a light-coloured, flat Corex or cardboard sheet to sow the seed on the surface of the compost; pour a small amount of seed on to the card, position the card close to the edge of the container and push off small amounts or single seeds at regular intervals on to the surface of the seed-sowing compost below.

As sowing progresses the board is then moved back $\frac{1}{4}$ in (5 mm) or so and the process repeated until the whole tray is sown or all the seed used up.

When sowing pots, a small pinch of seed taken between the thumb and forefinger and sprinkled over the surface will also give good distribution.

In both cases every effort should be made not to sow too thickly as this is wasteful and the resulting seedlings will be overcrowded.

4. Firm the seed by using the firming board or cover with seed-sowing compost as indicated on the packet, and if required place under a propagator at the germinating temperature recommended on the packet.

5. Cover the propagator with newspaper to give shade for at least fourteen days.

6. Water only if needed and then very lightly, using a very fine watering-can rose.

7. Once the first signs of germination are seen, reduce or remove the heat according to the instructions and start to vent the propagator a little more each day; after a week of gradual ventilation, most trays or pots of seedlings can be removed from the propagator.

8. Once the seedlings show signs of the second pair of leaves they are large enough to handle and can be pricked off – transplanted into individual trays or pots. Do not be tempted to move them too soon or to delay unduly; the timing of this stage is important if the young plants are to grow on well without undue disturbance.

9. Throughout the early stages, most seedlings will require some form of frost protection – ideally a greenhouse, but cold frames may be suitable, as will, to a limited extent, a window-sill – depending on the species or variety being sown.

10. As the time approaches for the seedlings to be planted in the garden they will have to be hardened off by gradually allowing them, over a week or so, to experience the outside temperature. Each day they are exposed for longer periods, so that their foliage slowly adjusts to the outside temperature; however, some will tolerate no frost, however slight, and care must be taken to identify these and protect them for as long as necessary.

Most seedlings respond to this treatment; it is most important to prevent the plant being 'shocked', thus making it slow to grow away in its new home, so timing is vital.

Seed sowing outdoors

Many seeds can be sown directly into the soil outdoors as long as the rules are followed.

Soil preparation

When sowing out of doors directly into the soil, preparation is of paramount importance and any site to be used for sowing should be at least single dug.

Often the growth of young seedlings is rapid in the first few weeks, so it is important to ensure that adequate plant foods are available in the soil; an application of a general fertilizer, such as Growmore, in late winter or early spring, is advised.

Before sowing, the cultivated soil should be broken down to a fine consistency (tilth) and any large stones and rubbish removed.

Sowing times
There are two times for sowing outdoors and most plants fit into one of these.

Mid to late spring sowing
At this time the following can be sown with success.

HARDY ANNUAL
Centaurea cyanus
  (Cornflower)
Consolida (Larkspur)
Eschscholtzia varieties
  (Californian Poppy)
Godetia, hardy annual varieties
  (Godetia)
Helianthus (Sunflower)
Iberis sempervirens varieties
  (Candytuft)
Lavatera varieties (Mallow)
Limnanthes (Poached Egg
  Plant)
Linaria (Toadflax)
Linum (Flax)
Matthiola (Stock)
Nasturtium, see Tropaeolum
Nigella (Love-in-a-mist)
Salvia sclarea (Clary)
Scabiosa (Scabious)
Tropaeolum (Nasturtium)

VEGETABLE PLANTS GROWN
FROM SEED
Beetroot
Broad Beans
Carrots
Celeriac
Celery
Celtuce
Chicory
Chinese Cabbage
Courgettes
Cucumber
Endive
French Beans
Leaf Beet
Lettuce
Marrow
Parsnip
Peas
Radish
Runner Beans
Salsify
Spinach
Spring Onions
Swede
Turnip

WOODY PLANTS
Trees, shrubs, climbers, Roses and conifers – but remember that the end result may be variable.

Early summer to midsummer sowing

SUMMER-, AUTUMN- AND
SPRING-FLOWERING
BIENNIALS
These are grown from seed
in year one and overwintered
outdoors to flower in year
two.

Althaea varieties (Hollyhock)
Aquilegia varieties (Columbine,
Monk's Cap)
Bellis perennis (Double Daisy)
Campanula medium (Canterbury
Bell)
Cheiranthus (Wallflower)
Dianthus barbatus varieties
(Sweet William)
Digitalis varieties (Foxglove)
Myosotis alpestris (Forget-me-
not)

Primula juliae 'Wanda' (Wanda
Primula)
P. variabilis (Polyanthus)
P. vulgaris hybrids (Ornamental
Primrose)
P. vulgaris varieties
(Primrose)
Verbascum bombyciferum
(Giant Mullein)
Viola × *wittrockiana* varieties
(Spring-, Summer- and
Winter-flowering Pansies)

VEGETABLES
Broccoli
Brussels Sprouts
Cabbage (edible and
ornamental)
Leeks

All the resulting plants, whether biennials or vegetables, are
dug up when large enough and replanted in their final growing
positions.

Sowing
Most seeds are sown in rows but hardy annuals can also be
broadcast sown.

SOWING IN ROWS
Once the soil has been single or double dug and brought to a
fine consistency (tilth) a garden line – made from two sticks or
canes, approximately 18 in (50 cm) long with a length of string
tied between the two, long enough to stretch across the sowing
area – is put in place and pulled tight to indicate the intended
sowing line.

Using the back of a rake or the edge of a hoe blade or even a
suitably sized piece of wood, a shallow indentation (a drill) is
drawn across the soil along the line of the string.

The depth will depend on the size of the seed – most small seeds only require a depth of $\frac{1}{4}$–$\frac{1}{2}$ in (5 mm–1 cm), with larger seeds such as Broad Beans requiring up to $1\frac{1}{2}$ in (4 cm).

The seed is now sown as thinly as possible to avoid wasting seed and thinning out later on. The drill is then filled in with soil to cover the seed.

A few seeds such as Onions respond to being lightly firmed in but not all do, so check the packet for instructions.

Once the seeds have germinated and the seedlings are 1–2 in (3–5 cm) high, they will require thinning to prevent overcrowding. The distance between seedlings after thinning will depend on the plant in question, but as a rule 1–$1\frac{1}{2}$ in (3–4 cm) is suitable.

Hardy perennials, sown in the spring, are normally left in position to grow and flower; biennials are lifted in mid to late summer when they are 3–4 in (8–10 cm) tall, and replanted in their final positions, normally some way away from the seedling growing area.

BROADCAST SOWING
Hardy annuals in particular can be broadcast on to the pre-dug and raked soil, and then lightly raked in and covered with soil. This well-proven method allows for an informal display and can, with a little pre-planning, be very attractive and cost-effective.

As with those sown in rows, the resulting seedlings require thinning out and these thinnings can often be planted elsewhere in the garden. The remaining seedlings are left untouched to flower *in situ*.

Identifying weeds amongst seedlings

When sowing outdoors in the soil there is always the possibility of weed infestation and distinguishing the seedlings from the young weeds may be difficult, particularly when the seed is sown broadcast. When sown in rows the seedlings can normally be identified by the regimentation of the rows. When sowing broadcast, it helps if a small number of seeds of each variety are sown in a short row, making identification easier as they germinate.

GRAFTING AND BUDDING

Grafting and budding are the most skilled of all gardening practices, and take the most time. Both involve joining together the cambium or growth layers of two different plants, the rootstock and the scion. The cambium layer is positioned just below the bark of all plants and is the only part of the plant, except the bud, that can produce new tissue.

These methods are used for various reasons:

1. A plant may not be able to produce its own roots with other propagation methods; Hamamelis (Witch Hazel) is a good example of this group.

2. A plant may only be able to produce weak roots, unable to support it over a number of years; this is the case with the weaker-growing Hybrid Tea and Floribunda Roses.

3. Plants which may grow well from seed, but do not come true to their parent, must be reproduced by vegetative means; if cuttings from these plants will not root, they must be reproduced by grafting or budding. Many varieties of garden trees belong to this group, as do the best forms of Wisteria.

4. With Apples, and to a certain extent Fruiting Cherries, the overall shape and size of the bush or tree can be controlled by selecting an appropriate commercially grown rootstock.

5. Grafting and budding are used a great deal to produce 'mop-headed' or 'toy' trees; the best-known examples are the standard or weeping Roses but a number of shrubs such as Viburnum, Cotoneaster, Salix (Willow) and Euonymus can also be grown this way.

6. To produce certain weeping trees such as *Prunus serrata* (Cheal's Weeping Cherry), Malus (Flowering Crab Apple), and Fraxinus (Ash) it is necessary to graft or bud on to compatible rootstock stems of the selected species.

7. In a few cases grafting or budding is used to eradicate a disease problem and to produce disease-free plants which can then be propagated by other methods to grow more problem-free plants.

8. Some nurseries use grafting or budding to speed up the time it takes to produce a saleable plant, either (*a*) grafting or budding plants on to a fast-growing compatible rootstock, so speeding up the rate of growth – Elaeagnus, large-leaved Cotoneasters and Syringa (Lilac) are good examples of this practice – or (*b*) grafting or budding, in particular, the tree forms of *Prunus serrata* (Japanese Cherries), such as *Prunus serrata* 'Kanzan', on to stems of *Prunus avium*. This practice is referred to as 'top-working'.

Rootstocks

These are rooted plants that are used for grafting and budding, grown for the purpose by specialists and then sold to the production nurseries for propagation.

To obtain suitable rootstocks for yourself you need a friendly nursery which may be willing to sell you a small number of the right species of rootstock for the plants you are attempting to propagate.

Rootstocks, apart from those used for the propagation of Apples and eating Cherries, do not limit the ultimate size of the plant; in fact, in many cases they may even increase it. This is because the rootstocks are propagated from seed and may therefore be variable in their influence on the final plant.

The ideal rootstock for grafting will be just thicker than a pencil; those used for budding can be up to twice this thickness.

Only certain scions and rootstocks are compatible, and the proposed pairing must be carefully researched before propagation begins. The following list gives most of the pairings normally used.

Species	Compatible rootstock
TREES	
Acer negundo varieties (Ornamental Box Maple)	*Acer negundo* seedlings
A. platanoides varieties (Norway Maple)	*A. platanoides* seedlings
A. pseudoplatanus varieties (Ornamental Sycamore)	*A. pseudoplatanus* seedlings
Aesculus varieties (Flowering Chestnut)	*Aesculus hippocastanum/A. carnea* seedlings

Amelanchier varieties (Snowy Mespilus)	*Crataegus monogyna* seedlings
Betula varieties (Birch)	*Betula pendula* seedlings
Caragana varieties (Salt Tree)	*Caragana arborescens* seedlings
Catalpa bignonioides 'Aurea' (Golden Catalpa)	*Catalpa bignonioides* seedlings
Crataegus varieties (Flowering Thorn or May)	*Crataegus monogyna* seedlings
Fagus, ornamental tree varieties (Beech)	*Fagus sylvatica* seedlings
Fraxinus, ornamental varieties (Ash)	*Fraxinus sylvatica* seedlings
Gleditsia, ornamental varieties (Honey Locust)	*Gleditsia triacanthos* seedlings and suckers
Laburnocytisus adamii (Pink Laburnum)	*Laburnum anagyroides* seedlings
Laburnum varieties	*L. anagyroides* seedlings
Malus varieties (flowering and fruiting Crab)	*Malus pumila* seedlings, cuttings or layers
Prunus (flowering and fruiting Cherries and ornamental Prunus)	*Prunus avium* seedlings or cuttings
Pyrus, ornamental varieties (Flowering Pear)	*Pyrus communis* seedlings or cuttings
Robinia varieties (Acacia)	*Robinia pseudoacacia* seedlings
Sorbus aria varieties (Whitebeam)	*Sorbus aria* seedlings
S. aucuparia varieties (Mountain Ash)	*S. aucuparia* seedlings

SHRUBS

Acer japonicum varieties (Full Moon Maple)	*Acer japonicum* seedlings
A. palmatum varieties (Japanese Maple)	*A. palmatum* seedlings
Berberis, difficult-to-root varieties (Barberry)	*Berberis thunbergii*/*B. t.* 'Atropurpurea' seedlings
Corylus avellana 'Contorta' (Contorted Hazel)	*Corylus avellana* layers

Cotoneaster, large-leaved varieties	*Cotoneaster bullatus* seedlings, cuttings or layers
Cytisus battandieri (Pineapple, Moroccan Broom)	*Laburnum anagyroides* seedlings
Cytisus varieties (Broom)	*Laburnum anagyroides* seedlings
Hamamelis varieties (Witch Hazel)	*Hamamelis virginiana*
Hibiscus syriacus varieties	*Hibiscus syriacus* seedlings
Rhododendron varieties	*Rhododendron pontica* seedlings, layers or cuttings
Syringa varieties (Lilac)	*Syringa vulgaris* seedlings or layers/*Ligustrum ovalifolium* cuttings
Viburnum carlesii and related forms	*Viburnum lanata* seedlings or cuttings

ROSES

Rosa, all groups	*Rosa canina* (Dog Rose) seedlings
	Rosa rugosa seedlings or layers
	Rosa Laxa seedlings
	Rosa Pfanda seedlings or cuttings

FRUIT

Malus (fruiting Apples)	A range of numbered and named rootstocks, each influencing the growth of the propagated tree to have a given size and performance; grown from layers, stools or cuttings
Mespilus germanica (Medlar)	*Crataegus monogyna* seedlings
Prunus avium varieties (fruiting Cherries)	*Prunus avium* seedlings
P. domestica (Plum) varieties	Plum St Julian A or Pixie layers, stools or cuttings
Pyrus (fruiting Pears) varieties	Quince C seedlings or cuttings

Vitis vinifera (fruiting varieties)

Vitis vinifera selected
seedlings

CONIFERS

Cedrus atlantica varieties (Cedar)

Cedrus atlantica seedlings

C. deodora varieties (Deodar Cedar)

C. deodora seedlings

Chamaecyparis, dwarf varieties
(Dwarf Cypress)

Chamaecyparis lawsoniana
seedlings

Juniperus, slow-growing or difficult-
to-root varieties (Juniper)

Juniperus communis
seedlings

Taxus, slow-growing or difficult-to-
root varieties (Yew)

Taxus baccata seedlings or
cuttings

Planting or potting rootstocks for grafting

Rootstocks for grafting can be prepared in two ways, either planted outdoors or in pots under protection.

PLANTING OUTDOORS IN GARDEN SOIL Between late autumn and early spring the rootstocks are planted in well-cultivated soil in rows, normally 3 ft (1 m) apart, with 12–18 in (30–50 cm) between each plant in the row. They are allowed to grow and establish a good root system until the following midwinter, when they are ready for grafting.

IN POTS FOR BENCH GRAFTING INDOORS In the spring the rootstocks are planted in pots, using a soil-based potting compost, but avoiding peat-based composts as these are diffi-cult to keep moist under grafting conditions and also the pots can lose their rigidity when being handled. Use the smallest pots available which will not cause unnecessary root restric-tion, as grafting takes place under cover and space is often at a premium; also the pots have to be handled and any extra weight can make this difficult.

The potted rootstocks are then stood outside in a sheltered place and kept watered and weed-free for grafting in the following late winter.

Planting rootstocks for budding

When the rootstocks are to be used for budding they are planted as for grafting out of doors (above), except that the planting distance in the rows is 9–10 in (23–5 cm) apart. They are ready for budding in the early summer or midsummer of the year following planting.

Rootstocks for top-working
The rootstocks are first, over a period of approximately two years, grown to the required height before being planted out in the autumn and winter, usually into well-cultivated soil in rows 3–4 ft (1–1.2 m) apart, with 2 ft (60 cm) between each rootstock in the row. Some are also now being planted into large 10–12 in (25–30 cm) pots and grown under the protection of a polythene tunnel to give some early production of propagating material.

Scions or scion wood

Scion or scion wood makes up the other half of the graft; it is the name given to the section of shoot taken from the parent plant, to be joined by grafting to the selected rootstock.

The scion, in the case of grafting, will be about the diameter of a pencil and will have grown in the previous year on the parent plant.

The scion, or bud wood, for budding is the same size but will have been produced in the current year on the parent plant. Whereas the whole scion is used for grafting, only the buds are used for budding.

Grafting

There are many forms of grafting but the following are the two most widely used.

Whip and tongue grafting out of doors
This is a traditional grafting technique still very much used today for grafting a wide range of trees and fruit and some selected shrubs. Although it can be used for bench grafting (grafting under cover), it is normally adopted for grafting out of doors on to rootstocks grown in the soil, rather than in pots.

During early spring rootstocks planted in the soil the previous late winter to early spring are cleaned from soil level upwards to a height of 12–18 in (30–50 cm) to remove any dirt or soil that could contaminate the graft union and prevent its growing together.

The graft is best made 10–18 in (25–50 cm) from ground level to stop water entering the graft union and also, in later life, to prevent the new tree from rooting above the graft in its own right and upsetting the root balance that has been planned, particularly in the case of Apples and Fruiting Cherries.

First a number of scions are cut with secateurs from the selected compatible parent plant. To ensure that the scions do not dry out before being grafted, only a small number is taken at any one time and these are stored in a wet cloth until required. Grafting should take place as soon as possible after the scions have been cut.

A scion is then selected as close as possible in diameter to that of the rootstock being grafted so that, when joined, both sides of the stems' cambium layers come into contact. Finding an exact match is not always possible and then a compromise has to be made, but one side at least must be in full contact.

Next the rootstock is cut with a sharp knife at the recommended height at an angle of 35° and just above a bud, with the cut sloping down and away from it. An upward sloping cut is then made on the opposite side to the bud, approximately $1\frac{1}{2}$–$1\frac{3}{4}$ in (4–4.5 cm) long. The cut starts at the lower end on one side and by the time it has reached the top, it has cut through two thirds of the diameter of the rootstock at a gentle angle, ensuring that at all times the knife is kept square to ensure the most level surface possible.

Next the upper end of the selected scion is prepared: a cut is made with a knife at an angle of 35°, just above a bud and sloping down from it. Scions are normally $2\frac{1}{2}$–$3\frac{1}{2}$ in (6–9 cm) long, depending on the bud formation. The lower end, the end to be grafted, is now cut just below a bud, again at an angle of 35° and sloping down from it. It is important that the buds chosen should be on opposite sides of the scion except where they are opposite each other on the stem and on these the grafting cut is made on the side of the scion, away from the buds.

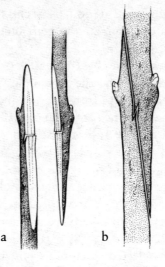

22. Whip and tongue grafting   (a) Prepared stock and scion
(b) Union between stock and scion before binding

Returning to the rootstock, a downward cut ¼ in (5 mm) deep is made into the face of the sloping cut, approximately one third of the distance from the top of it, to make a projecting tongue.

The scion is then matched with the rootstock and a mirror cut made into the scion, so that when they are brought together the surface of the cut and the tongues join together.

It is important that the surfaces come together without any gap. If a gap is visible, it is best to try again with a new scion, rather than try to cut them to fit. Once together, the union is bound with raffia and sealed with grafting wax or a pruning compound such as Arbrex to keep out water and dirt, which can prevent the graft union forming.

The grafts are left in this state until mid to late spring when the raffia ties are released and the new shoot is tied to a bamboo cane to be trained as a new tree or shrub.

Bench grafting (grafting in pots indoors)
Because of the more controlled environment, this form of grafting is often felt to be easier; however, you do need a greenhouse or working conservatory.

172

The grafting normally takes place from late winter to early spring when rootstocks, potted as already suggested, are brought into the greenhouse or conservatory approximately one month before they are to be grafted. This is done to induce the cambium layer to start into growth activity. Throughout the time that the rootstocks are under protection, it is obviously important to ensure that they are watered, but not overwatered.

Scions and rootstocks are prepared in exactly the same way as for whip and tongue grafting, but without the tongue being made.

They are then bound with raffia and the graft covered with grafting wax to prevent dirt or moisture entering the union. They are placed in a propagating case, normally at a temperature of 62–65°F (16.5–18°C) at an angle of say 35° to reduce the space required.

Normally, after two months, when a union is well-formed, the raffia can be removed and the plants stood upright outside in a sheltered area where they will grow very rapidly. They can be planted out in the following autumn.

Budding

Tee-cut budding
The stocks which were planted in the previous autumn are cleaned between early summer and midsummer. In the case of Roses, the short stem that will be used for budding is exposed from below soil level; these stems are normally much closer to the ground than with other stocks.

Once the stocks are cleaned and ready for budding, bud wood is then collected from the parent plant. This consists of a length of growth produced in the current season and with between three and ten buds along its length, depending on its age, size and species. These are collected in relatively small numbers so that they do not dry out while the process of budding is carried out, and during the process they should be kept covered with a wet cloth as much as possible or in a bucket of water.

The next stage is to make an upward cut in the skin or bark

173

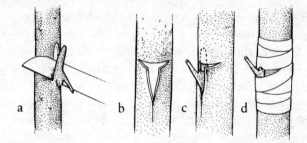

23. Tee-cut budding   (a) Preparation of bud
(b) Tee cut in stock   (c) Prepared bud inserted into stock
(d) Bud tied in to prevent movement and aid union

of the rootstock, approximately $1\frac{1}{2}$ in (4 cm) long, just through the skin. A horizontal cut is made across the top of the cut, around one third of the diameter of the stem, and centred on the upright cut; again it should be only skin deep. As the knife is drawn across the horizontal it is held at an angle of approximately 15°, which helps open the top of the cut.

A budding knife specifically designed for the purpose is normally used for this work. It has either an additional blade on the tail end or a shaped bone end; this is inserted into one side of the top of the vertical cut and slid downwards. This is then repeated on the other side of the cut, so that the skin can be levered open without tearing it. This exposes the cambium layer and allows the bud to be inserted.

The bud wood is held between finger and thumb, across the hand, and the knife inserted approximately $\frac{1}{16}$ in ($1\frac{1}{4}$ mm) below the selected bud starting from the top of the bud stick. (Each undamaged bud in turn, working downwards, can be used on a separate rootstock.) The knife is inserted approximately $\frac{1}{8}$ in ($2\frac{1}{2}$ mm) under the bud and then an upwards cut is made; once the knife is under the bud itself, it is possible to rip the remaining section of skin away.

The small section of wood behind the bud is removed, leaving the bud shield. This shield is pushed into the tee cut made in the rootstock, so that the bud is approximately halfway down the vertical cut, and any remaining tail of budwood growth is then removed along the line of the horizontal cut. The bud is bound in place with raffia or with plastic strip specifically designed for the purpose.

It is left in this condition for the next four to six weeks, after which it should clearly be seen that a callous or union has been formed between the bud and the rootstock. (If this is not obvious, then the process has to start again; a second attempt can be made on the opposite side.) Rootstock and bud are left for some eight to ten weeks after budding has taken place, and then the raffia can be removed.

In the following early spring the rootstock is cut off just above the point where the bud was inserted and this then allows the bud to grow away to form a new Rose, shrub or tree, as the case may be.

Chip budding

Chip budding is carried out between early summer and midsummer and is used for ornamental trees which are difficult to propagate by other means.

The rootstock is planted and cleaned in the same way as for tee-cut budding. A cut is then made between buds, downwards and inwards at an angle of 35° and to a depth of approximately $\frac{1}{4}$ in (5 mm).

The second cut is started $1\frac{1}{2}$ in (4 cm) above the first cut and

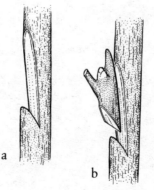

24. *Chip budding   (a) Prepared cut in stock*
(b) Prepared chip bud in position prior to tying in

descends from this point until it joins the lower point of the first cut, releasing a shield of bark. Whenever possible the cut is made on the reverse side to the bud.

The scion wood is selected and removed from the parent plant in the same way as for tee-cut budding; again the first downward-sloping cut is made at an angle of 35°, approximately $\frac{1}{4}$ in (5 mm) deep into the bud wood, $\frac{1}{2}$ in (1 cm) below the bud. A second cut is made approximately $\frac{1}{2}$ in (1 cm) above the bud and continued down behind the bud until it joins the lower horizontal cut. This will release a shield of wood with the bud in the centre. This shield is then placed in the cut in the rootstock, pushing the lower end into the cleft made by the downward cut on the rootstock.

The bud is then bound in position with raffia or specially designed plastic ties, and is allowed to grow on in exactly the same way as for tee-cut budding.

CHAPTER EIGHT

Pruning

Over the years I have come to realize that pruning is the job that causes the most apprehension, and it is therefore often delayed or avoided. Over a period of time this almost always causes unnecessary damage and reduced performance in the plants under our care.

This apprehension is born out of the belief that irreversible damage can be done to the shrub, tree, rose, etc., by pruning it. Of course this is not the case, as long as some simple rules are understood and followed. In most cases all that pruning achieves is a mirroring or speeding up of the plant's natural growth pattern.

However, if a plant is not pruned, the resulting decline in performance takes place over a number of years and often goes unnoticed until the plant is in such a poor state that it may be beyond recovery. On the other hand, if the recommended pruning is carried out correctly there is, of course, no way of knowing what would have happened if it had been omitted. If a plant is not pruned, flowers will decrease in size and number, or be completely absent, and fruiting too may fail in subjects such as Cotoneaster and Pyracantha (Firethorn). Leaves become smaller and, if the plant is grown for its foliage – as are shrubs such as *Berberis thunbergii atropurpurea* (Purple-leaved Barberry), *Cornus alba* 'Elegantissima' (Silver-variegated Dogwood) or *Sambucus racemosa* 'Plumosa Aurea' (Cut-leaved Golden Elder) – the main attraction is lost.

Smaller leaves means slower root activity and development, so less new growth will be produced and shrubs such as *Cornus alba* 'Westonbirt' (Westonbirt Red-stemmed Dogwood) and *C. stolonifera* 'Flaviramea' (Yellow-stemmed Dogwood) that are used in the garden for their winter stem effect will offer a diminished display.

Correct pruning is important; it is practised for the well-being of the plant in question and rarely causes any harm.

No pruning can reduce the true ultimate height of a plant variety when fully grown. The sweetly scented flowering shrub *Philadelphus* 'Virginal' (Mock Orange) grows ultimately to 13 ft (4 m) whereas *P.* 'Manteau d'Hermine' (Dwarf Mock Orange) will only reach 3 ft (1 m); both, if cut down to ground level, will over three or four years grow back to their normal heights. If, however, they are not pruned in the prescribed way, shoots will be produced at the ends of mature branches, so artificially increasing the height and spread.

If a shrub is cut to ground level, its flowering will be seriously reduced until it reaches its normal height again. Pruning ensures that plants grow to their most productive height and spread, and continue to produce renewed flowers, foliage and growth over many years.

Although my suggestions have been tried and tested over many years, very rare factors out of the gardener's control may, in a very small percentage of cases, temporarily counteract the effectiveness of the suggested procedures. These conditions include severe drought, excessive rain or abnormally hard winters. Late spring frosts can also influence the new growth of plants after pruning. However, in the long term, the risk of damage caused by not pruning is far greater.

After pruning the plants will require feeding to ensure that the correct balance of plant foods is present in the soil to encourage the new replacement growth. This feeding is best carried out in early to late spring, using an inorganic fertilizer such as Growmore, applied at the rate recommended in the instructions on the packet.

In addition to feeding, it is important to prevent competition from weeds and provide a lightly cultivated soil surface to allow the free passage of rainwater into the soil, so that the fertilizer is diluted and can be taken up by the root system.

The correct timing of the pruning is important to ensure that maximum use is made of the individual plant's natural growth pattern. In many cases this is after flowering; Weigela, Deutzia and Forsythia are good examples.

Some plants such as Potentilla flower throughout the spring, summer and early autumn, so these are pruned in early to mid spring, sacrificing some flowers but ensuring, on an ongoing basis, that new growth and flowers are produced.

Other shrubs are pruned in early to late spring to encourage attractive new foliage and shoots; *Cornus alba* 'Elegantissima' (Silver-variegated Dogwood) and *Rosa glauca/R. rubrifolia* (Purple-leaved Rose) are good examples.

In all cases the plants should have been established for more than three years before pruning starts and thereafter pruning should be carried out on an annual basis.

Other shrubs such as *Santolina chamaecyparissus* (Cotton Lavender), *Helichrysum angustifolia* (Curry Plant) and *Lavandula angustifolia* (English Lavender) need special care in the timing; nature's own signals in mid to late spring show when the pruning time is right. If these signs are ignored and the shrubs are not pruned, they will very quickly deteriorate. With this group of plants there is no need to wait before starting pruning – it is started in the first spring after planting and then carried out annually.

Shrubs such as *Hydrangea paniculata* 'Grandiflora' (Panick Hydrangea) and *Sambucus racemosa* 'Plumosa Aurea' (Golden Cut-leaved Elder) must be pruned in early to mid spring in the first spring following planting and the pruning continued on an annual basis; if it is not, the shrubs will probably die or deteriorate within eighteen to twenty-four months following planting or the last pruning.

With some slower-growing shrubs, such as Rhododendrons and Azaleas, pruning may be delayed for ten or twenty years after planting; once started, it is thereafter carried out biennially, so allowing time for new growth to be produced.

With some shrubs more than one pruning method may be advocated, with each method achieving a specific result which will show off one of the various characteristics of the plant – foliage, flowers or stems – to the best advantage.

I have also described the pruning of climbers and wall shrubs, including Clematis and Wisteria, and of all the different groups of Roses. Fruit trees and bushes will also be dealt with. Conifers can also be pruned to improve their overall size, shape, appearance and colour. Even perennial plants may require 'pruning' in some circumstances, and it can be very important to the plants' long-term well-being.

Trees in their early years can be improved in shape and, if a foliage variety, the size and colour of the leaves can be increased by pruning. They can also be pruned for specific uses such as pleaching, pollarding and to cover arches and walkways, and the pruning required to create these effects is covered later.

If a shrub, Rose or climbing plant has not been pruned for many years it may become overgrown and require rejuvenation pruning and details of how to achieve this are also given.

Pruning tools and their use

When using sharp tools health and safety must always be considered, and gloves and industrial eye protectors should always be worn. Children should be kept away from the area of operation.

Pruning knives

A good-quality pruning knife will be required, to remove thin weak shoots as well as to pare, or smooth off, the edges of pruning cuts that are larger in diameter than your thumb. This is done to assist the healing process and seal the cuts by aiding the production of a layer of new tissue by the growth cells in the cambium layer just below the bark. Once formed, this growth barrier can keep out infections such as canker on Apples and Pears, silver leaf on Cherries and Plums and fireblight on Cotoneasters.

In addition, Arbrex pruning compound should be applied to protect the cut from attack by fungus diseases such as coral spot. Whereas some would argue that this is no longer required, I believe it is particularly important on slower-growing ornamental trees, shrubs and climbers.

Secateurs

For larger cuts, secateurs will be required and these come in two types: *parrot bill*, where the upper, sharpened cutting

1. *Salix exigua* (Coyote Willow)

2. *Spiraea x bumalda* 'Anthony Waterer'

3. *Physocarpus opulifolius* 'Luteus'

4. *Chaenomeles speciosa* 'Apple Blossom' (Ornamental Quince)

5. *Pelargonium peltatum*
(Ivy-leaved Geranium)

6. *Salvia officinalis* 'Tricolor'
(Ornamental Sage)

7. *Lavandula angustifolia* 'Hidcote' (Old English Lavender)

8. *Fuchsia* 'Genii'

9. *Viburnum plicatum* 'Mariesii'

10. *Hebe* 'Midsummer Beauty'

11. *Ceanothus thyrsiflorus repens* 12. *Abelia x grandiflora* 'Francis Mason'

13. *Cornus kousa chinensis* (Chinese or Japanese Dogwood)

14. *Embothrium coccineum*
(Chilean Fire Bush)

15. *Hamamelis mollis* (Witch Hazel)

16. *Callistemon citrinus* (Australian Bottle Brush)

17. *Hosta fortunei* 'Albopicta'

18. *Iris unguicularis* (*I. stylosa*)
(Winter-flowering Iris)

19. *Astrantia major* 'Variegata'

20. *Polygonum affine* 'Donald Lowndes' and Pink Dwarf Aster

21. *Camellia japonica* 'Elegans'

22. *Skimmia japonica* 'Rubella'

23. *Rhododendron yakushimanum*

24. Mollis Azalea 'Apple Blossom'

SHRUBS THAT REQUIRE THE ONE THIRD METHOD
OF PRUNING

25. *Deutzia x kalmiiflora*

26. *Spiraea x arguta* (Bridal Wreath)

27. *Berberis thunbergii* 'Dart's Red Lady'
(Purple-leaved Barbary)

28. *Potentilla fruticosa* 'Abbotswood'

29. *Cornus alba* 'Spaethii' (Golden-leaved Dogwood)

30. *Buddleja* 'Lochinch'

31. *Cornus stolonifera* 'Flaviramea'
(Yellow-stemmed Dogwood)

32. *Santolina chamaecyparissus*
(Cotton Lavender)

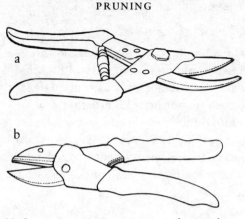

25. *Secateurs*   *(a) Parrot type*   *(b) Anvil type*

blade cuts down *across* the lower, unsharpened, anvil blade; and *anvil*, where the thinner, sharpened upper blade cuts down *on to* the lower, thicker and wider, unsharpened anvil blade.

It is said by some that the normally more expensive parrot-bill type makes a better cleaner cut and prevents bruising of the stem, but I have found that if both types are well maintained and kept sharp, there is little difference, except for the higher price of the parrot-bill type.

However, the following rules apply to both types to ensure a good clean cut and prevent damage to the secateurs. Firstly the upper, sharpened blade should always be on the top or front side of the cut so that the cut is made smoothly downwards or forwards and with the minimum of sideways movement. Secondly it is important never to attempt to cut material that is too thick: never try to cut shoots thicker than can be fitted between the blades when fully open and never nibble or attempt to cut a branch in stages from different sides. Also, never force the cut by placing sideways pressure on the secateurs as this is a major cause of permanent damage to both types of secateurs.

Long-handled loppers
Should the shoots be too thick for secateurs it will be necessary to use a pair of long-handled loppers, which have more leverage. These also come in two types, parrot and anvil, and the same rules of use apply as for secateurs.

Folding saws

As an alternative to loppers, and in some cases secateurs, my choice is to use a folding pruning saw; I find that with its 6–9 in (15–23 cm) blade it not only cuts the larger material and does it very cleanly, but because of its narrow and short blade it can reach into difficult confined spaces.

As it cuts on both strokes, backward and forward, care must be taken, as always, to prevent accidents from the very sharp teeth.

A good sharp folding saw can make as clean a cut as the best secateurs.

Bow saw

There may be times when the folding saw is not adequate for the job, and then a bow saw will be needed. Although it can sometimes be difficult to position due to its size, it is useful for the removal of larger branches, particularly on trees.

Chain saw

I advise strongly against using a chain saw, for not only can it be very dangerous when used by an untrained operator in confined spaces, but if used indiscriminately it can cause a great deal of damage to the tree or shrub being 'pruned'.

Sharpening of pruning tools

All tools should be kept clean and sharp, and if a lot of work is carried out in the garden each year, replacement tools, in particular secateurs, may be necessary. The sharpening of knives and secateurs is best done using a household or workshop chisel sharpening stone, which can be purchased from most DIY stores. It will normally have hard and soft sides and will be 4–5 in (10–12 cm) long, 1 in (3 cm) wide and $\frac{1}{2}$ in (1 cm) thick. Before use it should be moistened with water or a small amount of household oil. The cutting edge of the blade is drawn, three or four times, slowly and firmly over the stone at an angle of 25–35°, ensuring that the bevelled edge of the blade is facing down on to the sharpening stone. To finish off, one pass is made over the stone on the reverse side to remove any 'burr' – the small pieces of metal that may have formed.

If this sharpening process is carried out with a new knife or secateurs, the soft or smoother side of the stone is used. Sharpening should then be repeated at regular intervals during use.

Should the knife or secateurs have been neglected, three or four passes over the hard or rough side may be best, finishing off with two or three passes over the soft or smoother side, plus the reverse pass. If more than this is required it is probably best to purchase a new tool.

Loppers do not normally require sharpening, but from time to time passing the hard or rough side of the sharpening stone over the leading edge of the cutting blade may be of assistance and will help with the final cleanness of the cut.

Saw blades are best replaced as necessary, as to have them sharpened could cost as much, even if you could find somebody to do it.

Making the pruning cut

Whenever possible, cutting to above a bud is recommended. Buds are normally the raised points along a plant's shoots where the new side shoots, leaves and flowers will be produced. They may be arranged opposite each other or alternately along the length of the shoot, normally at regular intervals. They contain all the plant's potential for producing new side shoots, foliage and flowers in the spring, summer and autumn following pruning, so care is needed to avoid damaging them.

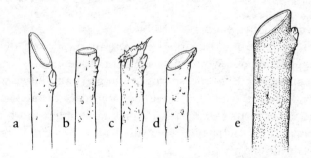

26. Pruning cuts (a) Wrong: angled towards bud
(b) Cut too square (c) Ragged cut will prevent healing of wound
(d) Bud damaged; cut is too close (e) Correct cut

When the plant is, say, more than three years old, the buds may be harder to see, having become camouflaged by the bark. But even if they cannot be seen, they are still there in a dormant state and once pruning has been carried out they will be induced to grow and produce new growth. When pruning, a calculated guess may have to be made as to their position.

If the buds can be seen, the cut should be made above and within $\frac{1}{4}$ in (5 mm) of the bud. If the cut is not made cleanly or at the right angle, there is always the chance of die-back; this is caused by rain entering through the pruning cut and inducing rotting, which can spread and cause further damage. Alternatively it can be caused by the pruning cut being made too high above a bud so that plant foods in the form of sugars are not used and all the surplus food above the bud will rot. Once the fungi have a hold, they spread down the stem in search of more food and start to kill the plant tissue in order to obtain food in a form they can use. With some species of shrubs, in particular Acers (Maples), coral spot fungus may gain a hold under these conditions, as will cankers of various trees in the Malus (Apple) family.

So a clean cut is made with a sharp pruning tool at an angle sloping away from the bud to ensure the run-off of rain, and just far enough above the bud to avoid it being cut or crushed. If the cut is larger in diameter than your thumb, it should be pared off (the edges of the cut trimmed) with a sharp knife and painted with Arbrex to prevent the entering of diseases.

Tree-pruning hygiene
To prevent the build-up of overwintering pests and diseases the application of a winter tar oil wash is good garden practice, to eliminate the eggs and spores of the pests and diseases that attack and spoil fruit. The wash also improves the appearance of the bark of trees or bushes by making it shine and for this reason it is very effective when used on ornamental trees as well as fruiting varieties.

The directions on the product should be closely followed and health and safety requirements complied with.

Personally I am not in favour of shredding pruned shoots,

as there is always a risk of spreading pest and disease infestation, nor do I like to use the shredded material for soil
mulching or improvement, for the reasons stated in Chapter 2.
All pruning material should always be removed and burnt as
soon as possible.

Removing large shoots and branches

If a large shoot is to be removed using a saw, folding or bow,
it is good practice to make the first cut 2 ft (60 cm) away from
the intended final cut, so removing some of the weight. To
help make a clean final cut, approximately a third of the
diameter of the shoot is cut with the saw from the underside
upwards. A cut is then started from the top, ensuring it is in
line with the lower one, and the remainder of the cut made.

Geographical differences in pruning times

Throughout the following text, reference is made to the timing
of pruning, based on the southern and central areas of the
United Kingdom. For those gardening in the south-west, the
work can often be brought forward by seven to ten days. In
the north, Northern Ireland or Scotland, it may need to be
delayed for a week or two, but in all areas, account should be
taken of weather conditions, and if in doubt wait until the
weather improves.

PRUNING SHRUBS

Reversion

Many variegated shrubs and some trees may revert: in other
words, the leaves will be all green, not variegated. This is a
natural reaction by the plant as a defence against starvation
and an attempt on its part to increase the area of green
productive cells in its leaves. The starvation defence may be
triggered by a natural deficiency of plant food in the soil, poor
root establishment or drought weather conditions which make
it difficult for the soil moisture to absorb plant foods.

All-green reversion leaves and shoots can appear at any time
throughout the growing season on a wide range of variegated

shrubs and trees, and are easy to identify. Once identified they should be removed, ensuring that the cut is made at a point below a variegated leaf, even if this means cutting a 'hole' in the overall shape of the shrub or tree. Any hole that is made will be filled with new variegated growth in the following spring.

As well as removing the reverted stem it is important to water the plant well; use of a general fertilizer such as Grow-more applied in mid spring will help to correct any future deficiency.

Not removing the reverted shoots, which are stronger than the variegated ones, can lead to a total takeover, and in a very short time the shrub or tree will be damaged beyond the point of no return.

The trees and shrubs that are most affected are:

TREES
Acer negundo, all variegated varieties (Variegated Box-leaved Maple)
A. platanoides, all variegated varieties (Variegated Norway Maple)
A. pseudoplatanus, all variegated varieties (Variegated Sycamore)
Gleditsia triacanthos 'Sunburst' (Golden Honey Locust Tree)
Liriodendron tulipifera 'Aureomarginatum' (Golden-variegated Tulip Tree)
Populus candicans 'Aurora' (Pink-leaved Poplar)
Robinia pseudoacacia 'Frisia' (Golden-leaved Acacia)

SHRUBS
Abelia grandiflora 'Francis Mason' (Golden-leaved Abelia)
Acanthopanax sieboldianus, all variegated varieties (Five-leaf Aralia)
Acer palmatum, variegated varieties (Variegated Japanese Maple)
Aralia elata, variegated varieties (Variegated Japanese Angelica Tree)
Buddleja davidii, variegated varieties (Variegated Buddleja)
Cornus alba, variegated varieties (Variegated European Dogwood)
C. alternifolia 'Argentea' (Variegated Pagoda Dogwood)
C. controversa 'Variegata' (Variegated Wedding-cake Tree)
C. mas 'Variegata' and the coloured-leaf varieties (Variegated Cornelian Cherry)
Cotoneaster horizontalis 'Variegatus' (Variegated Fish-bone Cotoneaster)

Daphne cneorum 'Variegata' (Variegated Daphne)
Elaeagnus × *ebbingei* varieties (Variegated Elaeagnus)
E. pungens varieties (Variegated Elaeagnus)
Euonymus fortunei, variegated varieties (Variegated Wintercreeper
  Euonymus)
E. japonica, variegated varieties (Variegated Japanese Euonymus)
Ilex × *altaclarensis*, all variegated varieties (Variegated Holly)
I. aquifolium, all variegated varieties (Variegated Holly)
Ligustrum lucidum, variegated varieties (Variegated Glossy Privet)
L. ovalifolium 'Aureum' (Variegated Golden Privet)
L. sinensis, variegated varieties (Variegated Silver Privet)
Pachysandra terminalis 'Variegata' (Variegated Spurge)
Philadelphus coronarius 'Aureus' (Golden-leaved Mock Orange)
P. c. 'Variegatus' (Variegated Mock Orange)
Prunus lusitanica 'Variegata' (Variegated Portugal Laurel)
Rhamnus alaternus 'Argenteovariegata' (Variegated Buckthorn)
Sambucus nigra, golden and variegated varieties (Variegated Elder)
S. racemosa, golden cut-leaved varieties (Golden Cut-leaved Elder)
Spiraea × *bumalda*, golden-leaved varieties (Golden-leaved Spiraea)
Weigela florida, golden and variegated varieties (Variegated Weigela)

Suckering

Many gardeners are aware of Rose suckers but other trees and
shrubs may also produce them and if they are not removed
they can outgrow the intended plant. Trees and shrubs on the
following list need careful watching; Roses are dealt with later,
p. 222.

TREES

Amelanchier (Snowy Mespilus), when grafted on to Crataegus
  (Thorn)
Caragana (Siberian Peashrub), ornamental varieties, both root and
  stem suckers
Catalpa bigninodes 'Aurea' (Golden-leaved Indian Bean Tree) – both
  soil and stem suckers
Cotoneaster, large-leaved varieties when grafted on to *Cotoneaster
  bullatus*, both root and stem suckers
Crataegus (Thorn), ornamental varieties when grafted on to *C.
  monogyna* (Thorn)

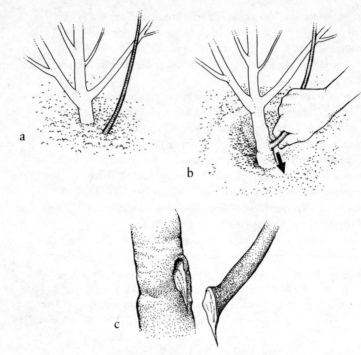

27. *Removal of suckers   (a) Sucker emerging from below soil level*
(b) Sucker dug out; downward pressure to rip out sucker
(c) Sucker wound, preventing any regrowth

Fraxinus excelsior 'Pendula' (Weeping Ash) – both stem and root
suckers
Malus (Ornamental Crab Apples)
Prunus serrulata (Japanese Cherry), in particular the weeping
varieties – both stem and root suckers

SHRUBS
Berberis linearifolia varieties when grafted on to *B. thunbergii*
atropurpurea
B. × *lologensis* varieties when grafted on to *B. thunbergii*
atropurpurea
Corylus avellana 'Contorta' (Contorted Hazel) – root suckers
Cotoneaster (large-leaved varieties), when grafted on to *C. bullatus* –
root suckers
Elaeagnus pungens varieties when grafted on to *Cotoneaster*
angustifolia – root suckers

188

E. × *ebbingei* varieties when grafted on to C. *angustifolia* – root
 suckers
Prunus triloba, when grafted as a shrub or on a stem as a small tree
- Syringa (Lilac), both species and hybrid varieties when grafted on to
 Ligustrum vulgaris or L. *ovalifolium* or *Syringa vulgaris*
Viburnum × *burkwoodii* varieties when grafted on to V. *lantana*
V. carlcephalum, when grafted on to V. *lantana*
V. carlesii varieties, when grafted on to V. *lantana*
V. × *juddii*, when grafted on to V. *lantana*
V. rhytidophyllum, when grafted on to V. *lantana*

To remove the suckers it is important to remove the soil from
the area where the sucker is located and confirm that it is
growing from below the graft or budding point (see Chapter
7). If it is, then it should be carefully ripped out, not cut, to
ensure that all possible sucker buds are removed; cutting always
leaves some buds that will regrow. If suckers are not spotted
soon enough the work can become a major task, so a careful
watch should always be kept.

With some of the trees the suckers may emerge from the
main stem, particularly on weeping Cherries, and there are
many examples, in gardens, of ruined trees where the sucker
has become dominant. Careful ripping out and covering with a
pruning compound such as Arbrex is again the best removal
technique, and watching and removing when young is always
best, creating less damage.

Territorial pruning

There is no substitute for planting at adequate distances to
ensure that no plant invades another's allocated space, but
where there is a problem, territorial pruning may be necessary.
At first sight it may seem that the need for this is obvious, but
in fact it is rarely adopted as a routine garden pruning practice,
which is sad, because if it was then many group plantings
of shrubs would grow together without causing each other
damage. By regular inspection and careful selective removal of
shoots that are infringing on their neighbours' growing space,
long-term damage can be avoided.

Removal can be done at any time on a 'when seen' basis and

there are very few shrubs on which it cannot be practised, except for some upright-growing conifers, and even here, if identified soon enough, it may be possible.

As to how much or what length of shoot should be removed, this will depend on the plant in question, but it is better to remove one third more than is at first thought necessary, to allow for the grow-back potential. If one of a pair of adjoining plants is less choice than the other, that is the one to prune hardest.

However, territorial pruning should never be seen as an alternative for the recommended long-term pruning method. In some cases territorial pruning may seem to contradict a specific pruning method, but as normally only a relatively small amount of material is removed, it will cause little or no harm.

One-third pruning method for shrubs

The reason for pruning shrubs is to keep the microscopic cellular tubes that are present in the stems clear of obstruction, so that they can carry soil moisture, containing the plant foods, from the roots to the buds and leaves. By the spring of the second year of growth, the stems will have become furred up with small deposits of calcium on the inside of the tube walls, impairing the flow of sap. This furring up is even worse in the third year but still does not cause any problems. In the fourth and subsequent years, however, the shrub's performance starts to deteriorate and as the years pass, the shrub loses more and more of its vigour and attraction.

At the same time, the density of the growths at the base of the shrubs means that no new shoots can grow, so the shrub counteracts this by producing superficial shoots from the upper ends of the main shoots, which increases the overall height, and as the original shoots become heavy and bend with the weight, the spread is increased.

The need for pruning rejuvenation on this group of plants is normally indicated by a severe decrease in the size of the foliage, often on one particular group of shoots. In addition, the leaves will be duller in colour and, in advanced cases, will start to turn brown. The size and number of flowers will also be reduced.

Age of shoots
Identifying the age of a shoot can be difficult but by careful inspection, in conjunction with the following descriptions, this should be possible.

ONE-YEAR-OLD SHOOTS
One-year-old shoots are sometimes referred to as 'previous season's growth'; in some older publications, words such as 'wood', 'growth', 'stems' or 'branches' may be used to describe shoots.

These shoots will not have flowered or show any signs of having done so. In most cases they will have no major side branches but towards late summer a few very short branches may form on some species. They will normally be smooth skinned and show few signs of having any bark. The skin will be shiny and brighter in colour than the older shoots, and as a general rule will be the thinnest.

TWO-YEAR-OLD SHOOTS
These shoots will have flowered for the first time and will have started to produce their first side branches. They will be duller in colour than the one-year-old shoots and the first signs of a normally grey bark will be visible. They will be thicker than the one-year-old shoots but not necessarily thinner than the three-year-old ones, and will have the overall appearance of being the most vigorous and strong.

THREE-YEAR-OLD SHOOTS
These shoots will have produced flowers for the last two years and will have a very branching habit. The bark will be fully formed and in most shrubs will be grey in colour, but these shoots may not always be the thickest.

FOUR-YEAR-OLD SHOOTS AND OLDER
These will have flowered for at least the last three years and

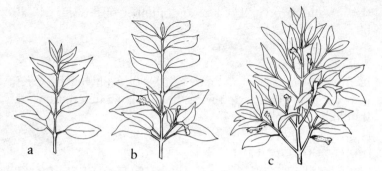

28. Shoots of different ages
(a) One-year-old shoot with no side shoots or flowers
(b) Two-year-old shoot with non-branching side shoots and
flowers   (c) Three-year-old shoot with branching side
shoots and flowers

will have a well-formed bark, particularly at the base. The first signs of dead side branches will be identifiable and the older the shoots the more these will be seen. Superficial strong growth may have started to develop from the upper ends and, depending on the age, will have started to bend outwards and downwards.

Position of flower buds and the wrong interpretation of pruning techniques

It is important to remember at this stage that, with this group of shrubs, particularly where the pruning is used to improve the flowers, the new flower buds for the following year, formed in the previous year, are situated mainly on the upper third to half of the shoot's length, so it is very important to retain this flowering material – in no way should it be shortened.

This explains why many shrubs fail to flower when wrongly pruned; if the wrong technique is repeated year after year, the shrubs may never flower successfully.

The use of the wrong pruning techniques often arises from the misinterpretation of the instruction, either verbal or written, that one third of the shoots should be removed. This is

192

mistakenly taken to mean that the upper third of any shoot, whatever its age, should be removed, but of course by doing this the misinformed pruner cuts away the next year's flowers.

Also, as has already been stated, no flowering shrub can be reduced effectively to less than its natural ultimate height and if attempts are made to do so, then all or most of the flowers will be removed, defeating the main reason for growing the shrub.

Where a shrub has been planted for more than three years – and not more than four – and assuming it has been planted correctly, it should be pruned by the one-third pruning method (see below), with certain variations in timing:

Three years after planting, whatever their age when planted, flowering shrubs are pruned after flowering, with the exception of Potentillas, which are pruned in mid spring just before the leaves start to form.

Shrubs grown principally for their coloured foliage are pruned in early to mid spring.

Where shrubs are grown for their ornamental stems, but the hard-cutting-back method is not used because the architectural shape of the shrub is required, the pruning is carried out in early to mid spring.

The only shrubs which do not respond well to this method are those in the Cytisus (Broom), Genista (Broom) and Ulex (Gorse) group of shrubs.

If a shrub's name is not known then this pruning method can be used without harm to the shrub and will produce better results than if it is left unpruned.

Carrying out the one-third pruning method
YEAR ONE

1. Inspect the shrub for any dead, diseased, damaged or broken shoots and if found, remove. It may be that as pruning

continues, more material of this type is identified and it too should be removed.

2. Clear any loose debris such as leaves and other rubbish from the base of the shrub; also remove any growth that is very weak and obviously of no value to the shrub.

3. Next, between ground level and approximately 18 in (50 cm) above it, count the number of main shoots and divide this number by three to give the target number of shoots – one third of the total – to be removed.

4. Identify the oldest wood and with the appropriate pruning tool cut away the selected shoot, at or as close to ground level as possible. Continue until the target number of shoots has been removed.

Care should be taken to ensure that when a shoot is being removed it is not pulled through the body of the shrub, breaking or damaging shoots and buds that are to remain.

On some occasions the balance of one-, two- or three-year-old shoots may not allow for the oldest shoots to be removed as low as one would like without removing a good two-year-old shoot, and in these cases a compromise needs to be made and the cut made higher than normal.

Where possible, shoots should be removed that open up the centre of the shrub to allow air and light in, which will not only ensure good future development but also go some way towards preventing build-up of pests and diseases.

Shoots that, when removed, will create space between the shrub being pruned and its neighbour, are worth considering first, as are shoots that cause an obstruction to, say, a path or in some way hinder cultivation.

The remaining shoots should not be shortened unless one of them is causing a real nuisance, as by so doing the flower production in the following year will be reduced.

YEAR TWO

All the same considerations that applied in year one apply in year two.

Last year's one-year-old shoots are now two years old and will have flowered; likewise last year's two-year shoots

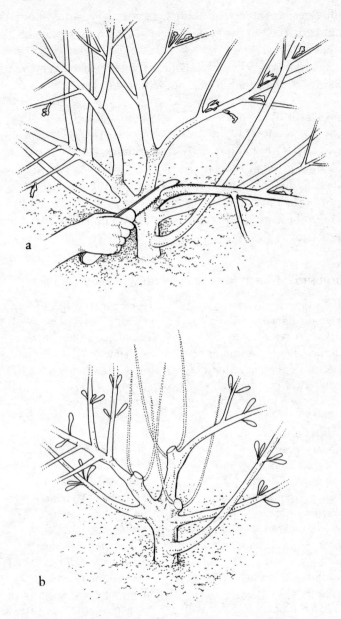

29. One-third pruning   (a) Cutting out a crossing shoot
(b) One-third of oldest shoots removed; future regrowth
indicated

will now be three-year shoots; new one-year-old shoots will have grown following last year's pruning, replacing those removed.

Again choosing the oldest shoots, one third are removed; the identification of the shoots should now be clearer.

YEAR THREE

Last year's one-year shoots are now two-year, the two are now three and both will have flowered and new one-year-old shoots will have grown to replace those removed in the previous year.

As before, after flowering, count, identify and remove one third of the oldest shoots.

From here on the process is repeated annually for the life of the shrub.

Shrubs that benefit from the one-third method

Abelia varieties (Abelia)
Abeliophyllum distictium†
  (Korean Abelia-leaf)
Abutilon, not tree-forming
  varieties (Trailing Abutilon)
Buddleja globosa and B. ×
  weyeriana varieties (Butterfly
  Bush)
Carpenteria californica†
  (Carpenteria)
Choisya varieties (Mexican
  Orange Blossom)
Deutzia varieties (Deutzia)
Diervilla varieties (Bush
  Honeysuckle)
Dipelta floribunda† (Dipelta)
Escallonia varieties (Escallonia)
Exochorda varieties† (Pearl
  Bush)
Forsythia varieties (Golden Ball)
Hebe, low and taller varieties
  (can also be hard cut back)
  (Hebe, Veronica)

Hypericum, shrubby varieties (St
  John's Wort)
Jasminum, shrubby varieties
  (Jasmine)
Kolkwitzia varieties (Beauty
  Bush)
Ligustrum varieties
  (Privet)
Lonicera, shrub and climbing
  varieties (Honeysuckle)
Mahonia aquifolium varieties
  (Mahonia)
M. pinnata† (Mahonia)
M. 'Undulata' varieties†
  (Mahonia)
Neillia varieties (Neillia)
Paeonia lutea ludlowii† (Yellow
  Tree Peony)
Philadelphus, including
  ornamental-foliage varieties
  (Mock Orange)
Physocarpus varieties (Nine-
  bark)

Potentilla varieties* (Shrubby Cinquefoil)

Pyracantha, when grown free-standing (Firethorn)

Ribes odoratum (Flowering Currant)

R. sanguineum varieties (Flowering Currant)

Rubus calycinoides (Ground-covering Bramble)

R. × tridel (Ground-covering Bramble)

R. ulmifolius (Fruiting Bramble)

Salix, low-growing varieties, but not very dwarf ones (Willow)

Spiraea × arguta (Spiraea)

S. × bumalda (Spiraea)

S. japonica varieties (Japanese Spiraea)

S. nipponica varieties (Nippon Spiraea)

S. thunbergii (Thunberg Spiraea)

S. × vanhouttei (Vanhoutte Spiraea)

Stephanandra incisa varieties (Cut-leaf Stephanandra)

S. tanakae (Tanaka Stephanandra)

Stranvaesia varieties† (Stranvaesia)

Symphoricarpos varieties (Snowberry)

Viburnum varieties (Viburnum)

Weigela varieties (Weigela)

* Pruned in late March. A limited number of flowers have to be sacrificed because during summer and early autumn it is rarely out of flower.
† Can also be allowed to grow unpruned but may deteriorate over fifteen years or more.

One-third method used to improve shoot and foliage effect

Using the same steps as for flowering shrubs and again starting three years after planting, but carried out annually in early to mid spring. When practised on the recommended shrubs this method can give one of the highest rewards in foilage performance, but may reduce flowering by up to one third.

SHRUBS

Abelia × grandiflora 'Francis Mason' (Golden-variegated Abelia)

Acanthopanax sieboldianus, variegated varieties* (Five-leaf Aralia)

Artemisia arbrotanum, and other shrubby varieties (Southernwood)

*Atriplex halimus** (Tree Purslane, Salt Bush)

Aucuba japonica varieties (Spotted Laurel)

Berberis dictyophylla, to improve stem colours (White-stemmed Barberry)

B. thunbergii varieties (Barberry)

Cornus alba, coloured- and variegated-leaved varieties†

in particular purple-leaved varieties (Red-barked Dogwood)

C. *stolonifera* 'Flaviramea'† (Yellow-stemmed Dogwood)

Corylus, purple- and golden-leaved varieties (Hazel, Filbert, Cobnut)

Cotinus, both purple- and green-leaved varieties (Smoke Bush)

Elaeagnus × ebbingei, both green and variegated varieties* (Elaeagnus)

E. pungens, both green and variegated varieties (Thorny Elaeagnus)

Leucothoë, both green and variegated varieties* (Drooping Leucothoë)

Ligustrum lucidum, both green and variegated varieties* (Glossy, Variegated Privet)

L. ovalifolium, both green and variegated varieties (Oval-leaved Privet)

Lonicera nitida 'Baggesen's Gold' (Golden Box-leaf Honeysuckle)

× *Mahoberberis aquisargentii** (Mahoberberis)

Philadelphus, both golden-leaved and variegated varieties (Mock Orange)

Prunus laurocerasus varieties* (Cherry Laurel)

P. lusitanica varieties* (Portugal Laurel)

Ribes sanguineum 'Brocklebankii' (Golden Flowering Currant)

Salix, silver-leaved varieties, except very slow growing ones (Silver-leaved Willow)

Spiraea × bumalda, golden-leaved varieties (Golden-leaved Spiraea)

Symphoricarpos, variegated varieties (Variegated Snowberry)

CLIMBING PLANTS: TO IMPROVE FOLIAGE COLOUR AND SIZE

Actinidia kolomikta (Actinidia)

Ampelopsis brevipedunculata 'Elegans' (Ampelopsis)

Aristolochia macrophylla, to improve size of leaf (Dutchman's Pipe)

× *Fatshedera lizei*, green and variegated varieties (Aralia Ivy)

Jasminum officinale, silver- and gold-variegated varieties (Jasmine)

Lonicera japonica 'Aureoreticulata' (Golden Variegated Japanese Honeysuckle)

---

* Can also be allowed to grow unpruned but may deteriorate over fifteen years or more.
† Will also improve colouring of stems in winter.

One-third pruning method when used for rejuvenation of overgrown shrubs

The one-third method is ideal for renovating overgrown shrubs and almost all respond to it. By its use the shrub is improved and flowering is maintained while the rejuvenation is taking place.

As before, it is feasible in most cases to cut the shrub hard back to within a few inches of ground level and let it regrow, but it will take at least three years to come into full flower again. Many shrubs can be treated by this method of hard cutting back but some resent it; the use of the one-third method avoids this trauma and possible loss.

Normally the pruning is carried out in the spring or after flowering, depending on the shrub in question; it is often found, however, that due to the volume of material to be removed in year one, it is better to carry out the first year's pruning in winter, so long as there are no hard frosts at the time.

If the first pruning is done in winter, no further pruning should be carried out until after flowering in the second spring following pruning; the one-third method should then be used annually for the rest of the shrub's life.

It may be that the balance of one-, two- and three-year-old and older shoots does not exist in years one and two, and if this is the case, then the thickest are removed for preference, remembering that the aim is to achieve an open centre to the shrub by removing any obstructing or crossing shoots.

After the removal of the older material, particularly in year one, the remaining shoots may be lax in habit and it is best to stake these; only shorten them as a last resort, as to do so will reduce the amount of flowers in the following year. This problem will decrease in year two and by the time of pruning in year three will have been eliminated altogether.

The improved appearance of the shrub over the three-year pruning cycle is dramatic, and once year three is completed, so long as the one-third method is used on an annual basis, the shrub should never reach the neglected stage again.

Many shrubs respond well to this rejuvenation but those shown on the list on p. 196 respond best.

Using the one-third method on slow-growing shrubs
With a few slow-growing shrubs – principally Rhododedrons, Azaleas, Kalmia and Pieris – that have been established for more than ten years, a two-year gap between each pruning stage will be required and once the three-stage cycle is complete they will not normally require pruning again for up to ten years.

The recommendation to create an open centre is more important with this group, as the new growth will need sunlight to encourage regrowth. Also dried blood at the rate of 4 oz (100 g) per square yard should be applied in mid spring, but because of the heavy canopy of evergreen foliage with Rhododendrons and the very solid and dense root development, the fertilizer should be applied to the soil in a band 18 in (50 cm) beyond the outer spread of the shoots and leaves.

Dog owners should be aware that dogs love to eat the dried blood, even when it is raked into the top few inches of lightly dug soil. To ensure that the fertilizer does its job in dry springs, some form of irrigation in late spring will be required to dissolve it and make it available to the shrub's roots.

The alternative is to cut an overgrown shrub hard back to within a few inches of ground level but it can take up to five or more years to grow back and even longer to flower.

With both methods, if new shoots are not being produced, washing the remaining shoots where new growth is required with a proprietory liquid fertilizer will often encourage shoot production, by stimulating dormant growth buds.

Hard cutting back
Hard cutting back as a necessity of establishment and longevity
With most subjects, the one-third method is to be preferred to

hard cutting back, but there are a number of shrubs that, if not cut back hard, are likely to die, either as young or mature plants.

Shrubs such as deciduous Ceanothus, some Buddlejas and Lavatera have microscopic tubes in the stem, which become furred up in a single year, and the stems therefore have to be removed annually if the shrub is to be long-lived and produce flowers and growth to its full potential. In the plant's natural environment this 'pruning' would be done by

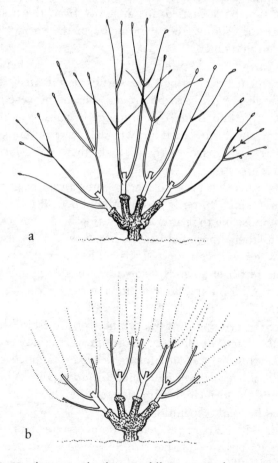

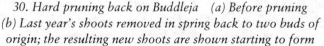

30. *Hard pruning back on Buddleja* (a) *Before pruning*
(b) *Last year's shoots removed in spring back to two buds of origin; the resulting new shoots are shown starting to form*

winter cold, so all that we are doing is acting as a substitute for the cold.

We could use the one-third method for almost any shrub, but hard cutting back is only suitable for certain varieties. Careful reference to the followings list must be made; further consideration has to be given to grey- and silver-leaved shrubs, which are covered in more detail later.

Age and timing of pruning

Hard cutting back carried out annually from the first spring after planting; should the planting be in the spring, pruning starts from that date.

From early to mid spring, once the winter weather appears to have turned to spring, the shrubs nominated for hard cutting back are ready to be pruned. Never, however, should we be tempted to bring the pruning forward, as this could induce the shrub into early growth and lead to damage from the winter cold, particularly to buds that have started into premature growth.

With shrubs that grow to reach a substantial height such as *Buddleja davidii* (Butterfly Bush) or Sambucus (Elder), it seems almost impossible that after hard cutting back they will again regrow to their unpruned height, but they almost always do. The new growth can be assisted with an application of an inorganic fertilizer such as Growmore or an organic fertilizer such as fish, blood and bone, following the instructions on the product.

Where the pruning is of importance for the establishment of the shrub, it will in all cases also improve the flowering. The one exception is the ornamental-leaved Sambucus (Elder), where the flowering will be reduced dramatically, if not eliminated, but the principal attraction of the shrub, the foliage, improved beyond recognition.

Height will be controlled to a point where it presents the shrub at its best productive size, but over a number of years this height will increase as a stool of pruned shoots is built up.

The shrubs on the following list benefit from this method.

Buddleja davidii varieties (Butterfly Bush)

B. fallowiana alba (Buddleja)

B. 'Lochinch', but not *B. alternifolia*, *B. globosa* or *B. weyeriana* (Buddleja)

Ceanothus × *delileanus* 'Gloire de Versailles' (California Lilac)

C. × *d.* 'Henri Desfossé' (California Lilac)

C. × *pallidus* 'Marie Simon' (California Lilac)

C. × *p.* 'Perle Rose' (California Lilac)
(But not evergreen Ceanothus)

Ceratostigma varieties (Shrubby Plumbago)

Cornus alba varieties (Red-barked Dogwood) to improve winter stems

C. stolonifera 'Flaviramea' (Yellow-stemmed Dogwood) to improve winter stems

Hebe, large-leaved varieties only (Veronica)

Hedysarum multijuga (Hedysarum), previous season's growth only

Holodiscus discolor (Ocean Spray)

Hydrangea arborescens varieties (Smooth Hydrangea)

H. paniculata varieties (Panick Hydrangea)
(But no other Hydrangea species)

Hypericum, shrubby varieties (Hypericum)

H. calycinum (St John's Wort)

Indigofera varieties (Indigo Bush)

Kerria varieties (Bachelor's Buttons)

Lavatera varieties (Tree Mallow)

Lespedeza bicolor (Thunberg Lespedeza)

Leycesteria formosa (Himalayan Honeysuckle)

Lippia cittodora (Lemon Verbena), previous season's growth only

Pachysandra terminalis varieties (Japanese Spurge)

Phygelius varieties (Cape Figwort)

Prunus glandulosa varieties (Chinese Bush Cherry)

P. triloba

Rhus varieties when grown as shrubs (Rue)

Rosmarinus varieties (Rosemary)

Rubus, white-stemmed varieties (White-stemmed Bramble)

Rubus deliciosus (Blackberry)

R. odoratus (Flowering Bramble)

R. spectabilis (Salmon Berry)

R. tricolor (Ground-covering Bramble)

Salix, except dwarf and low-growing varieties (Willow)

Sambucus, when grown as shrub for foliage effect (Elder)

Senecio varieties (Shrubby Ragwort)

Sorbaria varieties (Tree Spiraea)

Spiraea albiflora (Spiraea)

S. × *bumalda* (Spiraea)

S. douglasii (Spiraea)

S. *japonica*, golden-leaved forms
(Golden Spiraea)
S. *japonica* 'Shirobana' (Spiraea)
Tamarix, spring-flowering
varieties, after flowering;

summer-flowering varieties, in
mid spring before flowering
(Tamarisk)
Vinca (Periwinkle)

Making the cut

All the previous season's shoots should be cut to within two buds or 2–3 in (5–8 cm) of their origin; if possible, and if they can be identified, the cut should be made just above a bud, but the buds are not always identifiable and a calculated guess may have to be made. This pruning is then repeated on an annual basis for the remainder of the shrub's life, so forming a low stool of branches. In cases where a taller structure is required, or the shrub is to be fan-trained against a wall, a framework of older shoots can be built up, but they should not be more than 3 ft (1 m) in height; new shoots are then cut back to within 2–3 in (5–8 cm) of their origin from tihis framework.

Hard cutting back of silver- and grey-leaved shrubs and specified woody plants

With silver- and grey-leaved shrubs the timing of the pruning is important, to mimic the natural pruning done by winter and early-spring frosts. Many of these plants originate in regions of the world where they are partly or completely covered by snow in winter and so protected from frost damage, but as the snow melts in the spring, any exposed shoots are killed off. This process continues until a point is reached just above or at ground level, by which time all frosts are finished and no more damage will be done. New growth then starts and the plant again reaches its full height with fresh shoots that carry new, attractive foliage and flowers. This is the process that we should try to imitate by pruning and reducing the length of the shoots.

British winters are not hard enough to kill the shoots so they survive to the next year, but the pipes which carry the sap become furred up and are less productive. This builds up over two or three of years and the plant slowly becomes unattractive and may die.

Without the melting snow we need to use other signals and the most reliable way of doing this is to watch for the start of the new spring growth. Once this is seen, and is more than ½ in (1 cm) long, then pruning can start, normally with no problems. In some years this new growth may be seen in late winter and if this is the case you should wait until spring, as a hard frost might kill or damage any new growths which have been triggered by pruning, particularly as cover has been removed by the loss of the previous year's shoots.

Those that respond well to this method are:

Artemisia varieties, both green and grey (Southernwood)
Ballota varieties (Ballota)
Caryopteris varieties (Blue Spiraea, Bluebeard)
Dorycnium varieties (Dorycnium)
Eupatorium varieties (Joe-pye Weed)
Fuchsia, hardy varieties (Fuchsia)
Helichrysum varieties (Curry Plant)
Lavandula varieties (Lavender)
Microglossa albescens (Shrubby Aster)
Perovskia varieties (Russian Sage)
Phlomis varieties (Jerusalem Sage)
Romneya varieties (Californian Tree Poppy)
Rosmarinus varieties (Rosemary)
Ruta varieties (Rue)
Salvia, shrubby varieties (Common Sage)
Santolina, grey- and green-leaved varieties (Cotton Lavender)
Teucrium varieties (Shrubby Germander)

Hard cutting back to rejuvenate neglected shrubs and woody plants

Even though many shrubs and trees require hard pruning back to aid establishment and will die if they do not receive it, a few will survive. These survivors can be greatly improved by using the method to rejuvenate them. Often, however, because they have not been pruned before, they will have built up a woody structure and any hard cutting back will have to be to this structure, rather than close to the ground.

If the structure itself needs reducing, this is best done in mid spring. Of course the hard cutting back of the shoots is done as well. Pruning is then repeated annually.

Silver- and grey-leaved plants can be rejuvenated in the same way, waiting of course for the signs of new spring growth, and many old, woody and misshapen plants can be restored to their full glory. There is, however, a slight risk with Lavandula (Lavender) and Rosmarinus (Rosemary) that some very old plants may not recover.

The following shrubs respond well to this method:

Abelia varieties (Abelia, Glassy Abelia

Artemisia varieties (Southernwood)

Berberis,* except *B. linearifolia* or *B.* × *lologensis* (Barberry)

Buddleja (all varieties)* (Butterfly Bush)

Camellia* – slower to recoup, often up to five years (Camellia)

Ceanothus, deciduous varieties (California Lilac)

Ceanothus, evergreen varieties – can only be cut hard back to the main stem after spring-flowering, but there is a risk attached (California Lilac)

Chaenomeles varieties (Ornamental Quince)

Choisya varieties* (Mexican Orange Blossom)

Cistus varieties, but there is only a 50 per cent chance of success; prune late spring only (Rock Rose)

Cornus alba varieties (Red-barked Dogwood)

C. stolinifera 'Flaviramea' (Yellow-stemmed Dogwood)

Corylus varieties (Hazel, Filbert), except *C. avellana* 'Contorta' (Harry Lauder's Walking Stick), which should just be reshaped

Cotinus varieties (Smoke Tree)

Cotoneaster varieties (Cotoneaster)

Deutzia varieties (Deutzia)

Diervilla varieties (Bush Honeysuckle)

Elaeagnus varieties (Elaeagnus)

Escallonia varieties (Escallonia)

Euonymus varieties, except *E. alatus* (Spindle)

Exochorda varieties (Pearl Bush)

Forsythia varieties (Forsythia)

Fuchsia, hardy varieties (Hardy Fuchsia)

Garrya varieties (Tassel Bush)

Griselinia varieties (Broadleaf)

Hebe, large-growing varieties* (Veronica)

Hippophaë varieties* (Sea Buckthorn)

Holodiscus varieties (Ocean Spray)

Hydrangea arborescens varieties (Smooth Hydrangea)

H. paniculata varieties (Panick
Hydrangea)
Hydrangea, all other varieties
(Hydrangea)
Hypericum varieties (St John's
Wort)
Ilex varieties (Holly)
Jasminum varieties (Jasmine)
Kerria varieties (Bachelor's
Buttons)
Kolkwitzia varieties (Beauty
Bush)
Lavandula varieties – 50 per cent
chance of sucess (Lavender)
Lavatera varieties (Tree Mallow)
Leycesteria varieties (Himalayan
Honeysuckle)
Ligustrum, except slow-growing
varieties (Privet)
Lonicera, shrubby varieties
(Honeysuckle)
Mahonia aquifolium varieties
(Oregon Grape)
Olearia varieties (Daisy Bush)
Philadelphus varieties (Mock
Orange)
Phygelius varieties (Cape
Figwort)
Physocarpus varieties (Nine-
bark)
Potentilla varieties (Shrubby
Cinquefoil)

Prunus laurocerasus varieties
(Laurel)
P. lusitanica varieties (Portugal
Laurel)
Pyracantha varieties (Firethorn)
Rhodotypos scandens (White
Jew's Mallow)
Romneya varieties (Tree Poppy)
Rosmarinus varieties*
(Rosemary)
Rubus varieties (Fruiting
Bramble)
Salix varieties (Willow)
Salvia varieties (Common Sage)
Sambucus varieties, except very
slow growing forms (Elder)
Santolina varieties* (Cotton
Lavender)
Senecio varieties – 50 per cent
chance of success (Shrubby
Ragwort)
Spiraea varieties (Spiraea)
Stephanandra varieties
(Stephanandra)
Symphoricarpos varieties
(Snowberry)
Teucrium varieties* (Shrubby
Germander)
Ulex varieties (Furze, Gorse)
Viburnum varieties (Viburnum)
Vinca varieties* (Periwinkle)
Weigela varieties (Weigela)

* Either one-third or hard-cutting-back pruning methods can be used without
reducing flower numbers.

Using hard cutting back to produce brighter winter shoots
A number of shrubs will respond to hard cutting by producing
a crop of bright, new winter shoots.

Normally in early spring, just as the new season's leaf buds are opening, all shoots produced in the previous year are cut to within a few inches of ground level. On newly planted shrubs this is done in the second or third spring after planting so that they have time to establish a good root system first.

Older shrubs that have not been pruned in this way may take a year to adjust and in the year after pruning the stems may not be as strong as in future years; it may then be best to miss a year's pruning before setting up an annual cutting-back routine. However, once set up it can be repeated with confidence each year to very good advantage.

New shoots that are produced from the pruned shrub may stay green throughout the summer before ripening in late autumn, ready to provide their winter display.

Shrubs that respond to this method:

Cornus alba varieties (Red-barked Dogwood)
C. stolinifera 'Flaviramea' (Yellow-stemmed Dogwood)
Salix alba argentea, when grown as a bush (Silver Willow)

S. a. vitellina (Golden Willow)
S. daphnoides varieties (Violet Willow)
S. irrorata (Purple-stemmed Willow)

With this pruning method flowers and fruit on Cornus (Dogwoods) are sacrificed in favour of the new shoots. One bonus is that on all varieties the foliage size will be increased and this is particularly advantageous with the coloured and variegated-leaved varieties of Cornus.

Hard cutting back to improve leaf size

A number of shrubs, where the flowering effect is not of prime importance, respond well to hard cutting back all shoots in early to mid spring and produce new leaves that are much larger than if left unpruned or if the one-third pruning method is used: These are:

Cornus alba, variegated varieties (Variegated Red-barked Dogwood)

Cotinus coggyria, both green- and purple-leaved varieties (Smoke Bush)

Rubus odoratus (Flowering
  Bramble)

Sambucus nigra varieties (Elder)
S. racemosa varieties (Elder)

As with cutting back to increase stem display, the flowering
and fruiting effects are sacrificed on all.

Hard cutting back of selected trees

A number of trees have the same foliage-improvement potential. The overall height of the tree is dramatically reduced
while the pruning regime is being employed but once it stops
the tree will, if required, grow back to its full height over a
few years.

Care should be taken, however, when pruning trees: if they
have been grafted, only those shoots that are growing above
the point of grafting can be cut hard back, as the potential
growth below this point is only of the parent understock.

It is advisable to allow the tree to establish for up to three
years before starting the pruning.

The work is carried out in early to mid spring, and once
started it is best done on an annual basis but if, at a later date,
more height or a more natural shape is required, the shrub or
tree can be allowed to grow back to its former height.

Where the tree species can be purchased either as a bush or
with a stem, the pruning for the bush can be carried out just
above the graft union or 12–18 in (30–50 cm) above ground
level. Where the graft union is at the top of a stem, as in
Catalpa bignonioides 'Aurea', then the hard-cutting-back
method must be practised 8–12 in (20–30 cm) above the graft
union.

With *Populus* × *candicans* 'Aurora' and *Populus serotina*
'Aurea' it may be possible to cut the side shoots hard back to
form a columnar shape.

The trees that respond well to this pruning method are:

Acer negundo varieties (Box
  Maple)
A. platanoides, purple and
  variegated varieties (Norway
  Maple)

Catalpa bignonioides, only
  green-leaved varieties (Indian
  Bean Tree)
C. b. 'Aurea' (Golden-leaved
  Catalpa)

Paulownia tomentosa (Foxglove Tree)

Populus × *candicans* 'Aurora' (Balsam Poplar)

P. × *serotina* 'Aurea' (Golden Italian Poplar)

Robinia pseudoacacia 'Frisia'* (Golden Acacia)

* This species may be grafted at the top of the stem (top-worked).

As with all hard cutting back, flowers and fruits are sacrificed.

PRUNING CLIMBERS

Climbers, for the purpose of pruning, include both those plants that are self-clinging or twining and those that need extra support. This group of plants is often overlooked from the pruning point of view, but when pruning is carried out correctly, it is the most rewarding in terms of improvement, not only in flowering but in overall appearance.

Roses, Clematis, ornamental Vines and Wisteria are covered separately as they require more specific work.

This section does not include wall shrubs or fan-trained shrubs; for these the prescribed method of one-third or hard cutting back should be used, adapting it for the purpose if necessary.

Pruning of climbers should start three years after planting and should be done after flowering on a repeated annual basis. The task can look daunting at first sight as there is normally a mass of tangled shoots appearing to be growing all ways.

The objective is to remove one third of the total number of shoots, choosing the oldest shoots first. The count is done between ground level and 24 in (60 cm).

Once the shoots for removal have been identified, it is best to cut one and leave it for an hour or so. The foliage of the pruned shoot will wilt and this will distinguish it from the unpruned shoots. It can then be carefully removed, cutting it away piece by piece. Once this is done then the next selected shoot is cut, left to wilt and then removed, continuing the process until all that needs to be pruned is removed.

When carrying out pruning it is good practice to check the

condition of the supports as well and repair or replace them as necessary. The remaining unpruned shoots are then tied in to the support using soft fillis twine to prevent stem damage.

When pruning is finished the remaining unpruned shoots and foliage will look a little bedraggled but after twenty-four hours the climber will have adjusted its remaining foliage.

This pruning method is designed to encourage new basal shoots to form on an annual basis but they must be regularly checked and tied in when seen.

In mid spring each year feed the plant with an inorganic fertilizer such as Growmore, or organic fish, blood and bone at the rate recommended on the product.

A number of fungus diseases and pest infestations are reduced by pruning, in particular mildew on Lonicera (Honeysuckle). Even the disorderly *Jasminum officinale* (Jasmine) can be persuaded to become more manageable.

Flowering and fruiting is not impaired and in most cases is improved.

Actinidia kolomikta (Actinidia)
Aristolochia macrophylla (Dutchman's Pipe)
Celastrus orbiculatus (Staff Vine)
Holboellia varieties (Holboellia)
Jasminum varieties (Jasmine)
Lonicera varieties (Honeysuckle)
Passiflora varieties (Passion Flower)
Polygonum varieties (Russian Vine)
Solanum varieties (Potato Vine)
Stauntonia hexaphylla (Stauntonia)

Renovating old and overgrown climbers

The same procedure is followed as for regularly pruned climbers, the only difference being the overall size and the amount of rubbish that will be trapped between the mass of neglected and overgrown shoots. Therefore it is best to do the first year's pruning in the winter, the only problem being that there will be no wilting leaves to identify the pruned shoots. To overcome this, once the one-third count has been done and the shoots to be removed at or near ground level have been identified, the process of pruning should start from ground level, working upwards, taking care not to damage any shoots that are to be retained and removing any shoots that are in small pieces.

Due to the weight of the climber it may be necessary to tie in temporarily some of the shoots that are to remain to prevent them getting broken; then, once the work is finished, check the support and tie in the remaining shoots to it. No pruning is done after winter pruning until the second year, when pruning reverts to the one-third method and is carried out annually after flowering.

Again, the rejuvenated climbers need feeding each year with inorganic Growmore fertilizer or organic fish, blood and bone, at the rate recommended on the product.

Territorial and containment pruning on climbers
Where a number of climbers are grown side by side or in association with other plants it will be necessary to ensure that the strongest does not infringe on the territory of its neighbours. As a rule most climbers can be contained within a 6 ft (2 m) width and still produce a good foliage or flowering display. With established plants it is a good policy to check regularly and remove any shoots which may be encroaching on their neighbours' territory.

Pruning climbing plants back from windows and doors
Climbers planted against house walls very often obstruct the windows and doors. Close-growing, self-clinging climbers such as Hedera (Ivy), *Parthenocissus tricuspidata* 'Veitchii' (Boston Ivy) and *P. quinquifolia* (Virginia Creeper) are the main offenders. Assuming that in the first place they have been allowed a growing space of not less than 10 ft (3 m) in height and spread, it is good practice to cut back all growths by at least 24 in (60 cm) in early spring, away from any window, door or guttering which it may obstruct. This will provide a growing space for the new spring-produced shoots, although by midsummer the window or door may once again be reached.

CLEMATIS PRUNING

Anxiety over pruning is possibly expressed more frequently with Clematis than with any other group of plants; as well as worrying about harming the plant, people are understand-ably confused by the very wide range of species and hybrid varieties, and the number of different treatments required. But the different species and varieties can be separated into groups according to the season of flowering or the species, and this simplifies the pruning. There is also the potential use of the one-third method which, although not ideal for all the different groups, will go some way to improving the overall performance of any Clematis.

One-third method

This universal method is explained first because many of the Clematis in our gardens are not identified by name and there-fore the optimum pruning method cannot always be selected. However, it is always better to identify a Clematis, if you can, before pruning, and there are many illustrated reference books and nursery catalogues available which will assist.

If the species or variety cannot be identified, in mid to late spring, approximately three years or more after planting, count the number of main shoots between ground level and 18 in (50 cm) above it and divide by three. Once this target number is known, select the oldest first and cut as close to ground level as possible but being careful that no other main shoots are damaged or removed.

Identifying the oldest shoots is not always easy and often the pruner will have to revert to guesswork. There may be a forest of intertwined shoots, many of which are in fact dead, but by identifying a target number at the base, pruning them and very carefully removing the pruned sections piece by piece, the task can be successfully completed. Often only one or two shoots will require removing to achieve the required one third.

Once pruning is complete, the support should be checked and repaired or replaced if necessary and all remaining shoots carefully tied to it with soft fillis twine to prevent wind damage. The plant may look scruffy after pruning but it will soon generate new growth and an improved appearance. The pruning is repeated annually from there on.

Pruning *Clematis alpina* and *C. macropetala* varieties
Pruning will improve not only the flowering but also the overall growth and foliage appearance of all *Clematis alpina* and *C. macropetala* varieties.

After flowering in the spring all the previous year's shoots are reduced to within two to three buds 2–4 in (5–10 cm) of their origin, to be replaced by new shoots which will flower in the following spring.

With newly planted Clematis this pruning starts after flowering in the second year after planting.

This method should be practised annually and in preference to any other method, but if the plant has an architectural use in the garden, this may be extended to every other year, though not more, as the performance starts to deteriorate seriously after this time.

Pruning *Clematis armandii* and *C. cirrhosa* varieties
These varieties prefer to ramble over a large area and should not be pruned on a regular basis.

Every five to six years it is good practice to remove, to just above ground level, one third of the shoots, choosing the oldest. It is better to carry out the pruning after flowering to achieve the quickest regrowth and reduce flowering loss.

Pruning *Clematis montana* varieties
The very rampant *Clematis montana* varieties benefit greatly from the following pruning method, and even very old and neglected plants can be rejuvenated and brought back into full flower and foliage productivity.

Pruning is started some five to seven years after planting and repeated at five- to seven-year intervals thereafter. Just after flowering in the spring all the side shoots are cut back to

1–2 in (2.5–5 cm) of the main shoots, making sure none is missed.

To do this it is best to start from ground level and work carefully upwards, removing the side shoots as you go.

Once all the side shoots have been removed, the strongest three to five main shoots are selected and reduced in height to around 9 ft (2.7 m) from ground level and tied to the support in a fan shape, with any surplus being removed to as close to ground level as possible. The plant will now look completely naked and will not, of course, be covering the area it occupied before pruning.

However, within a few weeks buds will start to grow and new large leaves form; this is a real advantage with the purple-leaved varieties, particularly as the leaves will also be a better colour. In the following spring a mass of larger flowers will be carried and the Clematis will very quickly grow and cover the same area as it did before.

Large summer-flowering hybrid clematis and some species Clematis

The varieties that flower in early summer to midsummer produce their flowers on the two-year-old and older shoots, so it is important that these are retained. For this reason, no major shoots are removed. This particularly applies to the large double-flowering varieties because if the older shoots are removed the subsequent flowers will be single – but remember, of course, that the later flowers in this group are usually single.

The only pruning that needs to be done is to tidy up all shoot ends by removing the dead tips. It is better to do this in early spring, just as the last new buds start to open, so that any dead shoots are easily identified.

Once this tidying up has been done the shoots should be tied to the support in a fan shape as this arrangement will show off the flowers to their best advantage.

LARGE-FLOWERED DOUBLE
VARIETIES
'Beauty of Worcester', second
    flowers single
'Countess of Lovelace'
'Duchess of Edinburgh', second
    flowers single
'Glynderek'
'Louise Rowe', semi-double and
    double all at the same time
'Mrs George Jackman', semi-
    double
'Mrs Spencer Castle'
'Vyvyan Pennell', second flowers
    single

LARGE-FLOWERED SINGLE
VARIETIES
'Barbara Dibley'
'Barbara Jackman'
'Bees' Jubilee'
'Daniel Deronda'
'Doctor Ruppel'
'Ernest Markham'
'H. F. Young'
'Haku-ookan'
'Henryi'
'Lady Londesborough'
'Lasurstern'
'Lincoln Star'
'Marie Boisselot'
'Miss Bateman'
'Mrs Cholmondeley'
'Mrs N. Thompson'
'Nellie Moser'

'Niobe'
'Perle d'Azur'
'Rouge Cardinal'
'The President'
'William Kennett'

SPECIES CLEMATIS AND
SMALLER-FLOWERING
VARIETIES
Clematis campaniflora
C. *rehderiana*
C. *viticella*, C. *v.* varieties
    and hybrids belonging to
    the *viticella* group:
'Abundance'
'Alba Luxuriens'
'Albiflora'
'Caerulea'
'Elvan'
'Etoile Violet'
'Flore Pleno'
'Huldine'
'Kermesina'
'Little Nell'
'Madame Julia
    Correvon'
'Margot Koster'
'Minuet'
'Polish Spirit'
'Purpurea Plena
    Elegans'
'Royal Velours'
'Viticella Rubra'
'Venosa Violacea'

Hard cutting back of large-flowering hybrid Clematis and autumn-flowering species

Some varieties of Clematis flower on the shoots that are produced in the same year and it is important to prune them so as to encourage new flowering shoots to form or the plant will quickly deteriorate.

Even though this pruning may seem harsh, it should be carried out every year in mid to late spring, even in the first spring after planting.

All of the shoots that were produced last season should be cut down to within 12 in (30 cm) of their point of origin. From these new growths will form and quickly cover the area occupied before pruning commenced; they will produce flowers to the plant's full potential, supported by large, healthy foliage.

As the new flowering shoots grow they should be regularly tied in to their support with soft fillis twine to prevent wind damage.

The following large-flowered varieties are best treated in this way:

'Allanah'
'Ascotiensis'
'Belle Nantaise'
'Cardinal Wyszynski'
'Comtesse de Bouchard'
'Crimson King'
'Duchess of Sutherland'
'Ernest Markham'
'Fargesii'
'General Sikorski'
'Gipsy Queen'
'Hagley Hybrid'
'Jackmanii'
'Jackmanii Alba'
'Jackmanii Superba'
'Lady Betty Balfour'
'Lilacina Floribunda'
'Madame Baron Veillard'
'Madame Edouard André'
'Madame Grangé'
'Margaret Hunt'
'Marie Boisselot' (syn. 'Madame le Coultre')
'Perle d'Azur'

'Pink Fantasy'
'Sealand Gem'
'Serenata'
'Star of India'
'Twilight'
'Victoria'
'Ville de Lyon'
'Violet Charm'
'Voluceau'
'W. E. Gladstone'
'Warsaw Nike'
'Will Goodwin'

AUTUMN-FLOWERING SPECIES
CLEMATIS
Clematis × *jouiniana* 'Praecox'
C. flammula
C. f. 'Rubra'
C. orientalis
C. o. 'Bill McKenzie'
C. o. 'Burford Variety'
C. o. 'L & S 13342'
C. o. 'Sherriffii'
C. texensis

C. *t.* 'Duchess of Albany'   C. *t.* 'Pagoda'
C. *t.* 'Etoile Rose'   C. *t.* 'Princess of
C. *t.* 'Gravetye Beauty'   Wales'

Pruning perennial Clematis

There is a group of Clematis that die down to ground level in winter and regrow in spring. Sometimes, however, the winters are not cold enough to kill the growth above ground and when this happens it is important to prune to prevent the build-up of weak or old, non-productive shoots.

In the autumn it is best to cut the shoots back to within 12 in (30 cm) of ground level so that what is left acts as winter protection. Then in early to mid spring they are cut again to within 1 in (3 cm) or so of ground level, taking care not to damage any new shoots that may already be emerging. It is also good practice to provide some form of support at this stage which the new shoots can grow through, preventing wind damage later.

The principal varieties this method is practised on are:

Clematis × *durandii*   C. *i.* 'Hendersonii'
C. × *eriostemon*   C. × *jouiniana* 'Mrs Robert
C. *heracleifolia*   Brydon'
C. *h.* 'Crepuscule'   C. *recta*
C. *h.* 'Wyevale'   C. *r.* 'Purpurea'
C. *integrifolia*

PRUNING WISTERIA

Possibly the question most asked by the gardener is how to prune a Wisteria to make it flower. Before this can be described fully, one or two points must be explained and possibly the most important is the selection of the right Wisteria plant in the first place.

Wisteria grow very easily from seed but regrettably the resulting flowering, often some eight years after planting, is very variable, not only in the time they take to flower but in size and, more importantly, colour. Plants raised in this way should be avoided, even though they appear less expensive than the alternative, more reliable, grafted varieties.

To add to the confusion, even the basic form, *Wisteria sinensis*, may be grown from seed or grafted, and the only way to be sure is to purchase a grafted named variety or to ask the supplier which propagation method was used; if he does not know, do not buy.

Next the growing aspect: it is important that Wisteria is given a south- or west-facing position, for without it the shoots will not ripen and flower buds will not be formed.

You may have a newly planted Wisteria, say up to one or two years old, or a well-established Wisteria, planted some years ago but never pruned and somewhat out of control – a very daunting pruning task. Although the two ages require different pruning, the aim in both is to achieve a vine-like shoot formation on which the flower buds will form over the area allowed for its total maximum growth.

Pruning a newly planted Wisteria

In the late mid to late spring following planting (which should have been, most importantly, carried out as recommended in Chapter 1) pruning can start – or, more rightly, training can begin. A formation of horizontal shoots at regular intervals growing out from a central upright main shoot is the aim.

Even though it may seem harsh and it will appear that the height of the plant just purchased is being cut away, in early to mid spring of the year following planting the main shoot is cut back to within 18 in (50 cm) of ground level. Should the plant have more than one main shoot then choose the strongest and remove the remainder completely. If the main shoot is not 18 in (50 cm) tall, then just tip it, removing the terminal bud, but in all cases cutting it is important to prevent it from becoming dormant and shy of growing.

Normally when the plant is supplied it will have at least a 3 ft (1 m) bamboo cane supplied with it, which should be replaced with a 6–8 ft (2–2.5 m) one, and this should be tied to the horizontal support wires with soft fillis twine using a figure-of-eight knot (see Chapter 3).

In the spring and summer following the first cutting back at least one strong upright shoot will develop and as it grows it should be tied to the cane. If more than one develops the strongest is chosen and the others removed. By early summer the chosen shoot will have reached 6–12 in (15–30 cm) above the first training wire and is stopped at a bud 3–6 in (8–15 cm) higher than the wire. If it has not reached the first wire, pruning is best left until the spring of the following year.

From below the point at which the shoot is pruned a number of shoots will emerge. The first of these is tied vertically to the upright bamboo cane. The next two are tied left and right along the first horizontal training wires, and any surplus shortened back to 12 in (30 cm) in summer and then in winter reduced again to two buds or 2–3 in (5–8 cm) from the point of origin.

Should side shoots be formed off the selected horizontal shoots, these also should be shortened back to 2–3 in (5–8 cm) in the summer and winter; it is from these shortened back shoots (spurs) that the first flower buds will form for display in future years.

Depending on the weather and soil conditions the stopping of the central upright shoot may be required again once it reaches the next wire, and the resulting shoots should be tied in and trained as for the first wire.

In year two the plant is allowed to grow on until it reaches 6–12 in (15–30 cm) above the next wire, when the process is repeated. By now it may have gained enough root development to reach a number of the wire levels, and at each it is stopped and trained as before.

As the side shoots grow along the horizontal wires they are tied in and any surplus shoots on the main or side shoots are cut back in summer to 12 in (30 cm) from their point of origin, and reduced further in the winter to two buds or 2 in (5 cm).

In year three the same procedure is followed, shortening back the main shoot when it reaches the upper wires or possibly the full height required. The side horizontal shoots are tied in and any surplus pruned as before.

The main framework has now been formed and only the

horizontal side shoots will require further training and tying in.

Normally from year four onwards the Wisteria will be in flower, but without the training suggested it could be at least eight years and often longer before it comes into flower.

Routine training and pruning can now start and will be covered after the explanation of the pruning for an out-of-control Wisteria.

Always tie the shoots of the Wisteria to a bamboo cane or wires using soft three-ply fillis twine and the figure-of-eight knot described in Chapter 3.

Pruning an out-of-control and overgrown Wisteria

A Wisteria may have become overgrown from neglect, apprehension of causing damage or the sheer size of the problem. With the right approach, the plant can be brought back into full flower production and generally have its appearance improved, while at the same time bringing it under control and reducing the work required in the following years.

At the first inspection there will appear to be a maze of intertwining shoots that form no real pattern and the first task is to identify the ones that will form the main framework. Ideally this will be one major central shoot but more often two or even three have to be selected due to the lack of previous pruning and training. Care needs to be taken to locate any dead or partially damaged shoots that have been strangulated by the intertwining shoots or bad tying-in, and these are not always clearly visible at first sight.

As the pruning progresses, training wires, if non-existent or in poor condition, will need to be provided or replaced (see Chapter 3).

Starting at ground level and working upwards, the main shoot or shoots are tied to a 6–8 ft (2–2.5 m) cane, which in turn is tied to the support wire. In some cases this may be of a temporary nature until the pruning is complete. As suitable side shoots growing off the vertical shoot are located, they are tied out on to the horizontal wires. This may entail lifting, lowering or bending some to fill a particular position.

Any surplus side shoots are cut back to 12 in (30 cm) of their origin in the summer and further reduced to 2 in (5 cm) in winter. The process continues until the full height of the plant is reached. The selected side shoots are also trained and tied out until they cover as much of the area as required.

In some cases the pruned Wisteria may not cover the same area that it did before pruning but it will quickly make up any deficit in the following spring and summer as new side growths are formed.

A great quantity of surplus shoots will be removed but the pruner should not be alarmed.

The work can be carried out in late summer and autumn but as long as there are no hard frosts it can also be done in winter, and often this is the best time as the shoots to be retained or removed are more clearly seen.

The Wisteria is now ready to receive routine annual pruning.

Routine annual Wisteria pruning

From the main stems and horizontal side shoots, through spring and summer, numerous surplus side shoots (tendrils) will grow and it is the shortening back of all of these, each year, that produces the flower buds for future years.

Therefore the more shortening, the more flowers, but it takes upwards of two years for the remaining buds to form into flower buds. As the shortening is practised every year, 'flowering spurs' are formed, and care must be taken to ensure that these are not damaged in any way.

The pruning or shortening is best carried out in two stages, first reducing them to 12 in (30 cm) long in midsummer or late summer, and then finally to 2–3 in (5–8 cm), or two to three buds, in winter, at any time as long as the weather is not too cold. It should then be done annually.

ROSE PRUNING

There are two schools of thought as to when pruning of Roses (except climbers and ramblers) should be done. The first favours the autumn and the second the spring. Personally I prefer the spring, as there is always the risk of frost damage of early growth induced by autumn pruning. This does not arise with spring pruning.

The only exceptions to this are climbing Roses and ramblers, which I prefer to prune in early to mid autumn.

Of course the need to provide the Rose with food is as important as with any other plant; Roses require all the main plant foods, with plenty of potash, and, equally important, the trace elements manganese, magnesium and boron. The best way to provide these is to apply, in mid spring, a dressing of a proprietary rose fertilizer at the rates recommended by the manufacturer.

To improve growth, and thereby flowering, further, a liquid fertilizer should be applied just as the first flush of flowers are dying. As well as improving the overall performance it may induce a third crop of flowers on many varieties.

The combination of pruning and feeding can reduce the effects of disease such as black spot and mildew; they attack mainly old leaves on older shoots, and with pruning and feeding these are kept to a minimum.

Removing suckers
One of the best times to identify suckers on Roses is at pruning time, but of course a constant watch should be kept and they should be removed as soon as seen. Suckers are formed by unwanted shoots growing from underground stems and roots of the stock on to which the variety was budded (see Chapter 7).

Identifying the sucker can often be a problem: it will always, with the exception of standard Roses, originate from below ground and with careful inspection will be found to be growing from below the budding or grafted point or off a root growing some way from the Rose.

All suckers have different leaves from the main plant, as well as, in most cases, a different growth pattern.

The first instinct is to remove the sucker by cutting with a knife or secateurs but if this is done then in the next few weeks more suckers will be formed, because the sucker has been 'pruned' and so encouraged to branch and make more shoots. The best way to remove it is to rip it away at its point of origin, so removing all of the sucker shoot and any buds which might regrow. As long as the ripping out is done carefully and the resulting wound is kept as small as possible, no long-term harm will be done.

Suckers are common on standard Roses because the budding or grafting point is at the top of a single shoot of the host rootstock. Two main species of Roses are used: *Rosa canina* (Dog Rose), which has typical wild Rose leaves, and *Rosa rugosa*, which has light green, fleshy and deeply veined leaves. As the suckers are formed on the stem above ground and have distinctive foliage, they are more clearly identifiable. Removing them as young as possible, rubbing or ripping them off, is the best way to prevent regrowth.

Pruning shrub and species Roses

Many sources suggest that old shrub and species Roses do not require pruning but I have not found this to be true. Certainly the true species Roses such as *Rosa rugosa*, *R. alba*, *R. centifolia*, etc., will grow and flower without the help of pruning but pruning will improve their overall appearance and flowering ability and they will be more disease resistant.

Over the last fifty years more and more new varieties of shrub Rose have been introduced, being bred from the original species and today's range of varieties. Due to their hybrid parentage they are more like large Floribunda Roses than the original species, and therefore benefit in the long-term from following the suggested pruning.

The best time to start is three years after planting, but if the bushes have been established longer, this method can still be used to good effect.

From early to mid spring, all the shoots at or just above ground level are counted and once the number is known, one third of the total are selected to be removed, choosing the oldest first and removing them as near to ground level as possible. This will encourage new flowering shoots to grow up through the centre of the bush to replace those removed.

These new shoots will produce more and larger flowers and leaves, and this in turn will stimulate root growth, preventing the bush from deteriorating and increasing the length of its useful and attractive life. The more vigorous, healthy foliage will ward off many attacks of fungus diseases such as black spot and mildew, as well as preventing long-term damage from attacks of pests such as greenfly and blackfly.

In addition, using this pruning method on *Rosa glauca* (*R. rubrifolia*) will increase the size and colour of the purple foliage, making it more attractive.

Many shrubs and some species Roses can be grown as climbers on walls and other supports and the one-third pruning method works equally well under these growing conditions.

The many varieties of *Rosa moschata* and *R. hybrida*, of which *R. m.* 'Penelope' and *R. m.* 'Felicia' are good examples, can also be pruned in the same way as Floribunda Roses. This alternative method gives an overall reduced size, but increased flower production and size.

Feeding in mid to late spring with a specific rose fertilizer will further improve their performance.

Pruning Hybrid Tea Roses (large-flowered or bush)

In this group all the large specimen flowers are produced on the new shoots made in the same growing year, so the aim of pruning is to encourage and maintain the continued production of these new flowering shoots on an annual replacement basis.

At first sight it seems impossible to the inexperienced eye that after the following pruning, the Rose is able to regrow and flower to its full potential, but it is, and not to prune is to commit the bush to an ever-declining existence, producing smaller flowers in smaller numbers, with poor regrowth. After a number of years, it will finally die before its time.

When newly purchased Roses are planted in autumn or winter it is good practice to shorten the shoots to approximately 10–12 in (25–30 cm) long, unless of course the supplier has already done this for you. This shortening back will help establish the root system, particularly in exposed gardens where damage can be caused by wind rocking and not only the shoots but the roots may be torn by excessive movement.

Pruning should then be undertaken in early to mid spring. If the shoots of a number of bushes are observed, there will be seen to be thin (thinner than a pencil), medium (thicker than a pencil) and thick (thicker than one and a half to two pencils) diameter shoots. Any combination of these may be found on any particular bush.

Once the shoot sizes have been identified, the following pruning formula should be followed and used for newly planted and established Roses. All thin shoots should be cut to within one bud (1 in/3 cm) of their origin, medium to two (2 in/5 cm) and thick to three (3 in/8 cm). Using this formula will give the bush a more balanced shape and the potential for better flower production. The formula can be made a little less harsh by using the formula of thin, two buds (2 in/5 cm), medium, three (3 in/8 cm) and thick, four (4 in/10 cm). This will encourage more flowers but they will lose some of the Hybrid Tea flower size and shape.

Clean, correctly angled cuts, cutting above a bud, should be made, and there may be some advantage in choosing an outward-facing bud. Feeding with a specific rose fertilizer is also necessary to encourage vigorous new shoots.

Pruning Floribunda Roses (cluster Roses)

With this group the aim is to produce large sprays of flowers and the pruning is designed to encourage this.

These Roses should be pruned from early to mid spring, again according to the thickness of the shoots: thin shoots should be cut back to four buds (4 in/10 cm) from their point of origin, medium to six (6 in/15 cm) and thick to eight (8 in/ 20 cm). This will give the bush a balanced shape and good flower-spray production. Care with the correct pruning cut is important and an outward-facing bud should be chosen if possible.

Some shoots, of all three thicknesses, may not have made as much length as suggested in the pruning formula, and if this is the case, the shoot is cut back to the nearest suitable bud. Once pruning is complete, feed with a specific rose fertilizer.

Pruning half standard and standard Roses
The pruning of standard Roses is the same as for the grafted Hybrid Tea, Floribunda, shrub or species Roses, or climbing Roses (when used as weeping standards). The only difference is that they are grown on stems, although there may be a case for suggesting that the pruning should be slightly less harsh. Should the variety not be known, then except for climbers (weeping), prune as for Floribunda (cluster) Roses. There is a greater risk of suckers on standards and a careful watch should always be kept.

Pruning patio and ground-cover Roses
It is often suggested that these relatively new introductions need no pruning, but in my experience, if not pruned, they will, over a period of three to four years, slowly start to deteriorate.

The best approach is to allow them to grow for two years so they can establish; then each year, in early to late spring, count the number of shoots at or near ground level and, choosing the oldest first, remove one third of the total number as close to ground level as possible. Follow the pruning by feeding with a specific rose fertilizer.

Pruning miniature Roses
Again pruning is said to be unnecessary but if the following method is used, the bushes will live longer and will be more prolific in flower.

For the first one or two years after planting just remove the dead flowers. Then, in year three, in early to mid spring, carefully remove, as close to ground level as possible, one third of the total number of shoots, choosing the oldest first. This pruning is then repeated every other year, at the same period. Feed each year with a specific rose fertilizer.

If at all possible, purchase budded miniature Roses rather than those propagated by micropropagation, as the former are by far the longer-living and more prolific.

Pruning newly planted climbing and rambling Roses

When new climbing or rambling Roses are purchased for planting in autumn, winter or early spring, they should be inspected and any dead tips to the shoots removed; if left, die-back can spread.

In early to mid spring all shoots of newly planted rambling Roses should be cut back to within 2–3 ft (60 cm–1 m) of ground level to induce growing vigour, as in many cases they become dormant and refuse to produce any new growth if this is not done.

Climbing Rose varieties should just be trimmed to remove any dead tips as they do not have always the vigour to grow strongly and if pruned hard many varieties may revert and only grow as bushes.

Of course, all the usual rules of good planting apply – without it the desired regrowth will not be produced. (See Chapter 2.)

Pruning established climbing and unclassified Roses

Deciding whether an established Rose is a climber or rambler is often difficult and there may be no way of identifying the variety except when it is in flower – and even then it may not be possible.

With a climbing Rose, the following pruning method should be used to maintain a balance of new and old flowering shoots. Should the classification be unknown, then the method can be used as an acceptable compromise.

Pruning can start the year after planting and is repeated every year thereafter. The best time for pruning is in early to late autumn; the number of shoots at or near ground level should be counted and, choosing the oldest first, one third of the total are removed as close to ground level as possible. With some this may mean removing only a few shoots and sometimes only one. On some there may be very few or no new growths low down and in these cases a compromise may have to be made and the older shoots only pruned back to a young, strong-growing side shoot.

Very neglected or unpruned climbers may only have two shoots in total and in this case, remove the oldest.

If there is only one shoot, it may not be worth keeping the plant unless it is an irreplaceable variety or has sentimental value. In these cases it is worth taking a gamble and pruning the remaining shoot back to within 12–24 in (30–60 cm) of ground level in the hope that it will send out new shoots from below the pruning cut. About one in five do not, so there is a risk. Personally I would take it, however, because if successful the resulting new shoots will make a good foundation on which to build a new productive climbing Rose; if not, it would finally give up in any case. (Alternatively, you could take hardwood cuttings for propagation before pruning; see Chapter 7.)

For both strong and weak specimens, feeding in mid to late spring with a specific rose fertilizer will help to produce the good flowering shoots required.

Pruning established rambling Roses

When the Rose is known to be a rambler, the following pruning is recommended to retain and encourage as many of next year's two-year-old flowering shoots as possible.

In the early to mid autumn of the second year following planting, and when flowering is nearly finished, remove as many of the flowered shoots as possible, cutting them as close to ground level as possible. As a guide this will mean cutting away one third to half of the original total number. All the remaining new unflowered shoots are then tied to the supports, normally in a fan shape.

On neglected and unpruned ramblers there may be very little new growth and if this is the case then the oldest and weakest shoots are removed until about half the original total number of shoots remain.

There is always the temptation not to prune as to do so may entail removing a number of shoots of architectural importance, but it should be remembered that not pruning it will lead to a slow decline in the performance and long-term well-being of the rambler. In time the architectural effect will be lost if pruning is not undertaken and the shoots in question will die and at some time have to be replaced, so pruning is not a drawback.

Feeding in mid to late spring with a rose fertilizer is as important as always.

Increasing the flowering of climbing and rambling Roses

One aid to flowering is to bend and tie as many of the shoots as possible horizontally along the training wire supports to slow down the flow of sap; in time this will increase the formation of flower buds and the number of flowers produced.

Dead-heading Roses

At first sight the dead-heading of Roses may not seem to be pruning, but of course it is, because if done properly it can greatly enhance the flowering performance of all groups. The extent to which it will be done in practice will of course depend on the labour or free time available. Of course this 'pruning' does not apply to those varieties grown for their ornamental fruits such as *Rosa rugosa* or *R. moyesii* varieties.

Normally Rose flowers are presented in clusters and as soon as an individual flower dies or loses its attraction it should be removed, using fingers or secateurs. Once the whole cluster of flower buds is exhausted, the remaining skeleton of the cluster should be cut away. To do this, first inspect the shoot that supported the flower cluster and find the location of the buds. Select the second or third bud down from the old flower cluster and cut cleanly above the selected bud. All pruned material should be removed from the area and burnt to prevent the spread of pests and diseases.

PRUNING PERENNIALS

Pruning for winter protection

Cutting back the growth of perennials in late autumn may not seem to be pruning but it is.

'Pruning' or cutting back in autumn can help with winter protection and this help is important because today we can grow many plants that are not as hardy as the older, well-tried varieties. It used to be the practice to cut very hard back, almost to ground level, all shoots, in mid to late autumn, once the plant had finished flowering and was unattractive.

However, today it is thought best to leave 6–12 in (15–30 cm) of growth attached over winter so that an individual 'microclimate' is set up amongst the shortened-back shoots, providing winter protection to the plant's next season's buds, which lie just below the soil surface. Then in early spring the remaining growth is cut away. I realize that this entails two operations, but the protection given to the overwintering plants well outweighs the effort.

Most species of perennial plants respond well to this practice.

Pruning 'perennials' that are in fact sub-shrubs or semi-tender shrubs

A number of 'perennial' plants are in fact either sub-shrubs or semi-hardy shrubs and in winter are naturally killed to ground level. Often in our gardens the winters are not cold enough to kill off the growth above ground level, so we must 'prune' by cutting all the shoots hard back to within a few inches of ground level in mid to late spring, just before growth starts.

If this is not done, the tubes in the unpruned shoots fur up, become less productive and can, in a relatively short time, run out of energy altogether and die. With silver- or grey-leaved plants, watch for the first signs of new spring growth before pruning.

Plants that fit into this group are:

Astilbe varieties (Astilbe)
Artemisia varieties (Wormwood)
Clematis, perennial varieties (Clematis)
Euphorbia varieties (Spurge) – care must be taken with the sap, which is a skin irritant
Fuchsia, hardy varieties (Hardy Fuchsia)
Gypsophila varieties (Baby's Breath)

Lathyrus, hardy varieties (Everlasting Sweet Pea)
Osteospermum varieties (Osteospermum)
Penstemon varieties (Beard Tongue)
Ruta varieties (Rue) – care must be taken with the sap, which is a skin irritant
Salvia officinalis varieties (Sage)

231

Pruning perennials to 'cut and come again'

'Cut and come again' is a useful practice that can be adopted to increase the interest offered by some perennial plants. Once the flowers have finished and the foliage is looking shabby, they can be cut hard back to within a few inches of ground level. Although they look barren for a couple of weeks, the newly produced leaves carry the plant forward into the remainder of the summer and early autumn with new interesting leaves, and there is a chance, with some, of a second flowering.

The following are the principal perennial plants that respond to this treatment; the individual gardener may identify others.

Alchemilla mollis (Lady's Mantle)
Anaphalis varieties (Snowy Everlasting)
Astrantia varieties (Masterwort)
Epimedium varieties (Barrenwort, Bishop's Hat)
Euphorbia robbiae (Robb's Spurge)
Geraniums, most perennial varieties (Geranium)
Heuchera micrantha 'Palace Purple' (Purple-leaved Coral Flower)
Iberis sempervirens (Perennial Candytuft)
Lamium varieties (Dead Nettle)
Melissa officinalis varieties (Lemon Balm)
Mentha varieties (Mint)
Nepeta varieties (Catmint)
Tellima varieties (Fringe-cups)
Tovara virginiana varieties (Tovara)

PRUNING ALPINES

All alpine plants with carpet-forming habits benefit from being cut back after flowering. To do this place a tea or dinner plate on top of the alpine, choosing the size to fit the plant, and then cut back all protruding growth from around the outside. Remove the plate and lightly trim off the top. This will greatly enhance the shape, foilage and flowers of the alpine.

PRUNING FRUIT

The pruning of fruit is practised to increase the quality,

quantity and size of the fruit produced, and it can also improve the appearance of the plant from an architectural point of view. In some cases the fruit tree can be adapted by pruning and training to fulfil a specific ornamental role. Pruning may also help to control pests and diseases and it certainly helps in the overall management of fruit production.

It may seem at first sight that the advice given, especially for pruning newly planted fruit trees, is harsh and might harm the tree. This fear is completely unfounded; in fact, the reverse is the truth.

Pruning, as well as improving the shape and encouraging the production of fruit, helps to establish a good balance between roots and top growth in the critical first few months between planting and establishment.

Classification of fruit

Fruit is divided into specific groups, and these groupings are relevant to pruning methods; they are explained in the following notes.

Top fruit

Top fruit is a term given to all fruit produced on a tree rather than a bush, vine or cane, and can further be divided into the following categories, which have a bearing on the pruning used.

CLASSIFICATION ACCORDING TO FRUIT TYPE

Pip fruit Apples, Pears, Quinces and Medlars; fruit containing pip seeds.

Stone fruit Plums, Damsons, Greengages, Peaches, Nectarines, Cherries and Bullace; fruit containing stones.

Mulberries and Walnuts are also grouped under top fruit, but normally require no pruning to aid fruiting.

CLASSIFICATION ACCORDING TO FORM

There are six main trained tree forms, covering both pip and stone fruit, each requiring specific pruning techniques:

Bush   A shrub or small tree where branches grow from or near soil level or on a 2 ft (60 cm) high stem.

Half standard   A tree with a stem or trunk of at least 3 ft (1 m) and not more than 5 ft (1.5 m) with branch system above.

Full standard   A tree with a clear stem of 5 ft (1.5 m) minimum, and not more than 8 ft (2.5 m).

The height of a stem or trunk of a bush, half standard or full standard cannot extend once the trees are trained and it is important to select the right height for the planting position.

Horizontal or espalier-trained   Many wall-trained top-fruit trees are trained into a horizontal tiered shape to show off their beauty to the full and also to aid ripening of fruit. Support is required to maintain this shaping (see Chapter 3).

Cordon-trained   A single stem with short side branches (spurs) is trained and secured to a support by annual pruning. Support is required (see Chapter 3).

Fan-trained   Branches radiate from the base or trunk in a fan shape. Support is required, and annual pruning, to maintain this shaping. (See Chapter 3.)

To achieve the required shape, top fruit has to be trained; to avoid some of the stages of training the gardener can purchase pre-trained fruit trees at different stages of their development.

There is also the problem of the overgrown and neglected fruit tree which requires rejuvenation pruning, and this will also be explained in this section.

Most of the pruning methods will follow a formula that will vary in the formative years but will become an annual routine later.

Soft fruit

Soft fruit includes all the remaining fruit that is not grown as 'trees' but as bushes, vines and canes. The following grouping further describes the forms of training for soft fruit and has a bearing on pruning.

Bush Grown with a short stem (leg) of approximately 6–12 in (15–30 cm). The height of this stem cannot increase, once set. These include Red and White Currants and Gooseberries.

The word bush is also used for Blackcurrants and Blueberries, where no leg (or trunk) is formed and the shoots emerge from a central point below, at or just above ground level.

Bush fruits, except Blackcurrants, can be trained by pruning into mop-headed standards, cordon-trained and fan-trained forms.

Mop-headed standard A soft fruit bush that is grafted on to a short stem approximately 3 ft (1 m) in height, or alternatively is trained up from ground level. Gooseberries and Red and White Currants are often grown in this way.

Cordon-trained A single stem with short side branches is trained by annual pruning, and secured to a support. In some cases these may be single, double or even treble cordons, and they are not always trained to grow at an angle, as with top fruit. The main soft fruits grown in this way are Gooseberries and Red and White Currants.

Fan-trained With this shape the shoots radiate from the base or stem in a fan shape. Support and annual pruning are required to maintain this shaping. Red and White Currants and Gooseberries are the main forms of soft fruit that can be grown in this way.

Cane A cane has a shoot or number of shoots that grow and fruit on an annual basis and carry the foliage, flowers and fruit of the plant. These include Raspberries, Loganberries, Tayberries, Boysenberries, Blackberries and hybrid berries. They are normally tied to a support. (See Chapter 3.)

Vines These include Black and White Grapes, both dessert and ornamental, and also *Actinidia chinensis* (Chinese Gooseberry or Kiwi Fruit). They require specific pruning and are normally tied to a support.

Figs Figs may be grown indoors or outdoors, as a bush or fan-trained.

Strawberries are also included in this group, but of course do not need pruning.

Pruning top fruit

With all top fruit the first season's fruit crop must be sacrificed; removing the flower buds in the spring directs the energy of the tree towards establishment, rather than using it in the production of fruit.

With cordon, horizontal and fan-trained pip fruit, and all forms of stone fruit, the thinning of the fruit on established trees will improve the quality of the fruit and prevent undue pressure being placed on the tree.

Cordon, horizontal and fan-trained pip fruit which have been established for more than eight to ten years will need, in winter, their spur formations thinned by one third every five to six years to induce the ongoing production of flower buds.

The control, spread and eradication of pests and diseases is important, and common problems specific to a particular group, such as canker in Apples and Pears, must always be considered. Checking prior to pruning for dead, diseased or broken branches, and removing any found, is necessary with all types of top fruit.

Pruning young, newly planted top fruit

Top-fruit trees can be purchased in a number of sizes and the size will dictate the amount of pruning and training required.

The sizes, types and varieties required may not all be available from one source and the gardener may have to buy from a number of suppliers, and even then may have to make compromises. The younger the trees, the less expensive, but this saving must be weighed against the amount of training that will be required and the time the tree will take to come into full fruit production.

The youngest top fruit are 'maiden', or 'feathered' trees, but the pruning that is required to train these into a bush, half or full standard tree takes time and a certain amount of skill. There is also the problem of different tree shapes needing specific named or numbered rootstocks, and finding the right combination can sometimes be difficult. For those intending to attempt training from maiden or feathered trees, reference to the Royal Horticultural Society's *Encyclopedia of Practical Gardening: Fruit* is advised.

My advice is to purchase, wherever possible, either pre-trained bush, half standard or possibly full standard trees, although the latter are becoming increasingly scarce. Pruning should start in the year of planting, in the late autumn to late winter.

Select four of the main shoots that will form the start of the framework of an open-centred tree and remove completely any other shoots, pruning as close to the main shoot as possible. If the central leading shoot has not been removed by the nursery then this should also be reduced to the height of the tallest of the selected framework branches. The chosen four remaining framework shoots are now pruned by shortening back to within 12–15 in (30–40 cm) of the main stem, pruning to an outward-facing bud.

From this original pruning up to two or three shoots will emerge on each shoot. Choose the two strongest and remove the remainder; shorten one of the two by two thirds and leave the other to form one of the main branches.

From here on, one of a number of pruning systems can be adopted but I would recommend the renewal system, described later.

Pip fruit

Pruning established top fruit, and neglected bush, half and full standard trees

When pruning Apples and Pears and, if felt necessary, Quinces and Medlars, the main consideration is to open up the centre of the tree to let in light and air so that the sun can ripen the fruit. The following formula aims to do this and is common to all four pip fruits.

The work should be carried out in early to mid winter at any time the weather is not too severe, as cold may enter the open wound and cause stem tissue damage, which may in turn encourage the start of other diseases.

The pruning of established and neglected trees in this group is the same. With a neglected tree there will be times when it will have reached a point beyond rejuvenation and it is impossible to state here when that point is reached, but in my experience around 80 per cent of trees are reclaimable.

STAGE 1
Inspect the tree for any signs of canker – the fungus disease that can attack all four pip fruits in varying degrees by killing the bark and the tissues below and is identified by the eating away of both. If seen, treat by removing, if possible, the affected shoot or cutting away the affected area with a sharp knife if the attack has not completely encircled the shoot, and painting with an anti-canker fungicidal paint.

STAGE 2
Consider the overall tree shape and decide whether there are any main branches that are causing an obstruction to the surrounding area or to adjoining trees and buildings. If their removal is essential, cut these away first; if not, wait until you are sure.

STAGE 3
Identify the main branches that are obstructing the centre of the tree and decide which ones need removing to open up this area and let the sunlight in; consider the effect of removing them on the overall shape and on those that will remain. Then make the necessary cuts, bearing in mind the general advice given earlier (p. 183) on how a cut should be made.

STAGE 4
Inspect the remaining branches; if there are any that still cross, decide on which ones to remove to prevent further possible damage by rubbing, which leads to infection by canker. Take into account that the final aim should be to have the main branches 15–18 in (40–50 cm) apart. If two branches have been rubbing and are damaged, decide which of them is the sounder and therefore should remain. Of

course, if both can be removed, this would be the best option.

On large trees, say more than 16 ft (5 m) in diameter, it may be best to work on a section at a time, but taking into consideration the adjoining sections and the overall shape of the tree. Once all of these points have been considered make the selected cuts.

STAGE 5
Pare off the edges of all cuts that are larger in diameter than your thumb and paint with a pruning compound such as Arbrex.

If the tree is not an Apple, spray with an overwinter tar-oil wash at this stage, following the directions on the product, to kill overwintering pests and diseases.

From here on nothing more is normally required for neglected Pears, Quinces or Medlars, but Apples require further work, as follows.

The renewal system for Apples
There are many pruning methods for Apple trees, and reference to a publication specializing in the subject will assist those who wish to adopt other pruning systems. However, over the years I have found that the following renewal system will benefit all varieties of Apple trees, in most situations, particularly when they play a dual role, both fruiting and ornamental.

The gardener will discover that trees can be either tip bearing (fruiting at the end of the shoots) or biennial (fruiting more abundantly every second year), and normally the fruit buds will be borne on spurs. Rootstock vigour and tree shape also have to be taken into account when pruning. This is more difficult when the variety of Apple is not known. The 'renewal system' of pruning covers all these points and keeps the Apple tree in fruit, as well as keeping it healthy and of architectural garden merit over many years.

For Apples only, complete stages 1–5 above, with the exception of the winter wash. Then continue as follows.

STAGE 6

Inspect the shoots that are growing from the framework branches. It will be found that in most cases they will be growing in pairs, with just a few singles and possibly a small number of trebles. Very neglected trees may have very limited numbers of shoots and to induce their production it will be necessary to shorten the ends of the main shoots by 6–12 in (15–30 cm) so that in the following year new shoots will grow that can be brought into the renewal pruning system.

STAGE 7

Where pairs of shoots exist inspection will show that, in each pair, one of the shoots is stronger. This shoot is left unpruned to develop fruit buds for fruit production in two years' time. Fruit buds are formed along the shoots and at the ends in tip-bearing varieties. The weaker of the two is pruned back to two or three buds from the point where it joins the main shoot to produce two new shoots in the following spring.

On a few trees the shoots may be in threes; in this case remove the weakest completely and prune the remaining ones as if they were a pair.

Where there is only one shoot this should be cut back to two buds from its origin (to about 2 in/5 cm); it will produce two shoots in the following spring and these can then be introduced into the renewal pruning system.

There may be a number of strong upright 'water shoots' growing from the main branches, particularly on branches towards the centre of the tree. These are formed by the tree to absorb surplus energy and will, in some cases, grow to form branches. Unless they are required to make a new branch to improve the overall shape or balance of the tree, they should be removed by pruning back flush with the main branches.

STAGE 8

In the second year, in early to mid winter, the overall shape of the tree should again be worked on as in stages 1–5, although the work carried out will be greatly reduced in quantity, and stage 7 is repeated. The removal of the major branches in year one will have increased the production of 'water shoots' and all unwanted ones should be removed.

In the following spring the two-year-old unpruned shoots will flower and fruit, the shoots left unpruned the previous winter will set flower buds and the pruned shoots will again produce at least two shoots.

STAGE 9
The process continues at the same time in the third year, and stages 1–7 are repeated. In addition, the shoots left unpruned in the first winter, which have now fruited, are removed, as they will be replaced by those left unpruned in the second winter.

The tree has now been pruned for three years and the cycle of annual production of fruit buds and new growth has been established.

From here on the process is repeated every year and the Apple tree will always look healthy and attractive, rather than neglected and unproductive. It can now be sprayed with tar-oil wash to kill off over-wintering pests and diseases.

Pruning cordon Apple trees
Cordons can be grown from feathered maidens or pre-trained cordons; only the most popular varieties are normally available pre-trained and even these will be in limited numbers.

The trees are first planted at an angle of 35° against support wires as described in Chapter 3. The benefit of this is that the tree's growth and sap flow is slowed down by the angle of planting, and the tree starts to fruit earlier in its life, producing more fruit than it normally would for its overall untrained size.

The angle also means that more varieties can be planted in a confined space, so improving cross-pollination.

If feathered maidens are planted in autumn to early spring, all side shoots should be pruned back to four buds from the main shoot, but the leading shoot left unpruned.

In midsummer, all shoots more than 8–10 in (20–25 cm) long growing from the main shoot should be cut back to a bud

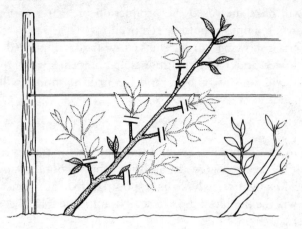

31. Pruning cordon fruit trees

3–5 in (8–12 cm) from the main shoot. Any shoots growing from the fruiting spurs which may be present are also reduced, this time to 1–2 in (3–5 cm) long, cut to just above a bud.

If a number of additional shoots are produced as a result of this pruning, as is often the case in wet summers or in areas with a high rainfall, these are again pruned to two or three buds from their origin. Once the main shoot has reached the top support wire it is pruned and stopped a few inches above the wire, and tied to it.

This pattern of pruning is then continued for the rest of the cordon's life.

After ten years or so the resulting fruiting spurs often become overcrowded and should be thinned out to leave one every 5–6 in (12–15 cm) along the main shoot. This pruning is carried out during the winter, except in severe cold weather.

Should cordons become neglected, the formula above will quickly bring them back under control but it may be necessary to remove substantial material to arrive back at the cordon's tight-growing formation.

Pruning horizontal-trained (espalier) Apples and Pears
Growing from the maiden stage can be be considered and this certainly costs less; however, it will take longer for the trees to

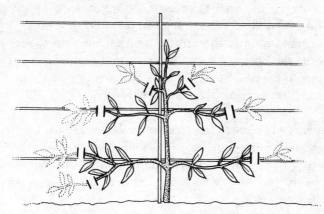

32. Pruning espalier-trained apples and pears

come into flower and fruit. Pre-trained trees with two and sometimes three pre-trained tiers of shoots are available in the popular varieties and it is this age of tree I would recommend planting. If younger trees are used, advice should be taken as to how to proceed.

Both young maidens and pre-trained trees will need support (see Chapter 3).

In the first early to mid winter following planting of two- or three-tiered trained trees, the horizontal shoots should be pruned back by approximately 20 per cent, normally leaving them 24–30 in (60–80 cm) long. The central upright shoot is pruned to stop its growth approximately 18 in (50 cm) above the highest horizontal layer of pre-trained shoots and any surplus shoots growing from the central or horizontal shoots are pruned back to within two or three buds of where they join the main shoot, to form fruiting spurs for the future.

If further horizontal shoots are required above the originals, these can be formed by tying in the new shoots as they grow from the 18 in (50 cm) of central shoot left after pruning.

Once the full requirement for horizontal shoots has been reached, the upward-growing shoots are simply removed in mid to late spring. At the same time, if the horizontal shoots have covered the area intended they are stopped by pruning the end 3–6 in (8–15 cm) to stop further lateral growth.

From midsummer to early autumn all the side shoots that grow off the horizontal and central shoot are pruned back to within 4–6 in (10–15 cm) of their origin, cutting to a bud. This formula is then repeated on an annual basis.

Pruning newly planted fan-trained Apples and Pears

Apples and Pears can be successfully grown as fan-trained trees to grow against a warm sunny wall where the ripening will be helped and where an architectural feature for the garden is required.

Growing from maiden trees is possible, but again I would suggest that, even though they are scarce in nurseries and garden centres, it is best to start with a pre-trained fan-shaped tree.

When the pre-trained tree is planted it will have from five to seven main shoots arranged in a fan-shape with a limited number of short side shoots.

In mid to late summer following planting, all side shoots should be pruned to within 4–6 in (10–15 cm) of the main shoots, cutting to a bud. This pruning is repeated each year but as the tree ages the early pruned shoots will have formed fruiting spurs and the side shoots are pruned back to the fruiting spur.

Once each of the fan-forming shoots has covered the in-

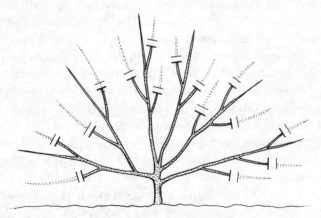

33. Pruning a fan-trained fruit tree

tended area it can be stopped, pruning it in winter to the required height by removing the upper portion, but this is normally not less than 12 ft (3.5 m) in height and spread so room must be allowed for this development in the first instance.

Stone fruit

Pruning newly planted Plums, Damsons and Greengages when grown as bush, half and full standard trees

As with pip fruit, maiden and feathered maiden trees can be purchased, but again, due to the time they take to develop and flower and the skill required, I believe that it is best to purchase the trees pre-trained as bushes or half standards – and possibly full standards, but these are very scarce.

Traditional sources suggest doing the first pruning after planting in spring but in view of the recent build-up of the unpreventable winter airborne fungus disease silver leaf I feel it is best to wait until the first midsummer following planting.

First remove any shoots that are growing from the main shoot (stem) which are unwanted and then shorten the remaining main and side shoots, leaving them approximately 12–15 in (30–40 cm) long and trying to form a balanced shape.

This process is repeated annually thereafter. In the winter when the weather is not severe apply a winter wash of Mortegg to the whole tree to help reduce disease and pest attacks.

Pruning neglected Plums, Damsons, Bullaces and Greengages

Often the gardener inherits a neglected Plum, Damson, Bullace or Greengage, which appears to have a mass of branches, often intertangled and possibly multi-stemmed. Before any pruning starts the following points must be taken into account.

To prevent attacks of silver leaf (a terminal, uncontrollable fungus disease) always prune after the end of May and before the beginning of August, as the spores of this fungus are wind-blown in winter, entering the plant through a wound, however small.

Plums in particular, and especially Victorias, are very susceptible and Damsons, Bullaces and Greengages can also be attacked. If a branch is broken by wind, the weight of fruit or some other accident, the affected shoot should be removed at once and burnt, and the cut painted with a pruning compound such as Arbrex.

Damsons, Greengages and Bullaces fruit best on mature shoots, so any pruning could upset their performance; they are probably better left unpruned, other than removing damaged crossing or rubbing shoots, which could provide an entry route for silver leaf.

The Plum tree may have a number of shoots originating from below ground level; these are probably non-productive suckers and should be removed by ripping them out (see p. 223). With Damsons and very old Greengages, however, the tree may well be on its own roots and the basal growth will be productive.

Pruning newly planted and mature fan-trained Plums, Damsons and Greengages

Training from feathered maidens is possible, but they are very difficult to obtain; even if a feathered maiden were available, I personally would start with a pre-trained fan-shaped tree.

The new tree should have been pruned back during its training by the nursery, and from this pruning three to five shoots will have developed. Beware of those that have not been pruned back as these are only maidens and can rarely be formed into good, productive, fan-shaped trees.

In the early spring of the first year following planting, the main fan-forming shoots should be pruned back by one third, leaving approximately 18–30 in (50–80 cm), depending on the starting size. Through the summer, as the new shoots develop, tie them out into a fan shape on bamboo canes which have been tied to the supporting wires. (See Chapter 3.)

In the second year, in the spring, watch for the start of any shoots that are growing towards the support or are growing forward, and pinch them out with your fingers or cut them off with secateurs as they develop. During early to mid summer, as new side shoots grow from the main shoots, the tips are pinched out once the shoots are 10–12 in (25–30 cm) long to just above a bud. The new shoots are tied to the support.

Once the fruit has been harvested these shoots are again

pinched back, this time to 5–6 in (12–15 cm). This operation is then repeated on an annual basis. If any shoot outgrows the allotted space, it is pruned to stop it, but pruning is always done in the spring and summer.

Pruning newly planted and mature fan-trained Peaches, Nectarines and Apricots

A word of warning first. As with Plums, the shortage of correctly trained fan-shaped trees means that the Peach or Nectarine tree you are offered may only be a feathered maiden. A fan-trained tree will have been pruned to within 12–18 in (30–50 cm) in the second year following grafting and from this cutting back will have arisen the first and main base shoots that the fan shape will be built on. Sadly many feathered, untrained maiden trees are sold as fan-trained trees, often at a price that reflects the work involved in producing a correctly trained tree. Because of this, I will describe the pruning from the feathered maiden stage: however, if a correctly trained fan-shaped tree can be found, I would suggest this is the best stage to start at.

YEAR ONE

The feathered maiden is purchased and planted in the autumn or early winter in the manner described in Chapter 2. If container-grown, the planting time can be extended into the early spring.

The planting times are governed, not by availability, but by the need to plant and be able to prune at critical times during the first summer, and by the time it takes the root system to provide the new growth that is required for further training.

In late winter or early spring, prune back the feathered maiden to approximately 24–30 in (60–80 cm) above ground level, making sure to prune just above a side shoot with at least two strong side shoots below the pruning point. All the remaining side shoots below the top one are then pruned back to within 1 in (3 cm) of the central shoot, pruning to a bud. Leaving the top side shoot unpruned helps draw the sap up from the roots and encourages new strong spring growth.

By early summer new shoots will have grown from the pruned side shoots; leave the top one and the lowest two, assuming one is growing to the left and one to the right or can be trained to do so. Remove all surplus side shoots and any smaller shoots that may have formed.

During midsummer, when the lower retained two side shoots are strong and obviously well-established, tie bamboo canes to the support wires at an angle of 35° and tie the retained horizontal shoots to the canes. Remove the retained top side shoot, pruning it back to just above the lower retained pair. The wire support system is explained further in Chapter 3.

YEAR TWO
In late winter or early spring, prune the retained lower pair of side shoots to within 12–18 in (30–50 cm) of the central shoot.

By midsummer, select four or five of the resulting new side shoots to left and right, so forming a fan shape. Remove all surplus shoots and tie those selected in a fan shape on to bamboo canes fixed to the support wires. The tree is now at the stage at which a pre-trained fan-shaped tree would be purchased.

YEAR THREE
Whether working with a trained feathered maiden or a pre-trained tree, in late winter prune the now established fan of shoots by one third, balancing the length of the remaining shoots to form a fan shape. By midsummer it should be possible to select side growths both above and below the main shoots of the fan. Side shoots should be encouraged to fan out every 3–5 in (8–12 cm) along the main shoots at a 35° angle. Both the side and main shoots are tied to bamboo canes fixed to the support wires.

During the summer, once all side growths are 18–24 in (50–60 cm) long, the tips or leading ends are pinched out; it is these pinched back shoots that will flower in the following year to produce the fruits.

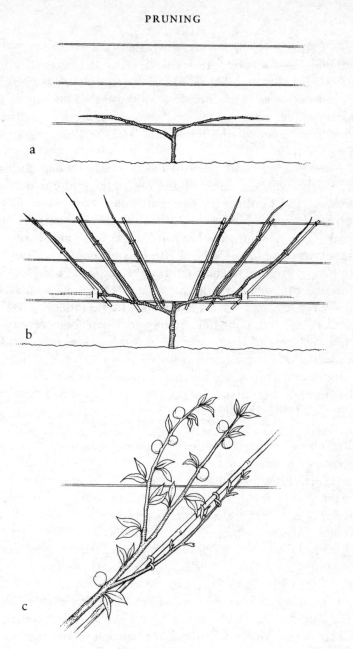

34. Pruning fan-trained peaches
(a) Year one   (b) Growth and pruning in the second year
(c) The new shoot is tied in; the fruited shoot will then be removed

249

YEAR FOUR AND THE FOLLOWING YEARS

In mid to late spring remove all forward- and backward-growing shoots as close to the main fan framework as possible; any with flower buds, including all those growing out of the sides of the main framework, should be pruned to within 2–3 in (5–8 cm) of the framework and the flower buds left intact to fruit.

After fruiting, select two of the new side shoots, one low down the existing side shoot and one in the centre to act as a reserve, and tie them in. Leave all other side shoots off the main fan-shaped framework to be the fruiting shoots for next year. Once new growths are formed on the pruned-back side shoots and they are 18–24 in (50–60 cm) long, pinch out the tips to encourage them to form the basis to continue the formula of pruning in the next year. All the harvested and fruited shoots are cut back to the main framework.

Once the tree is in full production it will be necessary to thin out some of the fruit once it is large enough to handle, and about 25–35 per cent is removed each year.

Bush or half-standard Peaches, Nectarines or Apricots rarely produce good results in Britain and are best avoided in all but the most favourable situations.

Renovating neglected Peaches, Nectarines or Apricots

Renovating a neglected Peach, Nectarine or Apricot is difficult, as many, if not pruned as suggested, grow in such a way as to make it very difficult to bring them back to the fan-trained shape, but it may be possible to practise the production and removal of the fruiting shoots on an overall misshapen tree as described for a correctly pruned fan-shaped tree.

Pruning to form bush Cherries

As more and more garden centres are selling feathered maidens as finished trees, which they are not, I will start the pruning of Cherries from the feathered maiden size, but wherever possible I would try to purchase a pre-trained bush, half standard or possibly, subject to availability, full standard tree.

Ideally the feathered maiden should be planted, staked and

tied in the autumn or at least before the end of early spring to allow it time to establish a good productive root system. It should be in excess of 5–6 ft (1.5–2 m) high and have at least five side shoots, ideally towards the top.

YEAR ONE

Just before the leaves show in the spring all the side shoots up to 24–30 in (60–80 cm) from the ground are pruned as close to the central stem as possible. This should normally leave five side shoots on the remainder of the central shoot; if not, reduce the distance from ground level at which side shoots are removed. Select the four best side shoots to form the basis of a branch framework and shorten back to the central shoot, leaving 15–18 in (40–50 cm) of shoot, but pruning in such a way that a balanced framework is formed.

Throughout, all the pruning cuts should be made as close above a bud as possible.

YEAR TWO

In the following mid spring prune the resulting shoots again to 15–18 in (40–50 cm) to build the framework. The tree is now at the age and of the formation that would be expected for a pre-trained tree.

YEAR THREE

From here on any side shoots growing from the central stem below the height of the main selected branches are removed in spring; however, if the growth consists of just a few leaves it is beneficial to leave these to help draw up the sap from the roots.

Just before the leaves form in spring, shorten the new shoots that were formed from last year's pruning, leaving 18–24 in (50–60 cm). Any secondary side shoots that are competing for space with the framework shoots should be shortened to 3–4 in (8–10 cm); those that are not competing for space can be left unpruned. Should any side shoots be growing into and blocking the centre of the tree, these are removed completely.

From here on very little pruning is required, except for

routine removal of any dead shoots or seriously crossing branches, and the final trimming of the central shoot to form a trunk.

Pruning to form half standard or full standard Cherries

The problem here is that the feathered maiden may not have the height required for the pruning, as suggested for the bush, to be carried out, so the first pruning in the spring following planting is to remove all the side shoots and support the central shoot with a bamboo cane until it reaches 24–36 in (60 cm–1 m) above the height of the stem length required. For half standards this is 3–5 ft (1–1.5 m) and for full standards 5–6 ft (1.5–2 m). Once these heights are reached and adequate side shoots have formed, then spring pruning is carried out as for bush Cherries, but at the greater height of the main shoot.

Pruning fan-trained sweet Cherries

Feathered maidens Cherries can, with some effort, be fan-trained for growing against walls and other frameworks. However, I prefer to start with a pre-trained tree.

YEAR ONE

At the time of purchase the tree should have been pruned back and, as a result of this pruning, three to five shoots will have formed on each side of the central shoot to form the fan shape. In mid to late spring following planting, all the main shoots are pruned back to leave them 18–24 in (50–60 cm) long.

From this pruning the number of main shoots forming the fan will double and each will require tying to the support wires. This is best achieved by first tying to the wire a bamboo cane of sufficient length to cover the space allocated for the size of the tree and then tying the shoots to the cane, so preventing damage by rubbing. The provision of the training wires is covered in Chapter 3.

YEAR TWO AND THEREAFTER

In the second spring and annually thereafter, prune back to the main shoot any small side shoots to prevent them maturing and overfilling the allotted spaces between the main shoots.

As the tree develops, in mid to late summer prune back to 10–12 in (25–30 cm) any side shoots that have formed and are not needed for the main framework.

Prune these shoots again in mid autumn by a further 5–6 in (12–15 cm). These two separate prunings will encourage them to form flower buds. At the same time, once the main shoots have reached the height required they are stopped by pruning back the leading shoot. However, it should always be remembered that a fan-trained Cherry will require a height and spread of not less than 10 × 12 ft (3 × 3.5 m).

Pruning fan-trained sour Cherries
Personally, as before, I would plant a pre-trained tree, but if you wish to start from a feathered maiden, follow the first stages of pruning for a fan-trained Peach, Nectarine or Apricot.

If a pre-trained tree is planted or when the feathered maiden reaches the same stage, the following pruning should be started in early spring.

YEAR ONE AND FOLLOWING YEARS
Prune back all framework shoots to within 18–24 in (50–60 cm) of their origin. Later, in late spring and summer, as the secondary side shoots grow, thin them out to 3–6 in (8–15 cm) apart along the framework shoots, removing any surplus.

After the fruit has been harvested, prune out the fruiting shoots back to the point where new secondary side shoots have formed. This pruning is then repeated annually.

Pruning soft fruit
Pruning newly planted Blackcurrants
The aim of pruning Blackcurrants is to form a bush where the shoots are produced annually from under or at the soil surface. Also, as the best fruit is produced on two-year-old shoots, the aim is to encourage the bush by pruning to produce a new crop of shoots each year to replace those that have fruited.

It is best to plant one- or two-year-old bushes between autumn and early spring, so that the root system has time to establish and produce the growth required.

Once the bush has been planted, all shoots are cut back to within 1–3 in (3–8 cm) of ground level. This of course sacrifices all the fruit for the coming year but it is very important to build up a good strong root system before fruiting is allowed to start, otherwise the number of new fruiting shoots may be reduced.

YEAR TWO AND FOLLOWING YEARS
By the summer of the second year the bushes will have formed a new crop of fruiting shoots which, after fruiting, are pruned as close to ground level as possible without damaging or removing any of the replacement shoots that have formed or will be forming. From here on this pruning is repeated annually in the same way and at the same time.

Pruning neglected Blackcurrants
With neglected and established unpruned Blackcurrants it is best to destroy the old bushes to prevent the spread of an army of pests and of disease problems. Blackcurrants are not grown as trained shaped bushes such as fan or cordon.

Pruning Red and White Currants: bushes
Red or White Currant bushes are one or two years old when purchased and the aim of pruning is to produce a round wine-glass shape on top of a 12 in (30 cm) stem (leg).

YEAR ONE
The new bush is best planted between late autumn and early spring to allow the root system to develop. The first pruning starts at any time after planting, assuming the weather is not extremely cold, and should be finished by late spring.

The one- or two-year-old bush will have up to four or five shoots at the top of the 12 in (30 cm) long stem. Any shoots below are cut away to ensure the stem is maintained. The stem is used to slow growth down and so aid the production of fruit. Each of the shoots on top of the 'leg' is pruned back to within 6 in (15 cm) of the stem, attempting to ensure that the pruning creates a balanced shape by cutting the strongest shoots a little less hard than the weakest.

YEAR TWO
In the early winter of the second year, the shoots produced by the first year's pruning are shortened by 50 per cent of their growth, but again attempting to cut to a bud in such a way that the length of the remaining shoot will form a balanced round shape.

YEAR THREE AND FOLLOWING YEARS
From early winter to late spring in the third year all shoots are again reduced as before but by now there may be some crossing ones and these are cut out and the bush pruned so as to open the centre. This process is then repeated every year.

Pruning Red and White Currants: cordons
YEAR ONE
One-year-old plants are best planted between late autumn and late spring for this type of training. Throughout pruning all cuts are made just above a bud.

At any time when the temperature is above freezing within the planting period, the lowest shoots on the central stem are removed to a height of 4–5 in (10–12 cm). Any other side shoots above this are pruned to within 1 in (3 cm) of their point of origin on the central stem, which itself is reduced by 50 per cent of its total length.

In early summer to midsummer the resulting new shoots are again reduced to 5–7 in (12–17 cm) from where they originate from the central shoot. The central shoot itself is not pruned and is left to grow, being tied to a 4–5 ft (1.2–1.5 m) bamboo cane tied to a system of support wires (see Chapter 3).

YEAR TWO AND FOLLOWING YEARS

In early winter all new side shoots are pruned back to 1–2 in (3–5 cm) from the point where they originate from the main side shoots. The leading section of the central shoot is also reduced to 5–6 in (12–15 cm) from the point where it grew in the previous year.

Finally, each summer, shorten the shoots produced from last winter's cuts and reduce to a length of 4–6 in (10–15 cm) from the main side shoots.

Pruning Red and White Currants: standards

Pre-trained standard Red and sometimes White Currants can be purchased; apart from the removal of any side shoots which may grow on the stem below the selected side shoot, the pruning of the side shoots is the same as when grown as a bush.

Rejuvenating neglected Red and White Currant bushes

To rejuvenate neglected bush Red and White Currants, in winter prune to create an open centre and prune back side shoots to within 5–7 in (12–17 cm) of the main stem. After the first year's pruning the bush should become more manageable and productive, and pruning can be continued as recommended for newly planted bushes.

Pruning Gooseberries: bushes

YEAR ONE

Normally one- or two-year-old bushes are purchased and planted from late autumn to late spring, to allow the plants to establish a good root system. The aim is to create a goblet-shaped bush on the top of an 8–12 in (20–30 cm) stem (leg) and to maintain this stem for the life of the bush.

Following planting, any shoots growing on the main shoot are removed to a height of 12 in (30 cm) and any remaining side shoots cut back to within 3–4 in (8–10 cm) of the main shoot.

YEAR TWO AND FOLLOWING YEARS
In the winter of the second year the stem is cleaned of any side
growths below the selected side shoots and the new shoots on
the side shoots are reduced in length to 3–4 in (8–10 cm). This
pruning is repeated annually thereafter.

It may be necessary to remove occasional crossing shoots
from the centre of the bush's framework to let in sunlight to
ripen the fruit.

Some varieties of Gooseberries have a weeping habit so
cutting to an upward facing bud will help counteract this. Of
course all shoots are cut cleanly to just above a bud. Care
should be taken when pruning Gooseberries as they have
numerous sharp thorns.

Cordon Gooseberries
Gooseberries can be grown as cordons in exactly the same way
as Red Currants, but it is important to chose a variety with an
upright habit and my choice would be 'Careless', avoiding
varieties such as 'Leveller' which may have a more weeping
habit.

Pruning standard Gooseberries
Pre-trained standards are available and make useful fruiting
and ornamental specimen mop-headed trees – they are often
used in the vegetable garden. Apart from keeping the stem free
of shoots, the pruning of the upper branches is the same as for
bushes (see Training Shrubs as Mop-Headed Trees, p. 273).

Rejuvenation of neglected Gooseberries
Neglected and unpruned bushes can be brought back into full
production by removing, in winter, shoots to open the centre
and then pruning the remaining side shoots in the same way as
for bushes; in the first year some side shoots may need to be
removed to counteract overcrowding.

Pruning Worcesterberries
This is a hybrid berry resembling a purple Gooseberry. It is
pruned in exactly the same way as the Gooseberry.

Pruning Blackberries, Tayberries, Boysenberries, Loganberries, John Innes Berries and Japanese Wine Berries

All in this group produce their crop on a cane; thorned and thornless varieties are both treated in the same way.

Before planting it is important to provide supports (see Chapter 3).

The new canes are planted from late autumn to mid spring, and are cut to within 8–10 in (20–25 cm) of ground level. From these pruned canes, between two and six new strong canes will grow in the late spring and summer but they will not fruit in the first year. There are a number of ways of training but all require the support of fences, walls or posts and wires; this is covered in Chapter 3.

METHOD ONE

In year one, all the new shoots are gathered together in an upright column and tied temporarily to the support. In the autumn of year one the new canes are spaced out in a fan shape and tied to the support wires approximately 12 in (30 cm) apart.

In year two the tied-in canes produced the previous year will fruit and a crop of new canes will be produced; these are again gathered together in a group in the centre.

After fruiting all fruited canes are cut out to ground level and the new canes spread out in a fan shape, approximately 12 in (30 cm) apart on to the support wires, ready to fruit next year. The process is then repeated annually. As the plants become more established it may be necessary to reduce the number of canes retained, removing the weakest first.

METHOD TWO

Instead of gathering all the new canes together in the centre, as they grow they are tied out into a half-fan shape, say to the left of the centre, and are harvested from this side. In the second year the new canes are tied to the opposite side, again in a half-fan shape. Once harvested, all fruiting canes are removed to ground level.

Rejuvenating neglected Blackberries, Tayberries, Boysenberries, Loganberries, John Innes Berries and Japanese Wine Berries

Rejuvenating a neglected or unpruned plant is simply a matter of removing any dead or fruited canes and retaining and tying in the new canes to a fan shape. This is done after fruiting or during the following autumn or winter.

Pruning Raspberries

Of all fruit, Raspberries are most at risk from disease, in particular Raspberry mosaic and reversion. Both of these problems are diseases that cannot be eradicated. Also, because Raspberries are propagated by simply dividing and removing rooted shoots, there is a very high risk that the new plants will carry the diseases. For this reason you should always buy plants which are certified as being free of these diseases.

Even if new plants are certified, there is a chance of cross-infection if there are infected plants already in the garden. Renovating neglected unpruned Raspberries is therefore strongly discouraged and careful regular inspections should be made for both diseases.

It is always best to plant, between late autumn and early spring, bare-rooted certified canes; always avoid any that are offered at other times as container grown.

Pruning of summer- and autumn-fruiting Raspberries consists of removing the fruited canes – the canes only produce a good crop once and if they are not removed they inhibit the production of strong new canes, depriving the plant of food and so reducing the overall fruiting capacity. The old shoots are in fact slowly naturally dying and the pruning just speeds up this process and redirects the energy to the new.

Before attempting to grow Raspberries it is important to provide supports, and this is covered in Chapter 3.

Pruning summer-fruiting Raspberry varieties

This group is the most widely planted, producing its fruit from mid to late summer, depending on the variety. The fruit is produced on canes grown the previous year so the aim of pruning is to maintain the replacement of the shoots each year.

YEAR ONE

New certified bare-rooted canes are planted 15–18 in (40–50 cm) apart in rows 6 ft (2 m) apart along the line of a post-and-wire support. Planting is done from mid autumn to early spring in well-prepared soil and it is recommended that planting outside these times should be avoided as the establishment of the plants, including the pruning, will be upset.

After planting reduce the canes to 9–10 in (23–5 cm) from ground level. In mid to late spring, just as the new canes are growing, reduce the old canes, this time to ground level.

As the new canes grow, tie them no closer than 4 in (10 cm) apart along the support wires, removing any surplus. No fruit should be expected in the first summer after planting.

YEAR TWO AND FOLLOWING YEARS

In late winter, prune all canes to 6–9 in (15–23 cm) above the top support wire or carefully bend them in one direction along the top wire. After fruiting, prune all fruited canes to ground level and tie in new canes to wires 4–5 in (10–12 cm) apart along the wires as they develop.

Remove any surplus canes, and any that have been produced outside of the main row, by digging them out; then destroy them.

This process is then repeated annually, so preventing a possible build-up of Raspberry mosaic and reversion diseases.

Pruning autumn-fruiting Raspberry varieties

These varieties fruit on the new shoots produced in the same year and as their name implies, they fruit in the autumn. They can be planted without support, in rows or in large clumps.

In late winter to early spring the newly planted certified canes are pruned to ground level, just as the first signs of new growth are seen.

New canes will grow and fruit on the top 15–18 in (40–50 cm) of the cane; as they do this in the autumn the canes should never be reduced in height until after fruiting. In early spring all the previous season's fruiting canes are cut to ground level; new canes will fruit in the following autumn.

Pruning outdoor fruiting Vines

Outdoor Vines may be grown for two purposes in the garden, for fruit production or for ornament, and in either case they will need wire supports (see Chapter 3).

YEAR ONE

Newly purchased plants are best planted – from mid autumn to early spring to allow for root establishment – 4–5 ft (1.2–1.5 m) apart along the line of the post-and-wire support, with a bamboo cane tied to the support and the base of the plant tied to the bamboo cane. When planted against a wall they should be at least 15–18 in (40–50 cm) away from it.

In early spring the vines (shoots) are pruned back to within 9–12 in (23–30 cm) of ground level but care is needed at this point to determine whether the plant is propagated from cuttings or grafted. The supplying nursery or garden centre should be able to give this information; if not, it is normally possible with close observation to identify the point of graft union. If grafted it is very important to prune 6–9 in (15–23 cm) *above* the graft union or the grafted variety will be lost.

During the spring, summer and early autumn allow a single vine to grow, removing any side vines as they appear and tying in to a bamboo cane which is tied in turn to the support wires.

In November prune back the resulting vine to 15–18 in (40–50 cm) from ground level.

YEAR TWO

From the spring to late summer allow three vines to develop and tie them to the support, removing any others that may develop.

In late autumn carefully bend and tie down the lowest two vines, one to the left and one to the right along the lowest support wire, and reduce them in length to 24–30 in (60–80

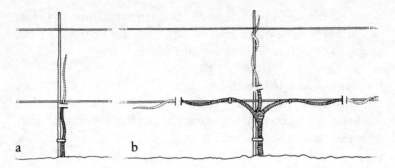

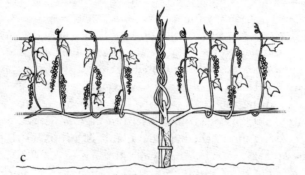

35. *Vine pruning* *(a) Year one*
(b) Growth and pruning in year two *(c) Year three*

cm). The remaining vine is pruned back to within 3–5 in (8–12 cm) above the first of the horizontal ones.

YEAR THREE AND FOLLOWING YEARS

From mid spring to late summer allow three to five vertical fruiting vines to grow from the horizontally trained vines. These are tied to the wires as they grow. Once they reach just above the top wire, which is normally approximately 4–6 ft (1.2–2 m) high, their tips are pinched out. Any lateral vines growing from them are also removed, as are any surplus ones.

Also tie in three vertical vines in a bunch in the middle for the next year's fruiting.

In early winter remove the two horizontal fruited vines and tie down their replacements. Prune the remaining vines as in

year two. Train the new vertical fruiting vines into position,
pinch and thin out as before in year two. From here on the
process is repeated annually.

Rejuvenating neglected fruiting Vines
Unpruned and neglected plants can be brought back to full
production by hard pruning back as described for year one,
and starting again.

Varieties of outdoor fruiting Vines
All are varieties of *Vitis vinifera*.

WHITE OUTDOOR FRUITING VARIETIES
'Chardonnay', 'Nimrod', 'Madeleine Angevine 7972', 'Madeleine
Silvaner 2851', 'Müller-Thurgau', 'Muscat de Saumur', 'Pinot
Blanc', 'Précoce de Malingre', 'Seyve Villard 5276', 'Siegerrebe'
and 'Traminer'.

BLACK OUTDOOR FRUITING VARIETIES
'Baco 1', 'Black Hamburgh', 'Brant', 'Léon Millot', 'Marshall Joffre',
'Millers Burgundy', 'Pirovano 14', 'Seibel 13053', 'Schuyler',
'Strawberry Grape' and 'Triomphe d'Alsace'.

Pruning outdoor ornamental Vines
YEAR ONE
Purchase a new plant and plant in the centre of the area to be
covered. If against a wall it should be planted at least 15–18
in (40–50 cm) away from it. Prune as for year one of fruiting
Vines; as the resulting vines grow select the strongest and tie to
the support wire.

Once it has reached 12–18 in (30–50 cm) above the first wire
support at 18 in (50 cm), prune it back to 6–9 in (15–23 cm).
From this pruning select three of the resulting vines. Tie two,
one left and one right horizontally along the wires. A third
shoot is tied vertically and each time the next support wire is
reached the pruning is repeated and the resulting new vines
tied in.

Depending on the height of the support it may be possible to
reach the top in one year, repeating the pruning as each level is
reached. If it is not, then it is carried on over into the next year.

YEAR TWO AND FOLLOWING YEARS

The horizontal vines are allowed to grow to cover the intended area and once they have filled it they are pruned to stop them. Side vines will be produced from the horizontals and once each of these is more than 15–18 in (40–50 cm) long they are stopped by pinching out the leading shoot; this continues throughout the summer.

In early spring each year, all side vines off the main horizontals are cut back flush with the vines to encourage flower buds and fruit production.

Varieties of ornamental Vines

Vitis coignetiae (Japanese Crimson Glory Vine)
V. vinifera 'Brant' (Brant's Vine)
V. v. 'Purpurea' (Purple-leaved Common Grape Vine)

Indoor Vines

Many Vines require protection and added heat to ripen their fruit so these varieties must be planted in a greenhouse or conservatory.

YEAR ONE

In late autumn or early winter, plant the new plant outside the greenhouse or conservatory in a position where it will have room to spread its roots over a wide area to obtain the food it requires. Lead the vine in through an entry hole as low down the structure as possible and which can later be effectively closed up.

In the early spring prune back to a point just inside the building.

Throughout the summer encourage a single strong vine to reach up to the end and highest point of the building, removing all other vines as they are formed.

YEAR TWO

By now the single vine should have reached its allotted height; if it has not then it should be given more time to do so.

When it has, stop the leading vine by cutting the leading bud out and from this stopping select the strongest vines from those that grow and tie one to each of the training wires that have been provided 18 in (50 cm) apart across the roof area allocated for the vine.

Once the vines have reached the end of their allocated wires they should be stopped by pinching out the ends. Any side vines, once 15–18 in (40–50 cm) long, are also stopped by pinching out.

YEAR THREE

In the early spring all side vines are pruned flush with the main roof vines to encourage fruiting. Any surplus vines that are produced on the main vertical vine are also removed when seen.

From here on the process is repeated annually, but there may be a need to prune back the roof vines to the vertical and retrain a new one every ten to fifteen years.

Varieties of indoor Vines
All are varieties of *Vitis vinifera*.

WHITE INDOOR VARIETIES

'Buckland Sweetwater', 'Chasselas d'Or', 'Foster's Seedling', 'Lady Hutt', 'Mireille', 'Mrs Pearson', 'Muscat of Alexandria', 'Syrian' and 'Trebbiano'.

BLACK INDOOR VARIETIES

'Alicante', 'Black Hamburgh', 'Frontignan', 'Gros Colmar', 'Lady Downe's Seedling', 'Mrs Pince's Black Muscat' and 'Muscat Hamburg'.

Rejuvenating a neglected or unpruned Vine
The aim should be to select main vines that are dispersed every 18 in (50 cm) apart over the available area and to remove all surplus vines. Once the framework is achieved then the reducing and hard pruning back of the side vines should start and they can be pruned to fit the purpose for which they are being grown.

Pruning Figs

Normally, in all but the most favoured gardens, it is impossible to grow good reliable crops of figs on free-standing trees. They should therefore be grown against a wall or fence.

No pruning can help a Fig to fruit or reduce its rate of growth if it is not planted properly and in conditions that closely mimic the poor soil of its native environment.

A planting pit approximately 3 ft (1 m) square and 30 in (80 cm) deep should be dug and surrounded with a brick or concrete retaining wall.

The bottom is then filled with 9–12 in (23–30 cm) of compacted brick rubble and the remainder of the pit filled with a mixture of 25 per cent coarse sand and 75 per cent good garden soil.

This arrangement prevents the roots reaching the surrounding garden soil and so restricts the take-up of excessive plant foods which would mean the production of shoots and leaves with little or no fruit. In addition the minimum wall or fence area required by a Fig is 12 ft (3.5 m) in height and spread and this must be taken into account.

YEAR ONE

Plant 12–18 in (30–50 cm) away from its support and allow it to grow for a year to establish a good root system. In the following early to mid spring tie one of the strongest shoots to the right and one to the left, cutting out any surplus.

Prune back the ends of the retained shoots to a length of 24–30 in (60–80 cm) from ground level and if these shoots fork, shorten each of the side shoots to the same length.

During early summer to midsummer tie the new growth to bamboo canes which are tied to the support wires as suggested in Chapter 3, in a fan-shaped formation.

Any shoots that are growing back to the support are removed completely, any growing forward are pruned to 2–3 in (5–8 cm) long, cutting to a bud.

YEAR TWO AND FOLLOWING YEARS

By the following early summer the Fig will be covering a large area of the support and the regular pruning that will be carried out every year thereafter can be started. In early summer thin out about 50 per cent of the side shoots growing from the main framework shoots and tie all remaining shoots to the framework as they grow, attempting to provide a shoot every 8–10 in (20–25 cm) over the area to be covered.

In early winter prune back all shoots that have fruited to within 1–2 in (3–5 cm) of the main framework. From these cut-back shoots new replacement shoots will form; this prevents the Fig from becoming leggy. All remaining side shoots should be thinned to allow for one every 8–10 in (20–25 cm) along the framework branches. Select first those shoots that are growing in line with the support and tie in all shoots that are retained.

Neglected and unpruned Figs are difficult to rejuvenate, particularly if the roots are not contained, but it may be worth cutting all the shoots close to ground level and when the new shoots grow, pruning them as recommended for newly planted Figs. Also contructing a pit around the roots, even if this involves cutting roots, may be of advantage.

PRUNING TREES

Even I would not attempt tree surgery, as of all the garden tasks this is one of the most dangerous and requires particular skill, not only for safety but also in the actual work being done. I always make sure that anyone carrying out this work for me is qualified and also has public-liability insurance.

However, there are a number of pruning methods that can improve the performance of certain trees for specific purposes and that we gardeners can carry out.

Pruning young trees

Sadly today young trees are offered for sale up to two years younger than they would have been in the past, due in the main to pressure by garden centres for a product that can be transported home at any time of the year in the family car.

The traditional role of the nurseryman was to train the tree from the feathered maiden stage to bush, half standard or full standard format, training that is very important to the future development of the overall shape, flower and fruit production, lifespan, damage limitation in severe weather conditions and garden interest.

In this section I will explain how to train a feathered maiden as offered today into a bush or standard format as the nurseryman would have traditionally done.

The feathered maiden will have a central shoot (stem) up to $5\frac{1}{2}$ ft (1.8–2 m) high; growing from this will be from three to ten or more side shoots.

The ideal time to plant a young tree is from late autumn to mid spring, whether dug from the nursery with no soil around its roots (bare-rooted), or containerized or container-grown. If either of the latter, the planting time can be extended into spring and summer, but the following suggested pruning should then be held over to the early spring following planting.

Top-grafted and weeping trees

Top-worked (top-grafted) and weeping trees have the required variety grafted on to a parent stem at some height above the ground. The graft union is usually clearly visible. With these the only 'pruning' consists of removing any suckers that are found growing below the graft.

Trees which may be top-grafted

The following trees may be grown by the top-worked method. Those marked * are almost always grown by this method.

Acer negundo 'Elegans' (Golden-variegated Box Maple)

A. n. 'Flamingo' (Flamingo Box Maple)

A. n. 'Variegatum' (Silver-variegated Box Maple)

A. platanoides 'Drummondii' (White-variegated Norway Maple)

A. p. 'Goldsworth Purple' (Purple-leaved Norway Maple)

A. pseudoplatanus 'Brilliantissimum'* (Shrimp-leaved Sycamore)

A. p. 'Leopoldii' (Leopold's Variegated Sycamore)

A. p. 'Prinz Handjery'* (Prince

Handjery's Shrimp-leaved
Sycamore)
A. p. 'Simon-Louis Frères'
(Variegated Sycamore)
Aesculus × carnea 'Briotii'*
(Scarlet Horse Chestnut)
Amelanchier lamarckii (Snowy
Mespilus)
Caragana arborescens
'Lorbergii'* (Siberian Pea
Tree)
C. a. 'Pendula'* (Weeping
Siberian Pea Tree)
C. a. 'Walker'* (Walker's
Weeping Siberian Pea
Tree)
Catalpa bignonioides 'Aurea'*
(Golden Indian Bean
Tree)
Cytisus, when grown as
standard* (Broom)
Fagus sylvatica 'Purpurea
Pendula' (Weeping Purple
Beech)
Fraxinus excelsior 'Jaspidea'
(Golden-stemmed Ash)
Gleditsia triacanthos 'Sunburst'
(Golden Honey Locust)

*Laburnocytisus adamii** (Pink
Laburnum)
Laburnum × watereri 'Vossii'
(Golden Chain Tree)
Malus 'Echtermeyer' (Weeping
Purple Crab Apple)
*Populus lasiocarpa**
Prunus, many flowering varieties
of all groups (Flowering
Almond, Cherry, Peach or
Plum)
Pyrus calleryana 'Chanticleer'
(Chanticleer Pear)
P. salicifolia (Willow-leaved
Pear)
Robinia pseudoacacia, all pink-
flowering varieties (False
Acacia)
R. pseudoacacia 'Frisia' (Golden
Acacia)
Sorbus sargentiana
Syringa 'Monique Lemoine'*
(Double White Lilac)
Ulmus wheatleyi (Golden-leaved
Elm)
Wisteria, when grown as a
standard

Top-working of trees is, thankfully, a practice on the decline, with only a very few British and Dutch nurseries using it.

All other young trees
Once it has been established that the young tree is not top-worked, the following pruning is carried out.

From early to late spring, two thirds of the total number of side shoots can be removed as close to the main shoot as possible, starting from ground level and working upwards.

To achieve a bush-trained tree, remove all shoots to a height of 2–3 ft (60 cm–1 m); for a half standard, to a height of approximately 4–6 ft (1.2–2 m); for a full standard, to a height of 4½–6 ft (1.4–2 m).

The central shoot is stopped at approximately 30–36 in (80 cm–1 m) above the first and lowest side shoots. It must be remembered, however, that once it has been removed, the height of the stem will not increase, nor should it need to do so. All retained side shoots are then pruned back to within 15–18 in (40–50 cm) from where they join the central shoot.

In some cases there may not be enough height of central shoot to achieve that required for half standard or full standard specification, for some lower-growing species may not achieve the necessary height in the first two years of growth. In this case, two thirds of the side shoots are removed and the retained side shoots are pruned, but the central shoot is allowed to grow for a further year or until the required height of stem is achieved.

In all cases the tree is staked and tied, and if necessary the support is temporarily used for tying in the new extension growth until it has reached the height required.

Where it has been necessary to grow on the central shoot, the pruning described for the first spring after planting is carried out in the spring of the second year.

This first pruning or training, whether it has taken one or two years, will help produce a tree with a conventional stem height and tree shape. If it is not done, you may end up with a multi-stemmed bushy tree with little or no shape or garden usefulness. A few trees – such as *Acer negundo*, variegated leaf forms (Variegated Box Maple), *Gleditsia triacanthos* 'Sunburst' (Golden-leaf Honey Locust), *Robinia pseudoacacia* 'Frisia' (Golden-leaf Acacia) and *Pyrus salicifolia* 'Pendula' (Willow-leaf Weeping Pear) – benefit from having shoots resulting from the first year's pruning pruned again in the following early to mid spring, with the shoots being reduced by one third to one half to encourage new colourful foliage. It can be repeated annually to good effect and will always increase the colour and size of the leaves. This pruning, although it is similar, is not pollarding; pollarding will be explained later.

If a young tree has been neglected for three or four years after planting, then the pruning described in this section can be brought into action and the overall shape improved.

Training shrubs as mop-headed trees

There are a number of trees that can be grown as mop-headed standards. Some, being grafted, are difficult for the gardener to raise and are better purchased; these are:

Acer japonicum varieties
(Japanese Maple)

A. palmatum varieties (Japanese Maple)

A. p. dissectum varieties (Cut-leaf Japanese maple)

Azalea, see Rhododendron

Cotoneaster horizontalis
(Fishbone Cotoneaster)

C. microphyllus

C. 'Skogholm'

Cytisus battandieri (Moroccan Broom)

C. praecox varieties (Warminster Broom)

C. scoparius varieties (Broom)

Euonymus alatus (Winged Euonymus)

E. fortunei, variegated foliage varieties (Wintercreeper Euonymus)

Hibiscus syriacus varieties (Tree Hollyhock)

Hydrangea paniculata 'Grandiflora' (Pee Gee Hydrangea)

Kalmia latifolia (Calico Bush)

Ligustrum lucidum (Glossy Privet)

Prunus × *cistena* (Purple-leaf Sand Cherry)

P. glandulosa (Chinese Bush Cherry)

P. triloba

Rhododendron, standards (Standard Rhododendrons and Azaleas)

Salix helvetica (Dwarf Silver Willow)

S. integra 'Albomaculata' (syn. S. 'Hakuro-nishiki', S. 'Fuiri-koriyanai') (Variegated Dwarf Willow)

S. lanata (Woolly Willow)

S. lapponum (Lapland Willow)

Syringa microphylla 'Superba' (Daphne Lilac)

S. velutina (Dwarf Lilac)

S. vulgaris varieties (Common Lilac)

Tamarix varieties (Tamarisk)

Viburnum × *carlcephalum*

V. carlesii varieties (Scented Spring-flowering Viburnum)

V. × *juddii* (Judd's Scented Spring-flowering Viburnum)

All of the above can form a woody stem, which, with the help of support in the form of staking and tying, will carry the

271

weight of the 'tree' on a single stem. It will take two to three years to make a useful architectural addition to the garden but is well worth the effort.

A young shrub from the following list, planted from mid autumn to mid spring and left to establish for one year, can be grown and trained as a mop-headed standard.

Buddleja alternifolia (Fountain Buddleja)
B. davidii varieties (Butterfly Bush)
B. fallowiana (*Buddleja fallowiana*)
B. globosa (Chilean Orange Ball Tree)
Buxus sempervirens varieties (Common Box)
Ceanothus, evergreen varieties (California Lilac)
Cornus alternifolia varieties (Pagoda Cornus)
C. controversa varieties (Wedding-cake Tree)
C. kousa varieties (Chinese Dogwood)
C. mas (Cornelian Cherry)
C. m. 'Variegata' (Variegated Cornelian Cherry)
Corynabutilon vitifolium (Flowering Maple)
Cotoneaster, all large-leaved varieties (Large-leaved Cotoneaster)
Elaeagnus, deciduous varieties (Deciduous Elaeagnus)
Elaeagnus × *ebbingei* varieties
E. pungens varieties (Thorny Elaeagnus)
Forsythia varieties (Golden Ball)

Genista aetnensis (Mount Etna Broom)
G. cinerea
Griselinia littoralis, only in very sheltered positions (Broadleaf)
Ilex × *altaclerensis* varieties (Altaclar Holly)
I. aquifolium varieties (Common Holly)
Laurus nobilis varieties (Bay)
Ligustrum ovalifolium 'Aureum' (Oval-leaved Privet)
L. sinense 'Variegatum' (Chinese Privet)
Magnolia varieties (Magnolia)
Osmanthus varieties (Osmanthus)
Phillyrea decora (Jasmine Box)
Photinia × *fraseri* 'Red Robin' (Photinia)
Prunus laurocerasus in variety (Cherry Laurel)
P. lusitanica varieties (Portugal Laurel)
Pyracantha varieties (Firethorn)
Viburnum × *burkwoodii* (Burkwood Viburnum)
V. opulus 'Sterile' (Guelder Rose)
V. plicatum varieties (Double-file Viburnum)
Weigela varieties (Weigela)

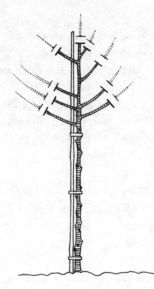

36. Pruning a young standard mop-headed tree

Training mop-headed standards

YEAR ONE

The selected shrub is planted *in situ* in the garden; in the second early to mid spring after planting all shoots are pruned to within 1–2 in (3–5 cm) of ground level. Through the spring and summer a number of very strong shoots will then be produced and the strongest of these, when all are about 18 in (50 cm) tall, is tied to a 5–6 ft (1.5–2 m) strong bamboo cane. All the remaining shoots are then removed.

The selected shoot is encouraged, by tying to the support cane, to continue to make more height until it reaches 24–30 in (60–80 cm) above the final height of the stem required. Any side shoots are removed as they are seen by rubbing off, except those above the intended stem height.

Once it has reached this height the central shoot is stopped by taking out the growing tip. In some species it may take one to two years to reach the height of stem required, and in this case the following pruning is delayed until it has.

YEAR TWO OR THREE

In the spring all the retained side shoots are pruned back by half to encourage more growth. By year three or four and in the following years, the normal recommended pruning for each shrub when grown as a bush should be practised. Normally these standard mop-headed trees need tying to a bamboo cane or stake support for the whole of their lives to prevent wind damage or breakage.

Pleaching

Pleaching is a method of pruning and training that has, to a certain extent, been forgotten, which is sad, because it has a useful role to play in garden design as a screening and dividing planting that establishes height more quickly than any other planting.

It entails growing a tree vertically and horizontally at the same time. Two types of finished effect can be achieved, flat or boxed, and both can be trained on short stems or from ground level.

A number of shaped tops and bottoms can be used if required, such as convex or concave. There is the opportunity to introduce gates, entrance-ways and windows, or plant in avenues and other geometric or serpentine formations and, more importantly, in confined places.

Quercus ilex (Evergreen Oak) is the only evergreen tree that can be used, but it is painfully slow to produce an effect of any size.

Pleached deciduous trees can very quickly form a visual barrier with their foliage, effective in late spring and summer and most of the autumn. After maybe five years, the pleached branches make a screen which lasts through the winter as well.

Winter interest can also be provided by the new red shoots of *Tilia platyphyllos* 'Rubra' (Red-stemmed Lime) and *Salix alba* 'Chermisina' (Red-stemmed Willow), or the yellow of *Tilia* × *euchlora* (Yellow-twigged Lime) and *Salix alba* 'Vitellina' (Golden-stemmed Willow), and these in the dead of winter can be a very useful garden bonus.

At first sight the following method may seem laborious and

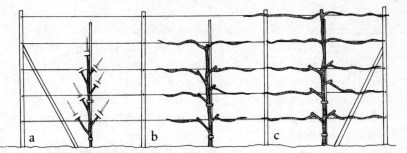

37. *Training pleached trees* (a) *Year-one pruning* (b) *Year two*
(c) *Results of year-two pruning in year three*

costly but when compared with a hedge or wall it works out
favourably on both counts.

Once the line of the pleached trees is decided, tennis-court
fencing angle-irons are erected; these are obtainable from most
agricultural and sports-ground suppliers. They have the advantage of being pre-drilled with holes for the training wires,
normally 18 in (50 cm) apart. They are relatively narrow and if
painted matt olive green can be difficult to see. Experience also
shows that they stay serviceable for the life of the pleached
trees.

One angle-iron is used at each end, some 4–5 ft (1.2–1.5 m)
from the last planted tree. The height will depend on the
desired height of the pleaching. Depending on the length of
the planting line, there will be a need for intermediate bracing supports after every third tree as well as at the ends; all
of these should be concreted into the ground for stability.

The trees will be planted with the normal planting care as
suggested in Chapter 2, 7–10 ft (2.2–3 m) apart along the
chosen line.

Choosing the right-sized trees is important. If you are purchasing from a nursery, letting them know the purpose the
trees will be put to should help you obtain, for preference, the
flat-sided trees that will work best for pleaching. They will be
feathered maidens with from five to ten side shoots, and if the
pleaching is to extend to the ground they should be clothed
with side shoots to as near to the ground as possible. They will

be 5–6 ft (1.5–2 m) tall and their stems $1\frac{1}{2}$–$2\frac{1}{2}$ in (4–6 cm) in diameter at 3 ft (1 m) from ground level.

Not all tree species and varieties are suitable for pleaching and those that have been traditionally used over the years are still the most reliable. These are listed below.

The numbers indicate the speed of growing and density of the various species, with the lowest number indicating the fastest and thickest.

Carpinus betulus (Hornbeam) – 3
Quercus ilex (Evergreen Oak) – 4
Salix alba 'Chermesina' (Red-stemmed Willow) – 2
S. a. vitellina (Golden-stemmed Willow) – 2
S. daphnoides (Purple-stemmed Willow) – 2
Tilia cordata (Small-leaved Lime) – 1
T. × *euchlora* (Yellow-twigged Lime) – 1
T. platyphyllos 'Rubra' (Red-twigged Lime) – 1
All other varieties of Tilia (Lime) could also be considered, except
　T. petiolaris (Weeping Lime).

The following have also been used to good effect:

Acer negundo, variegated-leaf varieties (Variegated Box Maple) – 2
A. platanoides varieties (Norway Maple) – 3
A. pseudoplatanus varieties (Sycamore) –3
Gleditsia triacanthos 'Sunburst' (Honey Locust) – 2
Laburnum × *watereri* 'Vossii' (Waterer Laburnum) – 2
Robinia pseudoacacia 'Frisia' (False Acacia) – 2
Sorbus aria 'Lutescens' (Whitebeam) – 2

Planting is best done between mid autumn and mid spring but can be done at other times if the trees are container-grown or containerized.

The support wire is the same gauge as that used for fencing, galvanized or plastic-coated, and fixed approximately 18 in (50 cm) apart from ground level upwards. If the trees are to be pleached from that level then all lower shoots are left on or, if 4 ft (1.2 m) from ground level, any surplus lower shoots are cut away.

Once planted, 6–8 ft (2–2.5 m) bamboo canes are tied to the support wires and the newly planted trees attached to them.

In the spring after planting all side shoots are pruned to within 3–4 in (8–10 cm) of the central shoot and this shoot is pruned by removing the top few inches. If no main shoot exists, bend the most suitable side shoot upwards. New growths will very quickly form strong side shoots and these are tied, one to the right and one to the left, to each of the training wires.

Occasionally these will be no shoot in the right place and one will have to be bent up or down to fill the gap. Should there not be one close to, this will cause no long-term problem as the species suggested all have the ability to grow additional shoots from the central shoot later in the summer. Tying-in is continued into the summer as the shoots become longer. A suitable shoot at the top is trained vertically and further side shoots will form from it. As the selected side shoots grow, further side shoots will grow from both the central shoot and the trained side shoots; these are pruned out once more when 6–9 in (15–23 cm) long, pruning them back to within 3–4 in (8–10 cm) of their origin and wherever possible to a bud. It is from these pruned-back shoots that more shoots will grow and form the thick screen of growth required.

The process continues through the next three to five years, selecting and tying in until the area intended is full. After this time it becomes a simple matter of pruning the sides and top in spring as if they were a hedge. With the coloured-stem varieties the spring pruning is most important if the full effect of the new shoots is to be seen through the winter.

Any design to top, underside or width is simply a matter of pruning and training where required once the growth is strong enough.

Training for arches and walkways

Interest in planting and training trees to form walkways and tunnels is increasing, and any gardener who has been privileged to see Rosemary Verey's fine Laburnum walkway at Barnsley House, Gloucestershire, whether in flower or not, has had a treat indeed.

Planting of the feathered maiden trees starts in the autumn, through winter and into early spring, and thought must be

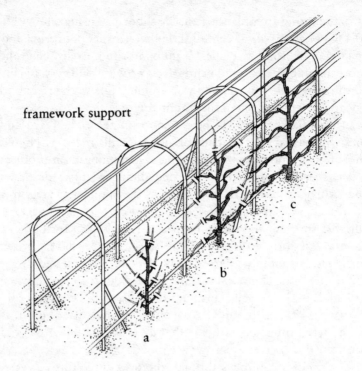

framework support

38. Arches and walkways   (a) First year's pruning
(b) Year two   (c) Results of year-two pruning in year three

given to providing a metal support on to which the trees will
be trained.

A number of proprietary frameworks are available but care
must be taken to ensure that the framework is strong enough
to carry the weight. Also, the framework does not have to be
too ornate as it will very quickly be covered by the trained
plants. Distances between the arch supports need not be less
than 6 ft (2 m) and can be as much as 12 ft (3.5 m).

Supports need to be held apart at the top and bottom with
metal bracing poles and in between these fencing-gauge,
plastic-coated or galvanized wires are stretched and secured,
approximately 18 in (50 cm) apart.

The chosen species of trees are then planted one to each
upright support.

In mid to late spring all side shoots are pruned, cutting to a bud to within 2–4 in (5–10 cm) of the central shoot. The top 6–8 in (15–20 cm) of the central shoot is removed and from this pruning new side and central shoots will appear; these are tied to the support wires so as to provide one to each wire on left and right, and at the same time increase the upward cover over the frame.

In the second year the tied-in side shoots have 6–8 in (15–20 cm) of their ends pruned back and the central shoot is again pruned, shortening it by 12–18 in (30–50 cm). The resulting new growth is tied in to the wires sideways, and upwards and over the top of the frame.

Each year any surplus side shoots, once they reach more than 18 in (50 cm), are pruned back to 4–6 in (10–15 cm) on a routine 'as required' basis.

By year three most of the framework will be covered; if not the process is continued until it is. From then on, all excess shoots are shortened when seen, or in one pruning session in mid to late spring.

The trees most suitable for arches and walkways are listed below. The numbers indicate the speed and density of the various species that might be used, with the lowest number indicating the fastest and thickest.

Carpinus betulus (Hornbeam) – 3
Laburnum × *watereri* 'Vossii' (Waterer Laburnum) – 2
Tilia cordata (Small-leaved Lime) – 1
T. × *euchlora* (Yellow-twigged Lime) – 1
T. platyphyllos 'Rubra' (Red-twigged Lime) – 1
   All other varieties of Tilia (Lime) could be considered, except *T. petiolaris* (Weeping Lime).

On occasions the following have also been used to good effect:

Acer negundo, variegated-leaf varieties (Variegated Box Maple) – 2
A. platanoides varieties (Norway Maple) – 3
A. pseudoplatanus varieties (Sycamore) – 3
Gleditsia triacanthos 'Sunburst' (Golden Honey Locust) – 2

Robinia pseudoacacia 'Frisia' (Golden False Acacia) – 2
Sorbus aria 'Lutescens' (Whitebeam) – 2

Apples, dessert and culinary varieties – 2
Pears, dessert and culinary varieties – 3

Pollarding

Pollarding is the art of pruning to encourage new lush production of shoots and foliage over a period of years or on a regular annual basis. In most cases this is a job for a professional tree surgeon, as more often than not it means working at heights and this can be dangerous for the untrained.

Pollarded trees are used as avenues, screens or individual or paired garden features. In the French colonnade system a number of trees are planted in closely ranked rows, often with the height of the trees uniformly varied to give geometric formations.

The trees are normally planted as half or full standards, although feathered maidens can be used and trained into the standard format. Planting distances will depend on the final use of the trees so no hard and fast rules can be given, other than to say that it must be remembered that they will require space, even under the pollarding routine.

The periods between carrying out the work will vary, but I like to do it when the shoots to be pruned are no more than 3 in (7 cm) in diameter as at this size the professional will find them manageable and this keeps the cost of the work down.

The range of trees that are conventionally used for this work includes the following:

Acer platanoides varieties (Norway Maple)
A. pseudoplatanus varieties, except slow-growing ones (Sycamore)
Aesculus hippocastanum varieties (Horse Chestnut)

Ailanthus altissima (Tree of Heaven)
Platanus × *hispanica* (London Plane)
Populus alba (White Poplar)
P. × *robusta* (False Lombardy Poplar)

P. × *serotina* 'Aurea' (Golden
  Poplar)

Tilia (Lime) – all varieties except
  T. petiolaris (Weeping Lime)

Pollarding trees for annual growth increase

Some trees respond to an annual pollarding. With these, the
term pollarding simply means the hard pruning back of all last
year's shoots either to or near ground level; this practice is also
sometimes called stooling.

The act of pruning hard all the previous year's growth
means that all new shoots carry foliage three to four times the
normal size, but as the shoots produced are young they
normally do not flower.

The method can be used to rejuvenate neglected shrubs and
trees as long as they are included in one of the lists of species
recommended for pollarding.

Pollarding pruning is normally done in early to mid spring
to ensure that decorative winter shoots can be enjoyed for as
long as possible.

The following trees can be treated in this way:

Acer negundo (Box Maple)
A. n. 'Elegantissimum' (Golden-
  leaved Box Maple)
A. n. 'Flamingo' (Pink-leaved Box
  Maple)
A. n. 'Variegatum' (Silver-leaved
  Box Maple)
A. platanoides 'Crimson King'
  (Purple-leaved Norway
  Maple)
A. p. 'Drummondii' (White
  Variegated Norway Maple)
A. pseudoplatanus 'Leopoldii'
  (Leopold's Variegated
  Sycamore)
A. p. 'Simon-Louis Frères'
  (Variegated Sycamore)
Catalpa bignonioides (Indian
  Bean Tree)

C. b. 'Aurea' (Golden Indian
  Bean Tree)
Eucalyptus, assuming they have
  adequate winter hardiness
  (Gum Tree)
Eucalyptus gunnii (Cider Gum)
Kalopanax pictus (Prickly
  Castor-oil Tree)
Liriodendron tulipifera (Tulip
  Tree)
Paulownia tomentosa (Foxglove
  Tree)
Populus candicans 'Aurora'
  (Variegated Balsam-scented
  Poplar)
Rhus typhina varieties
  (Sumach)
Robinia pseudoacacia 'Frisia'
  (False Acacia)

Salix alba (White Willow)   S. a. vitellina (Golden Willow)
S. a. argentea (Silver Willow)   S. daphnoides (Violet Willow)
S. a. 'Chermesina' (Scarlet   S. matsudana 'Tortuosa'
    Willow)   (Contorted Willow)

Pruning conifers

Of all the plants we grow in our gardens, conifers are the most overlooked as regards pruning, yet they can benefit greatly from it. Although pruning cannot in the long term contain the ultimate size of a specific variety or reduce an over-sized specimen growing in too small a space, it can improve the early shape and promote the annual production of a halo of colourful spring growth.

One word of warning: only Taxus (Yew) has the ability to make new growth from the main shoots; with any of the others, if the shoots (fronds) are pruned back beyond the green point, there is no chance of new growth.

Feeding all conifers with dried blood at the rate of 4 oz (100 g) per square yard in late spring will also improve the overall foliage colour.

One point that often causes concern is the tendency for the inside growth of many conifers to die out. This is their natural growth pattern and is caused by the annual new growth being produced at the outer ends of the shoots; after a year or two, the centre will become defoliated due to the lack of light. It is this natural action that pruning uses to improve the conifer, encouraging the new shoots to be more branching.

All conifers, but particularly Chamaecyparis leylandii varieties, can cause dermatitis – if you have a sensitive skin it would be wise to wear gloves when pruning them.

Upright-growing conifers
The main aim is to encourage the production of new growth and improve the shape of most young conifers.

To achieve this the outer foliage is lightly shaved in mid to late spring with a very sharp knife – great care is required to avoid accidents – using a stroking action and working up from the bottom towards the top and around the whole circumference of the conifer.

Often conifers produce more than one leading shoot and it is good practice to remove the weakest and retain just one to avoid the later spreading of more than one upright central shoot.

The main species that respond to this type of pruning, both in their slow-growing and larger-growing varieties, are:

Chamaecyparis (False Cypress), Cupressus (Cypress), Juniperus (Juniper), Libocedrus (False Cedar), Taxus (Yew), Thuja (Western Red Cedars).

Spreading types

Here a real improvement can be achieved to the shape, density, colour and longevity of the spreading conifer. Also, although only a slowing effect, the overall size can be contained for a few years.

From the mid to late spring following planting all shoots produced the previous season should be reduced in length by 50 per cent, using secateurs to make the cuts.

This pruning will induce new shoots to form behind the cut, so increasing the number of shoots, and as these new growths are the most colourful, the overall appearance is improved. Any upward-growing shoots can be pruned harder, even as much as 75 per cent, but never, in any case, cut back beyond the green leaves (fronds).

The following conifers can be treated in this way:

Chamaecyparis (False Cypress), spreading varieties
Cedrus (Cedar), spreading varieties
Juniperus (Juniper), spreading varieties, including *J. squamata* and
   J. × *media* 'Pfitzeriana', which respond extremely well.

Renovating neglected and overgrown conifers

One frequent problem is that a conifer has grown too large for the area it is growing in and therefore is causing an obstruction. This is difficult to deal with, but there are one or two pruning techniques that might be considered.

As already stated, apart from Taxus (Yew), no conifer can make new leaves (fronds) from the areas of shoots where they no longer exist; Taxus can be cut very hard back in the early to mid spring and will quickly start to grow attractive new branch and foliage cover.

UPRIGHT-GROWING CONIFERS

Here there are two possible courses of action. The simplest is to remove all the lower shoots from the central shoot (stem), working up from ground level to a height of 10–12 ft (3–3.5 m) if necessary, so giving the conifer the appearance of a tree. This practice works well where space is restricted near ground level, such as alongside a drive or path.

With soil improvement around the base, as described in Chapter 1, an underplanting of suitable plants for such conditions can then be established.

With many species of conifers, in particular Chamaecyparis, Juniperus and Taxus when they are more than ten years old, their central upright shoots, if more than one, may start to separate and spread, particularly if they have not been pruned from an early age or have been subjected to heavy snowfalls which have not been removed as soon as possible after settling. Here pruning is not the answer and we need to resort to wiring in (see p. 68).

REDUCING THE SPREAD OF SPREADING CONIFERS

In particular *Juniperus* × *media* and *J.* × *m.* 'Pfitzeriana', when they become exceptionally large, can be reduced.

The tendency is often just to prune the outer branches back and this does no good at all because it is from these branches that further growth is quickly produced, often stimulated by the pruning. Much better to remove a complete layer of growth – it is surprising how quickly the conifer can be reduced in spread and sometimes height by doing this.

Careful observation in spring will show that the lower branches are the most spreading, so if the lowest one or two layers are removed as close to the central short shoot as possible, the conifer will be reduced greatly in its spread without raising the underside enough to cause it to look out of place or giving it a cut-back appearance.

To a certain extent this practice can also be used to reduce the height, by careful selection of the tallest principal shoots. Using the technique described above for shortening back the leading shoots in the spring on an annual basis will also help to thicken up and contain the growth to a certain extent, although in the long-term the conifer will grow again to its original or ultimate size.

CHAPTER NINE

Winter Hardiness and Protection

The range of plants now available to us is ever-widening, as is the movement of plants between nurseries and garden centres within Great Britain and abroad. Plants from farther afield, however, may not be fully hardy in the conditions we can provide, and so may be susceptible to winter damage.

Every plant has its own geographical region where it grows naturally and can cope with the weather it experiences. We attempt to expand these regions to include our own gardens and by so doing expose the plants to a whole range of different growing conditions. The aim of this chapter is to look at hardiness and attempt to understand the changes, and then relate this knowledge to protecting our plants over winter.

It is wrong to consider only the effects of winter damage, as hard frosts in the autumn and spring can also cause severe damage to the foliage, stems and flower buds of garden plants.

A wet autumn following a hot summer can encourage plants to produce new growth which does not have time to ripen and will not have formed a protective bark or skin to shoots or evergreen foliage.

We talk of 'die-back' as if it were a disease, but in most cases it is not a disease at all but the effects of winter cold on unripened shoots.

Some plants that are considered slightly tender and 'difficult' in Britain may in their native conditions experience temperatures as low as our own, if not lower. The reason that they may be damaged here is that our summers and autumns are wetter and there is no time for their growth to ripen.

Wind plays a role in the amount of damage caused by frost and cold, by accelerating the fall of temperature and the rate at which it collides with the plant. A moderate frost can quickly become severe and so cause great damage to plant growth. We call this the 'wind chill' factor and it is one of the worst winter weather elements that British gardeners must combat; later we will discuss ways in which the wind can be reduced, thereby protecting our plants.

It is not possible to be dogmatic regarding climate, as in many situations there is a microclimate that maintains year round a mean temperature higher than the surrounding areas.

Cities are an example of this. Take London for instance: inside the M25 orbital motorway the temperature can be 3–4 Celsius degrees higher than outside it, and therefore a wider range of plants can be grown.

The sea also has great influence on hardiness and its beneficial influence can be seen twenty-five miles inland in the south. In the west this could increase to as much as thirty-five miles, and even in the east and north, the ten or fifteen mile strip by the coast might be more hospitable to a wide range of plants.

In the garden, the slope of the land and its closeness to water can present the possibility of frost pockets. These are areas in the garden where the cold air, unless interrupted, rolls downhill and builds up at the bottom of slopes or is generated by the effect of heat being lost from water cooling rapidly at night, causing areas of sustained frost. Without the slope of the land or the presence of a water feature the same garden might have been almost free of frost.

Winter cold and the geographical planting location can have a measurable effect on the plant's ultimate size and flowering time. Take a Lupin planted in Cornwall for instance: it could reach a height of 4 ft (1.2 m) and flower in mid June. The same plant in Scotland may only grow to 2 ft (60 cm) and flower three or more weeks later.

In many gardens there are areas that are naturally protected or face south or west, and using these areas for suspected tender plants can widen the range of plants we grow.

Frost

Correctly we should say frost and cold, as the two combined, often aided by the wind, cause the most damage, due to the severe cold freezing the moisture in the cells of branches, stems and shoots, and, if evergreen, the foliage.

Starting normally in a single plant cell close to the surface of the plant tissue, the moisture crystallizes and the cell's sharp-pointed ends puncture the adjoining cells, freezing their contents and setting up a very rapid chain reaction that moves through larger areas of plant tissue.

The degree of damage depends on the age and height reached by the plant and, in the case of the stems, on the thickness of the skin or bark. With leaves, either evergreen or new spring-produced foliage, the thickness of the leaf skin or cuticle is also a controlling factor.

When a plant we normally consider hardy is protected in winter in a greenhouse or plastic tunnel and then purchased and planted in the garden before the tissue of the stem or leaves is thick enough, then it takes only a frost of 1–2°C to cause damage and possibly kill the new plant.

Damage to new spring-produced stems, leaves and flowers, even with minor falls in temperature, can be devastating if the conditions are right, and many plants such as Hydrangeas and Pieris are damaged in this way.

In autumn and spring it is air frosts that cause most damage to stems, leaves, flower buds and flowers. Container-grown plants in late winter are also at risk for these air frosts may penetrate the sides of the container, causing root damage and ultimately death; container-grown Camellias and bulbs often succumb in this way.

Ground frost can have the same effect close to soil level and is often more devastating in the extent of the damage caused to stems. Ground frost damages not only by killing tissue but by dehydrating the plant. Underground buds and roots as well as evergreen foliage are damaged. In the south the worst months are January and February and in the north, December and March can also be times of risk.

But real problems start when the soil reaches a temperature of minus 8–10° Celsius for more than fifty to sixty hours non-stop. Moisture in the soil becomes solid and is denied to evergreen plants, which, even though it is winter, are still losing small amounts of water from the leaves. In some cases even deciduous plants lose small amounts of moisture through their stems and this must be replaced.

Once this intake of moisture is interrupted by the moisture in the soil becoming solid, the plant begins to dehydrate and as it does the tissue collapses, causing stem, leaf and flower damage which can lead to plant death.

Thankfully these conditions are only experienced in the south once every five to ten years and in the north plants should be chosen for their greater hardiness. Damage is still possible, however, and even the hardiest of plants, if the conditions are severe enough, will be affected.

Wind and frost protection will help and we will look more closely at this in a moment, but the most important thing to do in these cases is to release the frozen moisture trapped in the soil. Once the conditions have been in force more than sixty hours, carefully pour very hot water on to the soil surface in close proximity to the base of the plant over an area 3 ft (1 m) in diameter, but avoid pouring the hot water on to the plant's stems. This releases the moisture in the soil by creating a localized thaw and the roots can again take in the moisture and stop the process of dehydration.

However, the operation must be repeated each day until a natural thaw arrives. Covering the soil with an old carpet or some other material such as straw will also help keep the frost from locking up the moisture again.

Mulching with organic material around the base of plants in autumn before the bad weather comes will to some degree prevent frost penetration in the first place and is useful in protecting roots from frost damage, but in very severe cold even this may not be enough.

Although these conditions are infrequent, they can cause severe damage, not least the opening up of small lesions in the stems of a number of trees and shrubs; in the case of Prunus (Cherry), these can allow the spores of the winter-active silver leaf fungus to enter the stems and infect the tree. Laburnum, Oak (Quercus), Rhododendrons and many other woody plants can all have their stems split by very cold weather, which could lead to their ultimate death. The root systems of ericaceous shrubs and other plants can be damaged or destroyed under such weather conditions.

General winter protection

Severe winter conditions and damage is exceptional, but there is a need to consider providing more general winter protection to those shrubs and climbers that are less hardy and may be damaged by cold even in an average winter.

The temptation is to treat the shrub with tender loving care and wrap it up tightly at the first sign of cold, say in early autumn; straw, blankets and polythene sheeting are often seen wrapped around plants.

This, at first sight, might seem sensible, but the danger is that the plant's buds will start to develop prematurely from late winter onwards, and when, in the warmer days of early spring, the protection is removed, the shrub is left open to damage by spring air frosts, even as late as early summer.

Protection is best when it is set up to form a microclimate around the plant and usually prevents the temperature within the protected area from falling below 3–4°C.

To achieve this, plastic netting 4–4½ ft (1.2–1.4 m) high of small gauge – ⅛ in (2.5 mm) or less – is ideal. It can be purchased from most garden retailers for wind- or frost-break use; alternatively hessian sacking can be used to good effect. Both are supported by strong 5–5½ ft (1.5–1.8 m) high stakes or poles driven into the ground.

The netting can be used to surround an individual shrub or young tree completely but it should be no closer than 2½ ft (80 cm). Larger areas need protection only along the cold-weather sides, i.e. the north and east.

In the south the protection does not need to be in place until Christmas – a month sooner in the north – and in both cases can be removed once the worst of the winter weather is over in mid spring. It can then be rolled up and stored until required for the next winter.

The screening is just enough to protect the plants by breaking the frost-laden wind but without producing growth and will protect the plant under most average winter conditions. If the winter is exceptionally severe the plant will be damaged anyway, even if it is wrapped up like a Christmas turkey.

We may be able to provide permanent protection by planting wind-breaks or internal hedges that filter the wind year round and reduce its speed and force, or prevent the rolling downhill of cold air, so eliminating potential damage in frost pockets.

We can also, with plants that are not normally hardy, propagate each year by taking cuttings in the previous summer and growing them under protection over winter to replace any losses.

Plants that should be considered tender

The plants in the following lists are those that might be considered to be at risk in winter conditions in Britain, in all but the most southerly or sheltered gardens.

TREES
Acacia varieties (Wattle)
Albizia (Silk Tree)
Arbutus varieties (Strawberry Tree)
Catalpa bignonioides 'Aurea' (Golden Indian Bean Tree)
Eucalyptus, all varieties except *E. gunnii* (Gum Tree, Sweet Gum)
Kalopanax
Laurus nobilis varieties (Bay Tree)
Paulownia tomentosa (Foxglove Tree)
Prunus persica (Peach)
Sophora japonica (Japanese Pagoda Tree)
Styrax japonica (Japanese Snowbell)

SHRUBS
Abelia, most varieties (Abelia)
Abutilon megapotamicum varieties (Trailing Abutilon)
Acanthopanax sieboldianus varieties (Five-leaf Aralia)
Andromeda polifolia (Bog Rosemary)
Aralia elata varieties (Japanese Angelica Tree)
Azara varieties (Azara)
Ballota pseudodictamnus (Ballota)
Buddleja crispa (Butterfly Bush)
B. fallowiana alba (Butterfly Bush)
Callistemon (Australian Bottle Brush)
Camellia
Carpenteria californica varieties (Carpenteria)

Caryopteris varieties (Blue Spiraea, Bluebeard)

Cassinia leptophylla fulvida (Golden Heather)

Ceanothus, deciduous evergreen varieties (California Lilac)

Ceratostigma varieties (Shrubby Plumbago)

Cestrum varieties (Bastard Jasmine)

Cistus – small-leaved varieties are more hardy than large (Rock Rose)

Cleyera (Cleyera)

Clianthus puniceus varieties (Lobster's Claw)

Convolvulus cneorum (Silver-leaved Convolvulus)

Cordyline australis varieties (Cabbage Tree of New Zealand)

Coronilla varieties (Coronilla)

Corynabutilon vitifolium varieties (Flowering Maple Abutilon)

Crinodendron hookerianum (Lantern Tree)

Cytisus battandieri (Moroccan Broom)

Daphne varieties (Daphne)

Desfontainia spinosa (Desfontania)

Dorycnium hirsutum (Dorycnium)

Elsholtzia stauntonii (Elsholtzia)

Embothrium varieties (Chilean Fire Bush)

Eriobotrya japonica (Japanese Loquat)

Erythrina crista-galli (Coral Tree, Coxcomb)

Eucryphia varieties (Brush Bush)

Euonymus japonicus varieties (Variegated Japanese Euonymus)

Fabiana varieties (Fabiana)

× Fatshedera varieties (Aralia Ivy)

Fatsia japonica varieties (Castor Oil Plant)

Feijoa sellowiana varieties (Guava)

Fremontodendron californicum, until over 4 ft (1.2 m) high (Fremontia)

Fuchsia, hardy varieties (Hardy Fuchsia)

Griselinia littoralis varieties (Griselinia)

× Halimiocistus varieties (Halimiocistus)

Halimium varieties (Halimium)

Hebe, in particular large-leaved varieties (Veronica)

Hebe cupressoides and similar types

Hedysarum multijugum

Helichrysum varieties (Helichrysum)

Hoheria varieties (Hoheria)

Hydrangea aspera (Rough-leaved Hydrangea)

H. quercifolia varieties (Oak-leaf Hydrangea)

H. sargentiana (Sargent's Hydrangea)

H. serrata varieties

H. villosa

Indigofera varieties (Indigo Bush)

Itea ilicifolia (Holly-leaf Sweet-spire)

Lavandula stoechas (French Lavender)

Lavatera varieties (Mallow)

Leptospermum varieties (Tea Tree)

Leucothoë varieties (Drooping Leucothoë)

Ligustrum lucidum, variegated varieties (Glossy Privet)

Lippia citriodora (Lemon Verbena)

Lomatia varieties (Lomatia)

Microglossa albesceus (Shrubby Aster)

Myrtus varieties (Myrtle)

Nandina domestica varieties (Sacred Bamboo)

Olearia varieties (Daisy Bush)

Osmanthus delavayi, under extreme conditions (Osmanthus)

Parahebe varieties (Parahebe)

Perovskia varieties (Russian Sage)

Phlomis varieties (Phlomis)

Phormium varieties (New Zealand Flax)

Pittosporum varieties (Kohuha)

Phaphiolepis umbellata (Indian Hawthorn)

Plumbago capensis varieties (Leadwort)

Rhamnus alaternus 'Argenteovariegata' (Buckthorn)

Ribes laurifolium (Flowering Currant)

Rosmarinus varieties (Rosemary)

Ruta varieties (Rue)

Salvia, shrubby forms (Common Sage)

Santolina varieties (Cotton Lavender)

Solanum varieties (Solanum)

Sophora tetraptera varieties (New Zealand Laburnum)

Teucrium varieties (Shrubby Germander)

Trachycarpus fortunei varieties (Chusan Palm)

Viburnum tinus 'Variegatum' (Laurustinus)

Vitex agnus-castus (Chaste Tree)

Yucca varieties (Yucca)

Zenobia pulverulenta (Dusty Zenobia)

CLIMBERS

Billardiera longiflora (Billardiera)

Clematis florida 'Sieboldii' (Apple Berry)

Decumaria barbara (Decumaria)

Eccremocarpus scaber varieties (Chilean Glory Flower)

Lapageria varieties (Lapageria)

Lonicera splendida (Spanish Honeysuckle)

Mandevilla varieties (Achillean Jasmine)

Passiflora caerulea varieties (Passion Flower)

Rhodochiton atrosanguineus (Purple Bells)

Rubus henryi bambusarum (Rubus)

Schisandra varieties (Schisandra)

Schizophragma hydrangeoides (Japanese Hydrangea Vine)

Solanum varieties (Potato Vine)

Sollya fusiformis (Australian
Bluebell Creeper)
Stauntonia hexaphylla
(Stauntonia)
Trachelospermum varieties
(Trachelospermum)
Tropaeolum speciosum
(Flame Vine)

Wattakaka sinensis
(Wattakaka)

ROSES

Rosa banksiae 'Lutea' (Banksian
Rose)

Plants that use winter cold to help them branch

Plants that have been damaged by winter cold will show signs
of stem die-back. In a few instances this will be a form of
natural pruning, encouraging the plant to branch, and there is
no need to do anything about frost-damaged shoots in these
cases, though they can be removed if they are unsightly. The
following is a selection of plants in this group.

TREES
Ailanthus altissima (Tree of
Heaven)
Catalpa bignonioides varieties
(Indian Bean Tree)
Cercis siliquastrum (Judas Tree)
Hydrangea paniculata (Panick
Hydrangea)
Koelreuteria paniculata (Golden
Rain Tree)
Rhus typhinus varieties
(Sumach)
Robinia pseudoacacia varieties
(False Acacia)

Tetradium varieties

SHRUBS
Amorpha varieties (False Indigo)
Cotinus varieties (Smoke Tree,
Burning Bush)
Hydrangea arborescens varieties
(Tree Hydrangea)
H. paniculata varieties (Panick
Hydrangea)
Indigofera heterantha varieties
(Indigo Bush)
Perovskia atriplicifolia varieties
(Russian Sage)

Removing frost-damaged shoots

When die-back is identified on frost-damaged plants (not those
that use it naturally – see previous section) all damaged shoots
should be removed to at least 6–12 in (15–30 cm) beyond the
first signs of visual damage, even if this entails spoiling the
overall shape of the plant for a short period in the spring.

The reason for this is that if there are visual signs of frost damage to stems or foliage, it can be assumed that there will be secondary damage further down the stems, which, if not removed, will lead to poor growth and even more die-back once it starts to grow, since the shoots and buds are partially damaged and cannot perform their role fully. Valuable energy is being used by these unproductive shoots which would be better directed into new growth.

Even with this drastic pruning, the plant, once growth starts in spring and early summer, will quickly regain its former size, since its root system is geared to supporting the plant as it was before the damage was caused.

Spring frost damage

Plants will frequently be damaged as they start to grow in the spring, and not only the leaves but the flowers can suffer. Today, with our reliable tea-time and evening weather forecasts, even if we are unable to sense a frost by watching the weather, they are normally predicted for us.

Until recently it was difficult to find a material which we could use to protect our plants under these conditions and which was strong, yet light enough not to damage the plant's new young growth while protecting it from spring frosts. Many of us may have built plastic covers or draped the plant with net curtains, which helped to some degree, but we now have the non-woven, chemical-free, polypropylene-fibre frost protection sheets that are sold through nurseries and garden centres under a number of brand names. Some are more expensive than others so shop around for the best price. These have all the protection properties we need, as well as the advantage of letting rain through, while not becoming heavy and physically damaging the plants, should the forecast be wrong or the weather change. But if snow falls the sheets must be removed as soon as possible or the collected weight of the snow can cause breakage.

Trees can be protected while young, but after a time it obviously becomes impossible, due to their size. However, although cosmetic damage may be caused when the plants are larger, it is not normally terminal.

The following are examples of plants often damaged by spring frosts.

TREES

Acer pseudoplatanus 'Brilliantissimum' (Shrimp-leaved Sycamore)

Arbutus unedo varieties (Strawberry Tree)

Catalpa bignonioides varieties (Indian Bean Tree)

Cercidiphyllum varieties (Cercidiphyllum)

Davidia involucrata (Handkerchief Tree, Dove Tree)

Liriodendron tulipifera, in particular *L. t.* 'Aureo-marginatum' (Tulip Tree)

Paulownia tomentosa (Foxglove Tree)

SHRUBS

Abelia chinensis

Acanthopanax sieboldianus varieties (Five-leaf Aralia)

Acer japonicum varieties (Japanese Maple)

A. palmatum varieties (Japanese Maple)

Buddleja varieties (Butterfly Bush)

Cornus alternifolia 'Argentea' (Pagoda Dogwood)

C. controversa 'Variegata' (Wedding-cake Tree)

Crinodendron hookerinum (Lantern Tree)

Drimys varieties (Winter's Bark)

Fatsia japonica varieties (Castor Oil Plant)

Fuchsias, hardy varieties (Hardy Fuchsia)

Griselinia varieties (Broadleaf)

Hibiscus varieties (Tree Hollyhock) – particularly the flower buds

Hydrangea varieties (Hydrangea)

Laurus nobilis (Bay)

Magnolia varieties, specifically when young or in flower (Magnolia)

Philadelphus coronarius 'Aureus' (Golden Mock Orange)

P. c. 'Variegatus' (Variegated Mock Orange)

Pieris varieties (Lily of the Valley Shrub)

Piptanthus laburnifolius (Evergreen Laburnum)

Pittosporum varieties (Parchment Branch)

Stachyurus varieties (Stachyurus)

Syringa persica varieties, particularly the flowers (Persian Lilac)

Viburnum tinus 'Variegatum', particularly the new growth (Laurustinus)

CLIMBERS

Abutilon megapotamicum varieties (Trailing Abutilon)

Actinidia chinensis varieties (Chinese Gooseberry, Kiwi Fruit)

Ampelopsis glandulosa
  brevipendunculata 'Elegans'
  (Ampelopsis)
Aristolochia macrophylla
  (Dutchman's Pipe)
Berberidopsis corallina
  (Berberidopsis)
Clematis armandii (Evergreen

Clematis)
Wisteria varieties, under extreme
  conditions (Wisteria)

VEGETABLES
Potatoes
French Beans
Runner Beans

BEDDING

Tender perennials, and most other bedding before the end of April.
The month of May can also be difficult, and protection should be
considered for all bedding plants: *Begonia semperflorens* and
Zinnias are particularly susceptible.

Protecting perennial plants over winter

In addition to an autumn mulch, if the previous season's
shoots are cut to within 8–12 in (20–30 cm) from the ground in
autumn they form a localized microclimate at the base of the
plant, which protects the next season's buds just below the
soil.

Once mid spring is reached and before signs of new growth
are seen, the remaining old shoots are finally cut to within 2–3
in (5–8 cm) of ground level.

This is a tried and true method, and damage to many
perennial plants will be avoided if it is practised.

Protecting flowers and flower buds of Magnolias and Camellias

Magnolias and Camellias are best planted where they do not
get the early morning sun; this prevents cells in the flowers,
which may be frozen, from thawing out too rapidly and
therefore being ruptured. The situation chosen should be free
from direct sunlight from dawn until midday.

In extreme frost conditions damage will be caused but in
moderate conditions there is a good chance of avoiding it.

Protecting the root stools of Gunnera and Rheum

Gunnera manicata (Giant Rhubarb). The large leaves are cut down in autumn and a layer of dry straw is placed over the root crown; the leaves are then placed upside down on the straw and left in place to form a 'tent' or roof. This will give protection until mid spring, when the covering can be removed to allow the new shoots to grow away. Other ornamental and fruiting rhubarbs (Rheums) benefit from covering; normally straw is heaped up over the crown.

Hardy Fuchsias

Placing bracken or dry wood ash or, in very cold gardens, dry straw, over and between last year's shoots on hardy Fuchsias will protect the underground buds from frost damage. Remove the protection in mid to late spring and prune the Fuchsia hard as soon as signs of new spring growth at ground level are seen.

Protecting outdoor planted containers

All outside planted containers should be moved together into a sheltered corner of the garden, surrounding the pots with straw or other insulating material and covering the tops with non-woven, chemical-free, polypropylene-fibre frost protection; in this way both the plant roots and the pots themselves are protected. This protection is normally needed from Christmas to early spring. See also Chapter 10.

In more northerly areas protection may be required from early winter until mid spring, but the pots should be inspected from time to time for any signs of growth, particularly with bulbs, and these removed from protection as necessary to show off their display. They will still need temporary protection should the conditions warrant it.

Protecting flower buds of Peaches and wall-grown Nectarines

Historically this has been done using bracken or conifer-fronds but it is an art and there is the risk of encouraging premature growth.

A clear polythene sheet or non-woven, chemical-free, polypropylene-fibre screen can be erected in front of the wall-trained Peaches and Nectarines and a small plastic or glass roof over the top can be of value. The screens should be erected approximately 12–18 in (30–50 cm) in front of the trees, in such a way as to allow them to withstand the effects of wind. They should be kept in place from midwinter to mid spring.

Growing tubes for young trees

These are possibly beneficial but normally work best on indigenous species such as Oak (Quercus), Ash (Fraxinus), Norway Maple (*Acer platanoides*), Sycamore (*A. pseudoplatanus*) and other strong-growing trees. They are not so beneficial to ornamental varieties and there have been some cases of premature growth and then die-back due to late frost. Also disease and pest build-up can be a problem.

Protecting Cordylines, Phormiums and Yuccas outdoors

Cordylines (Cabbage Tree of New Zealand), Phormiums (New Zealand Flax) and Yuccas can have their leaves gathered together and either held with a strong elastic-band or tied with raffia, so protecting the central bud, but this should be done in late autumn when the foliage is dry and released as soon as possible in the spring. It is important that they are not held together longer than necessary as they may grow internally within the bound leaves and this can cause problems.

In cold gardens, however, the plants may not be hardy enough to survive even with this treatment, and it may be better to grow them in containers and move them inside in winter.

Protecting plants in store or growing in a cold greenhouse, conservatory or plastic tunnel

The use of non-woven, chemical-free, polypropylene-fibre frost protection, draped over growing plants in cold greenhouses or plastic tunnels over winter, will give added winter protection.

In late winter and early spring this will also help protect

newly germinated seedlings, young cuttings and plants, and will offer 2–4 Celsius degrees of additional frost protection, as well as reducing heating costs.

In autumn and winter the material can also be draped over boxes of Dahlia tubers, Chrysanthemum stools and Geraniums and Fuchsias that are being overwintered as stock plants.

Controlling the environment of alpines and very slow growing conifers and shrubs

Some of the choicer alpines, very slow-growing conifers such as Juniperus and low-growing shrubs such as Daphnes benefit from having a small glass or clear plastic structure erected above them with adequate air space passing beneath to keep them cool while diverting rain and severe cold away from the plants.

The rain and frost together can be a killer as far as these plants are concerned. Such plants should be grown in the first place in well-drained soil with additional sand or very small gravel added. A layer of gravel placed over the soil surface will protect them even more.

CHAPTER TEN

Planting Containers and Hanging Baskets

After preparing container-grown plants for the Chelsea Flower Show for almost three decades, one would have thought that the novelty of this form of growing would have worn off – but no, with today's ever-increasing range of container-friendly plants, I find myself filling more and more each year, not only in the spring for summer colour but in the autumn for interesting winter and early spring display.

In my early years spent as a garden boy and later on as an apprentice, I learnt many tips which, with slight amendments, are proving more and more useful today. In the following notes I will try to bring these tried and tested techniques up to date, to fit in with today's gardening needs.

Container-grown plants increase the colour and interest of the garden and can be grown in the smallest of spaces.

Pots and containers

The description 'pots and containers' can cover almost anything that will hold enough potting compost to enable plants to grow: not only the conventional tubs, pots, troughs and window-boxes sold in garden shops, but more off-beat containers, such as a child's broken wheelbarrow, a chimney-pot or even a Boy Scouts' tea urn.

Whatever the container, there are a number of considerations that should always be taken into account if plants are to grow successfully:

1. That it is of adequate size to contain enough potting compost to sustain the plants grown in it through their full growing seasons. In general terms the container should be no less

than 10 in (25 cm) deep and wide. However, the larger (within reason), the better the display.
2. That the container has adequate drainage holes.
3. That it is frost-resistant or can be made so, to prevent damage to the container and stop penetration of frost through the sides in winter, which can kill plant roots growing within.

Types of containers
Conventional containers are now constructed or manufactured out of a wide range of materials, including:

Terracotta (clay pots)	Peat products
China or glazed ceramic	Plastic
Concrete	Stone
Glass fibre	Wood, including troughs and
Paper products	barrels

In fact an ever-changing and widening range of materials, designs and finishes is becoming available – the choice is yours. (But remember the criteria listed above.)

Uses for container-grown plants
1. For the growing of a short-term flowering display, seasonally planted in spring for summer flowers and in autumn for winter and spring flowering, each requiring selected suitable plants.
2. To grow a range of plants that require specific soil conditions which may not exist in the garden, for example, acid soil for ericaceous plants such as dwarf Rhododendrons and Azaleas, well-drained sandy soil for grey-leaved plants and many bulbs, etc.
3. To grow plants in areas where no soil exists yet plants are required for floral display, such as balconies and small yard areas, or to decorate a front entrance to private or commercial premises.
4. To extend the range grown and isolate specific plant groups so that they are shown off to better effect; in particular, alpines and bulbs fit into this group.

5. To grow non-winter-hardy plants, so that they can be moved into the protection of a frost-free conservatory or greenhouse in winter; Datura, Camellia and citrus plants (Oranges and Lemons) are good examples.

6. To act as a short-term holding area for plants that will later be given a permanent planting position in the garden, or for plants that have arrived before a planting area is ready.

7. For use in garden design, to act as dividers on patios, as covers for manholes, to hide eyesores such as dustbins, or to highlight steps and entrance-ways, etc.

8. To allow for a changing display of plants, week by week, not only in public places such as hotels and public-houses, but in the garden.

9. To create a particular atmosphere, for example, cool and clean, hot and sunny, flowery and pretty. Even a regional slant is possible: a Mediterranean feeling can be created by choosing grey-leaved plants and other Mediterranean-type plants, for example.

10. To allow more plants to be grown in town and city gardens where access to the soil may not always be possible.

11. For the cultivation of tender plants in conservatories and greenhouses, where no access can be gained to the soil but the plants in question require a protected environment to grow.

In fact, containers will fill any role where plants are required and the surrounding area is unsuitable or hostile for plant growth, both indoors and out.

Types of potting compost

Purchasing the right potting compost in which to grow the plants is important. Never attempt to use garden soil, as it is not of the right composition and can contain harmful insects and diseases that rapidly build up in a container environment.

There are a number of potting compost formulas offered by different producers; these can be grouped according to their make-up, each having advantages and disadvantages, as follows.

303

Peat-based potting compost

These offer the potential of quick lush growth but may dry out faster in dry weather and become too wet in rain. When used outdoors they may need more attention to watering and feeding compared with other types. Because of this, they are specifically not suitable for use in outdoor winter-flowering containers.

John Innes No.3 Potting Compost; soil-based potting composts

These are used where plants are to be grown for a number of years in containers where a stable, semi-consolidated potting-compost mixture is important to sustain long-term plant growth.

Possibly still one of the best, but care must be taken to purchase only those produced by members of the John Innes Manufacturers' Association and showing their mark of approval. It is usable and manageable in both summer and winter as a potting compost and is strongly recommended.

However, beware of the recently introduced Universal John Innes Potting Compost; it is said to be suitable for all work but I find this difficult to believe as John Innes composts were formulated in the first instance to fulfil a number of specific roles, not for multiple use.

J. Arthur Bower's standard potting and seed-sowing compost

Throughout this book I have attempted not to use brand names. Gardening products are supplied by many firms and the secret, in most cases, is to shop around and find the best value for money.

However, J. Arthur Bower's Seed and Potting Compost, in my mind, stands alone in its suitability as a container compost. I have used it for over twenty years, both commercially and privately, and in all that time it has remained constant in quality and performance and has produced good results in winter and summer containers, both indoors and out. In fact, I have achieved Chelsea Gold Medal standard plants with it.

It stays moist yet well-drained, holds plant foods and generally encourages plant development. The only possible minus is that it is rightly, because of its guaranteed quality, slightly more expensive than other potting composts.

Coir-based potting compost
Much development is taking place in the formulation of different potting composts using non-peat-based mixtures, and coir is possibly the first of many. My own experience with products now available is that they dry out very fast and are hard to remoisten once they do; their chemical and structural characteristics are continuously changing while in use and this may cause problems with plant growth when used for long periods in containers.

However, their open texture may make them a good candidate, due to the heat insulation they offer, for use in winter containers, in particular when planting bulbs.

Potting composts specifically formulated for acid-loving plants
Most manufacturers offer 'lime-free' potting composts, designed for use when growing ericaceous plants such as Azaleas, Rhododendrons and Camellias, which dislike lime or calcium in the soil. These are useful, but make sure you are not just purchasing a packaged bag of peat with little else added in the way of fertilizer, and paying for the privilege.

I personally would put my money on J. Arthur Bower's Ericaceous Compost for all-year-round use and success.

Potting composts for specific groups of plants
Potting composts are now advertised specifically for use in containers or hanging baskets, but I would check the price and formula carefully to see whether they offer any advantage over the general types already described.

Bulb fibre
Bulb fibre is basically peat, although those based on coir are worth considering. It has a very specific use and contains charcoal and oyster shell to keep it sweet and stop the build-up of harmful soil salts which can damage bulb growth. Its use in the main is as a potting compost for bulbs grown in

containers indoors such as Hyacinths, Tulips and Narcissus (Daffodils).

Tips for purchasing and using potting composts

1. Select the correct potting compost for the season, environment and plants you are intending to grow.

2. Inspect the bag for age: any fading of the printing suggests that the compost has been held in stock for too long; potting compost should be used as soon as possible after manufacture.

3. Potting composts in their bags attract moisture from the air in wet weather and lose it in dry, so the compost will vary between wet and dry. Should it appear excessively wet or, worse still, as sometimes happens, contain green slime or moss, then return it to the retailer for a replacement or refund. Do not buy compost that has not been stored under cover.

4. Purchase your potting compost for spring use in mid to late winter as at this time of year it is often on special offer. If you are purchasing more than one bag at this time, see if you can negotiate a discount.

5. Try, if possible, to store it in a dry, frost-free place at normal room temperature so it is not 'cold' to the plants' roots when you finally come to use it. Never store it where plants are growing – such as in a greenhouse – as it can become an ideal home for the development of pests and diseases.

6. Never change the potting compost formula by adding additional material such as garden soil, peat or sand, except possibly for moisture-retaining polymer granules. Adding soil from the garden, or more peat or sand, will change the structure, which has been carefully developed by the manufacturer; this can lead to a host of problems, not least the introduction of weeds, pests and diseases, which have been eradicated from the purchased potting compost by sterilization.

Potting up a container

The following procedure can be used for both permanent and short-term containers:

1. Select a suitable container and the correct potting compost. Add water-retaining polymer granules to the compost as recommended on the product.

2. Ensure that there are drainage holes in the bottom of the container unless it is a bulb bowl for Hyacinths, where, if bulb fibre is used, no drainage holes are necessary.

3. If vine weevil is a problem and causing damage in your garden, place inside the bottom of the container a layer of non-woven, chemical-free, polypropylene-fibre frost protection (floating cloche or frost-protection material), to cover the drainage holes in the base of the container and prevent the adult vine weevil from entering. This will also keep out worms, small soil slugs and woodlice, which can cause damage.

4. Next place a 2–3 in (5–8 cm) layer of drainage material in the bottom of the container. Broken pots, brick, gravel or stones can be used, but my own preference is for broken up or small pieces of polystyrene packaging. I find that this material keeps the soil warm at the bottom of the pot and holds moisture and plant foods, and that plant roots infiltrate it and use it as a reservoir for both.

5. In the past, outdoor containers in winter were few and those that there were had thick sides able to resist frost penetration. Today the trend is to all-year-round use, but the containers are much thinner-sided and many of these do not insulate the plant's roots sufficiently against winter frost, as anyone who has attempted to overwinter outdoors Camellias and Narcissus (Daffodils) will know.

Traditionally winter containers, even those thick enough to withstand cold, were lined inside with old newspaper or straw; today we can improve on this by using the bubble insulating plastic intended for lining greenhouses or for packaging. A layer of this material will keep out 3–4 Celcius degrees of cold as well as acting in summer as an insulation against excessive heat or moisture loss.

6. Moisten the potting compost prior to use to avoid the need for heavy watering once the plants have been added.

7. One to two hours before planting them in the container, water the plants to be used in their growing pots. This will allow them to be removed without difficulty and prevent root

damage, as well as ensuring they have water in the early hours following planting.

8. Next fill the container with potting compost to a level that allows the plant's upper soil level to be 1–2 in (3–5 cm) lower than the upper rim of the container, measuring from time to time with the plant still in its original pot until the correct level is found. When more than one plant is to be used, adjust for the deepest pot first and then add more potting compost as smaller plants are added.

9. Remove the pot without disturbing the soil around the roots and make any final adjustments to the levels.

10. Fill the container with the potting compost 1–2 in (3–5 cm) below the top of the container.

11. Water well.

12. This watering will settle the surface of the soil. The resulting space should be infilled with more potting compost until it is 1 in (3 cm) below the top rim of the container.

13. Personally I do very little firming. I prefer to leave the potting compost open so that roots can travel freely through it and establish quickly.

14. Provide a mulch of organic material over the surface. I find that using cocoa shell, 1–2 in (3–5 cm) deep, just reducing the depth to ½–1 in (1–3 cm) directly around the base of the plants, prevents weeds, reduces water loss, keeps potting compost cool in summer and mostly frost-free in winter, while deterring attacks of surface-travelling slugs and snails.

15. Do not water for twenty-four hours unless it is really required. With restricted watering, the roots of the plants are encouraged to grow and spread throughout the container rather than remaining within the limits of the pot they were grown in.

16. If vine weevil is a problem in the garden, a film of insecticide glue can be applied to the upper outside rim of the container; alternatively, double-sided carpet tape or Sellotape can be used but it is more unsightly. Either will trap the adult insects and prevent them from laying their eggs in the container to feed on your plants later.

17. Finally the container is raised up on small stones or blocks up to $\frac{3}{4}$ in (2 cm) high so that air can pass freely under the container and prevent a vacuum from forming between the base of the container and the surface it is standing on. (If a vacuum is formed, it will impede the drainage.)

Management of a container

The routine care and management that should be carried out if the plants growing in containers, both long- and short-term, are to stay fully productive, is as follows.

Watering

Water plants regularly as required; this may mean watering in summer when light rain is experienced. Under-watering stops growth, the plants take time to recover and valuable displays are lost. Over-watering has the same effect and is more likely to lead to death.

If possible, water with rainwater, in particular those plants requiring acid soil conditions, as much domestic tap water is alkaline. Also, in many areas a licence is required or a charge made for the use of mains water in the garden.

Feeding

When grown in containers plants cannot go searching for the full range of plant foods they need regularly – all that they require has to be brought to them, so feeding is a key factor in success.

It is best to feed in spring and summer with a balanced, nitrogen, phosphate and potash liquid fertilizer for general mixed container plantings. Use a higher-nitrogen liquid ferti-lizer for long-term foliage plants such as Buxus (Box), conifers and perennial plants such as Hostas, to improve their vigour and foliage colour. (The ratio of plant foods in a fertilizer is shown on the packaging.)

Feed in the spring and summer at least once a week; I prefer to do this if possible on a regular day so as not to forget. Start at the end of May and stop at the end of July with permanent planting but continue until the end of September with summer short-term bedding. Normally winter bedding plants need only one liquid feeding at the beginning of March as a pick-me-up, assuming a new potting compost was used when the plants were potted in the autumn.

Turning
With both short- and long-term plantings it is useful to turn the containers a few inches each week to take full advantage of the plants' flowering and foliage performance, and also to prevent the plants growing one-sided.

Repotting permanent plants
To keep permanently container-grown plants at their most productive, once a year in early March, one of the following repotting or topping-up techniques should be carried out.

The principal reason for this is to encourage the growth of new roots and to give them room to develop fully. If this is not done then there is simply nowhere for the roots to grow and the plant becomes pot-bound; in other words, the roots are suffocated by their own mass.

Once a year scrape out all the surface potting compost until the roots of the plant are clearly exposed, but not broken, and then infill with a suitable new potting compost.

Every second year, in early March, remove the plant from the container, keeping the soil ball intact, and rub off and reduce it in size by up to a third, if possible, both on the outer edges and on top. Then repot using a suitable new potting compost.

Every third year, again in March, carry out the second-year operation but also provide and repot into a new container 2 in (5 cm) larger in diameter and depth than the first.

These procedures are repeated on a regular basis throughout the plant's life and will keep it in first-class condition. Failing to do this will quickly have the reverse effect.

Plants for permanent planting
Most shrubs, trees, conifers, perennials, Roses and climbers will survive in containers but few will thrive and grow to any substantial size. Their full potential is rarely achieved and the lifespan is considerably reduced. As long as this is accepted, all

types can be grown in containers, but some do better than others.

Those plants that need to make new annual growth to grow and flower should be avoided in favour of those that only need to produce limited new growth to perform well and interestingly, either by flowering or more likely with their foliage displays.

Remember that, once containerized, the plant rarely makes a great deal of additional height and should be chosen carefully for height and shape in the first instance.

The following plants do well for permanent container planting; they can tolerate the conditions and offer interest for a good number of years:

TREES

Acacia dealbata (Mimosa) – will require winter protection

Caragana arborescens 'Lorbergii' (Siberian Pea Tree)

C. a. 'Pendula' (Weeping Siberian Pea Tree)

C. a. 'Walker' (Walker's Siberian Pea Tree)

Cotoneaster 'Hybridus Pendulus' (Weeping Cotoneaster)

Gleditsia triancanthos 'Rubylace' (Purple-leaved Honey Locust)

G. t. 'Sunburst' (Golden-leaved Honey Locust)

Laurus nobilis (Bay) – when grown on a stem as a tree

Prunus cerasifera 'Nigra' (Purple-leaved Plum)

Sorbus aria 'Lutescens' (Whitebeam)

Viburnum opulus 'Sterile' (Snowball Tree), when grown on a stem as a standard

Weigela in variety – when grown on a stem as a standard

SHRUBS

Acer japonicum varieties (Japanese Maple)

A. palmatum varieties (Japanese Maple)

Aucuba varieties (Himalayan or Japanese Laurel)

Azalea, dwarf varieties (Japanese Azaleas)

Buxus sempervirens varieties (Box)

Callistemon varieties (Bottle Brush) – will require winter protection in cold gardens

Camellia varieties (Camellia)

Corokia varieties (Wire-netting Plant)

Elaeagnus, evergreen varieties (Evergreen Elaeagnus)

Euonymus fortunei varieties (Evergreen Bittersweet)

E. japonica varieties (Japanese Euonymus)

Fatsia japonica varieties (Castor Oil Plant)

Griselinia littoralis varieties (Broadleaf)

Ilex varieties (Holly)
Ligustrum varieties (Ornamental
    Privet)
Osmanthus heterophyllus
    varieties (False Holly)
Phormium varieties (New
    Zealand Flax)
Pittosporum varieties
    (Parchment Bark) – will
    require winter protection
Rhamnus alaternus

'Argenteovariegata'
(Evergreen Variegated
Buckthorn) – will require
winter protection in cold
gardens
Rhododendron, dwarf varieties
    (Dwarf Rhododendrons)
Rosmarinus varieties (Rosemary)
Viburnum tinus (Laurustinus)
Yucca varieties (Yucca)

CONIFERS
Most slow-growing (dwarf) and spreading conifers are suitable.
However, taller growing varieties will soon lose their fresh, soft
foliage.

FRUIT
Figs and Strawberries are possibly the only two fruits to do well and
produce the fruit expected. Dwarf Peaches may, in very favourable
gardens, produce fruit, but are not reliable. Citrus fruits such as
Oranges may be worth considering but will require winter
protection.

PERENNIAL AND ALPINE PLANTS
Most perennial and alpine plants do well in containers.

CLIMBING PLANTS AND ROSES
These have been omitted from the listings as they very rarely grow
to anywhere near their full potential and, in the case of climbers,
rarely reach a fraction of their expected height and are often
disappointing in their long-term performance.

Short-term plantings
Seasonal short-term plantings of bulbs, bedding plants and
hardy and tender perennial plants have been popular since
Victorian times. The operation and management needed to
keep the displays in tip-top condition have already been covered; suggestions are made here for plants that may be used
for specific seasonal displays.

The plantings are divided into two groups, winter flowering
and summer flowering.

Winter flowering

More correctly this should be late autumn and spring flowering, although, depending on the weather, they may flower in
winter too. The containers are planted in the autumn and left
in the open over winter.

However, in exposed gardens or in very cold periods, it is
advisable to bring the containers together in a sheltered corner
and surround them with straw or some other insulating material to prevent frost and cold damage. The tops can also be
covered with non-woven, chemical-free, polypropylene-fibre
frost protection material to prevent cold, frost-laden wind
damage.

Plants can be chosen from the following:

BIENNIALS FOR OUTDOOR USE

Aquilegia varieties (Columbine
or Granny's Bonnet)
Bellis perennis varieties (Daisy)
Brassica meracea sabellica
varieties (Ornamental Kale)
Campanula media varieties
(Canterbury Bell)
Cheiranthus × *allionii* varieties
(Siberian Wallflower)
C. cheiri varieties (Wallflower)
Dianthus barbatus varieties
(Sweet William)
Myosotis alpestris varieties
(Forget-me-not)
Primula polyantha varieties
(Polyanthus)
P. vulgaris (Primrose)
P. 'Wanda' (Specie
Primrose)
Matthiola (Stocks)
Viola varieties (Viola)
Viola cornuta varieties (Horned
Violet)
V. × *wittrockiana* (Winter-
flowering Pansy)

BULBS AND CORMS FOR
OUTDOOR USE

Allium aflatunense (Giant
Flowering Onion)
Allium, dwarf forms in
variety (Dwarf Flowering
Onion)
Anemone blanda in variety
(Greek Windflower)
Anemone, de Caen varieties (de
Caen Windflower)
Anemone, St Brigid varieties (St
Brigid Windflower)
Bulbocodium (Spring Meadow
Saffron)
Chionodoxa varieties (Snow
Glory)
Crocus (Autumn-flowering
Crocus)
Crocus, large-flowering varieties
(Large-flowered Crocus)
Crocus species in variety (Crocus
species)
Endymion nonscriptus (Bluebell)
Eranthis hyemalis (Winter
Aconite)

313

Erythronium, in variety (Dog-toothed Violet)

Freesia, double, in variety (Double Freesia)

Freesia, single, in variety (Garden Freesia)

Fritillaria imperialis varieties (Crown Imperial)

F. meleagris varieties (Snake-head Fritillary)

F. persica (Persian Fritillary)

Galanthus nivalis (Snowdrop, single and double)

Hyacinthus orientalis, unprepared varieties (Garden Hyacinths)

Iris, Dutch hybrid varieties (Dutch Iris)

Iris reticulata varieties (Dwarf Iris)

Ixia varieties (Corn Lily)

Muscari armeniacum (Grape Hyacinth)

Narcissus varieties (Daffodil, single and double)

Narcissus dwarf/species varieties (Dwarf Daffodil)

Ornithogalum nutans (Drooping Star of Bethlehem)

Oxalis adenophylla (Wood Oxalis)

Puschkinia varieties (Striped Squill)

Ranunculus varieties (Bachelor's Buttons)

Scilla campanulata varieties (Squill)

S. sibirica varieties (Siberian Squill)

Sparaxis varieties (Wandflower)

Triteleia varieties (Spring Star-flower)

Tulipa

Darwin varieties (Darwin Tulip)

Double early varieties (Double Early-flowering Tulip)

Dwarf *greigii/kaufmanniana* varieties (Dwarf Tulip)

Early-flowering varieties (Early-flowering Tulip)

Lily-flowering varieties (Lily-flowered Tulip)

Multi-headed/ fringed/ novelty varieties (Multi-headed Tulip)

Parrot varieties (Parrot Tulip)

Species varieties (Specimen Tulip)

Triumph types (Triumph Tulips)

BULBS FOR INDOOR USE

Indoor Narcissi including the following varieties: 'Bridal Crown', 'Cragford', 'January Gold', 'Paper White', 'Paper White Double', 'Soleil d'Or'; *Hyacinthus orientalis* cultivars (prepared Hyacinths for forcing) and many of those suggested for outdoors.

Plants, bulbs and corms suitable for summer containers

SUMMER BEDDING PLANTS

Ageratum varieties (Floss Flower)

Antirrhinum varieties (Snapdragon)

Argyranthemum frutescens (Marguerite)

Aster varieties (Frost Flower)

Aurinia saxatilis (Yellow Alyssum)

Begonia semperflorens (Fibrous-rooted Begonia)

Calceolaria 'Sunshine' (Slipper-wort)

Calendula varieties (Scotch Marigold)

Campanula carpatica varieties (Carpathian Harebell)

C. isophylla varieties (Star of Bethlehem)

Dianthus varieties (Bedding Carnation)

Celosia varieties (Cockscomb)

Coleus varieties (Flame Nettle)

Cosmos varieties (Cosmea)

Dahlia merckii varieties (Bedding Dahlia)

Dianthus varieties (Garden or Bedding Pinks)

Dianthus barbatus, annual varieties (Sweet William)

Fuchsia varieties (Lady's Eardrops)

Gaillardia varieties (Blanket Flower)

Gazania varieties (Treasure Flower)

Geranium varieties (Garden or Zonal Geranium)

Geranium, Ivy-leaf varieties (Ivy-leaf Geraniums)

Gerbera (Transvaal Daisy)

Godetia varieties (Farewell to Spring)

Heliotropium varieties (Heliotrope)

Impatiens varieties (Busy Lizzie)

Impatiens, New Guinea varieties (New Guinea Busy Lizzie)

Ipomoea varieties (Morning Glory)

Kochia scoparia (Burning Bush)

Lathyrus odoratus varieties (Sweet Pea)

Lavatera trimestris, annual varieties only (Mallow)

Lobelia cardinalis varieties (Cardinal Flower)

Mesembryanthemum varieties (Livingstone Daisy)

Mimulus varieties (Monkey Flower)

Nasturtium, see Tropaeolum

Nemesia varieties (Nemesia)

Nicotiana varieties (Tobacco Plant)

Nolana varieties (Chilean Bellflower)

Petunia hybrid varieties

Phlox varieties (Bedding Phlox)

Portulaca (Purslane)

Rudbeckia, annual varieties only (Black-eyed Susan)

Salpiglossis (Painted Tongue)

Salvia varieties (Salvia or Sage)

Senecio maritimus varieties (Cineraria)

Tagetes erecta (African Marigold)

T. patula (French Marigold)
T. signata varieties (Tagetes)
Tanacetum coccineum
   (Pyrethrum)
Tropaeolum majus varieties
   (Nasturtium)
Zinnia varieties (Zinnia)

SUMMER-FLOWERING BULBS
AND CORMS
Achimenes varieties (Hot-water
   Plant)
Babiana varieties (Baboon Root)
Begonia
   Double varieties (Double-
     flowered Begonia)
   Giant-flowered varieties
     (Giant-flowered Begonia)
   Non-stop varieties (Non-stop
     Begonia)
   Pendula varieties (Hanging
     Begonia)
Begonia crispa varieties
   (Crinkled-edge Begonia)
B. fimbriata varieties (Fimbriata
   Begonia)
B. multiflora varieties
   (Multiflowering Begonia)
Brodiaea (Californian Hyacinth)
Calla varieties (Arum Lily)
Canna varieties (Indian Root)
Dahlia
   Anemone-flowering varieties
     (Anemone-flowered Dahlia)
   Ball varieties (Ball Dahlia)
   Dwarf Bedding varieties
     (Dwarf Bedding Dahlia)
   Mignon varieties (Mignon
     Dahlia)
   Pompon varieties (Pom-pom
     Dahlia)

Eucomis (not hardy out of
   doors all year) (Pineapple
   Flower)
Freesias (outdoor) (Outdoor
   Freesias)
Galtonia candicans (Summer
   Hyacinth)
Gladiolus callianthus
   (Acidanthera or Peacock
   Flower)
Gloriosa (not hardy out of
   doors) (Climbing Lily)
Iris, Dutch
Ixia (Corn Lily)
Lilium
   Asiatic hybrids varieties
     (Asiatic Lily)
   Mid-Century Hybrids varieties
     (Mid-Century Lily)
   Oriental hybrids varieties
     (Oriental Lily)
   Species varieties (Species Lily)
   Trumpet type varieties
     (Trumpet Lily)
Nerine bowdenii varieties
   (Nerine)
Ornithogalum thyrsoides – not
   hardy out of doors
   (Chincherinchee)
Oxalis, tender varieties
Sinningia speciosa (Gloxinia)
Sparaxis varieties (Wandflower)
Sprekelia varieties (Jacobean
   Lily)
Tigridia varieties (Tiger Flower,
   Mexican Shell Flower)
Tritonia varieties (Blazing Star)
Vallota varieties (Vallota)
Zephyranthes (Rain Lily,
   Zephyr Lily)

TENDER PERENNIALS
Abutilon varieties (Flowering
  Maple, Parlour Maple)
Argyranthemum frutescens
  (Marguerite)
Brachyscome (Swan River
  Daisy)
Convolvulus mauritanicus (Blue
  Convolvulus)
Diascia varieties
Dimorphotheca varieties (Cape
  Marigold, Star of the Veldt)
Felicia amelloides (Blue Daisy)
Gazania (Treasure Flower)
Helichrysum varieties (Straw
  Flower, Straw Daisy)
Heliotropium (Heliotrope or
  Bloodstone)
Lobelia richardii (Tender
  Perennial Lobelia)
Lotus berthelotii (Trefoil)
Lysimachia varieties
  (Loosestrife)
Malvastrum varieties (False
  Mallow)
Nepeta, variegated – not
  hardy all year (Variegated
  Catmint)
Portulaca varieties (Purslane)
Scaevola varieties
Sedum varieties
Thunbergia alata (Black-eyed
  Susie)
Verbena peruviana varieties

HERBS
Angelica (*Angelica archangelica*)
Apple Mint (*Mentha* ×
  rotundifolia)
Basil (*Ocimum basilicum*)
Bay (*Laurus nobilis*)

Borage (*Borago officinalis*)
Caraway (*Carum carvi*)
Chervil (*Anthriscus cerefolium*)
Chives (*Allium schoenoprasum*)
Coriander (*Coriandrum
  sativum*)
Cotton Lavender (Santolina
  varieties)
Curry Plant (*Helichrysum
  splendidum*)
Dill (*Anethum graveolens*)
Fennel (*Foeniculum vulgare*)
Feverfew (*Tanacetum
  coccineum*)
Feverfew, Golden (*Tanacetum
  parthenium*)
French Tarragon (*Artemisia
  dracunculus*)
Garlic (*Allium sativum*)
Horseradish (*Armoracia
  rusticana*)
Hyssop (*Hyssopus officinalis*)
Lavender varieties (Lavandula)
Lemon Balm (*Melissa officinalis*)
Lemon-Scented Verbena (*Aloysia
  triphylla*)
Lovage (*Levisticum officinale*)
Marjoram varieties (*Origanum
  vulgare*)
Onion, Tree (*Allium cepa*,
  Proliferum group)
Onion, Welsh (*Allium
  fistulosum*)
Parsley, French (*Petroselinum
  crispum*)
Pennyroyal (*Mentha pulegium*)
Rosemary varieties (*Rosmarinus*)
Rue varieties (Ruta)
Sage varieties (Salvia)
Savory, Summer (*Satureia
  hortensis*)

Savory, Winter (*Satureia montana*)
Sorrel (*Rumex acetosa*)
Southernwood (*Artemisia abrotanum*)
Spearmint (*Mentha spicata*)
Sweet Cicely (*Myrrhis odorata*)
Thyme (Thymus)
Woodruff (*Asperula odorata*)
Wormwood (*Artemisia absinthium*)
Yarrow (*Achillea millefolium*)

VEGETABLES
Aubergine (*Solanum melongena*)
Bean, Dwarf French (*Phaseolus vulgaris*)
Lettuce (*Lactuca sativa*)
Melon (*Cucumis melo*)
Onion (*Allium cepa*)
Pepper, Sweet (*Capsicum annuum*)
Tomato (*Lycopersicon esculentum*)

In fact most vegetables can be grown successfully in containers and the above is meant as a selection only.

Container ideas from the past

Keeping and maintaining the containers attractive all the year round was an important task for the head gardeners of the past and we can still use their methods to advantage today.

Spare inner containers
Many of the containers in the garden had up to five inner containers in which the seasonal plant displays were planted. As each display finished a follow-up one was ready to be substituted. The five separate displays in order of use might be:

1. Spring-planted summer bedding
2. Spring-planted Lilies for mid to late summer use
3. Early-autumn-planted Ornamental Kale or Cabbage for autumn and early winter use
4. Evergreen shrub or conifer for winter; these were normally maintained year round
5. Autumn-planted winter and spring-flowering biennials and bulbs for early to late spring display.

Central inner spot plant
With this method the minimum diameter of the upper rim of the container should be not less than 12 in (30 cm).

318

The container is filled, but instead of a plant being planted in the centre a 6–8 in (15–20 cm) pot is sunk into the potting compost with its top edge 1–2 in (3–5 cm) below that of the main container.

In the gap between the main container and the inner pot, small-leaved, green or variegated Ivies (*Hedera helix* varieties) are planted and will soon grow over and down the outer side of the container, and can remain for a number of years.

Up to five or more 6–8 in (15–20 cm) interchangeable inner pots are planted for seasonal interest. The planting for these might be as suggested for seasonal planting, pp. 313–17, but there is no limit to the range the gardener might choose.

This has the added advantage of being cost-effective, with the Ivy (Hedera) making a good foil for almost any plant used in the central pots.

Multi-level bulb planting

Using containers with a depth and upper rim diameter of not less than 12 in (30 cm), a succession of interest with little input of effort or experience can be achieved.

Once drainage and, if required, vine weevil barriers are in place, a layer of potting compost 3–4 in (8–10 cm) deep is added and a layer of Narcissus (Daffodil) bulbs are planted 1 in (3 cm) apart in the compost.

A further 4 in (10 cm) of potting compost is added and dwarf Tulip bulbs planted on it 3 in (8 cm) apart.

The container is now filled to the top and lightly firmed, and then spring-flowering biennials such as Wallflowers and Polyanthus are planted 6–8 in (15–20 cm) apart; finally a ring of large-flowering Crocuses are planted 1–2 in (3–5 cm) apart around the inner rim of the container.

In late January/early February the Crocuses flower and then the Narcissus (Daffodils) in March/April. At this stage check that the leaf and flower shoots of the Daffodils do not loosen the roots of the biennials as they emerge – if they do, firm the biennials back in. Once the Narcissus have finished flowering their foliage can be gently worked in among the biennials, so as not to become unsightly, but left intact to help build up the

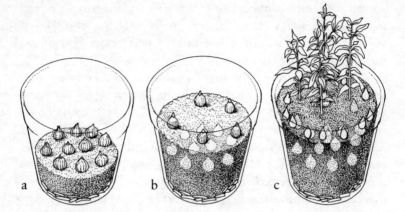

39. *Multi-level bulb planting* (a) *Drainage, potting compost and daffodil bulbs* (b) *Second layer of potting compost plus tulip bulbs* (c) *Third layer of potting compost plus crocus corms and bedding plants*

bulbs for the next year. The next to flower are the Tulips and again, once finished, their foliage is lost in the biennials, which are the last to flower.

From one potting operation the container has offered interest from late winter to late spring without any extra effort. However, the story does not stop there. In late spring the tops of the Crocus will have died down and the biennials finished flowering. These are then removed, along with the top layer of potting compost, and the Crocus are planted in the garden. Wallflowers join the compost heap; other biennials, such as Polyanthas and *Bellis perennis* (Daisy), can be planted out in the garden for next spring.

The potting compost is removed down to the tops of the Tulip bulbs and replaced with new. Both the Tulips and Narcissus (Daffodils) are left in the container to flower in the following spring. Summer bedding is now planted to grow and flower through the summer.

Come mid to late autumn, when the summer bedding is finished and has been removed, the soil down to the level of the tops of the Tulips is again renewed and new Crocuses and winter biennials purchased and planted in the container for the process to start all over again.

I have found that this procedure can be repeated for two years without deterioration of the Daffodils or Tulips and it may be possible to continue longer, or the bulbs can be removed and planted in the garden.

Hanging baskets, wall baskets and mangers

As well as planting for the summer, many gardeners also plant baskets for winter and early spring displays. All the points regarding potting compost, feeding, watering and management apply with hanging baskets and similar containers (see pp. 303–10). There are a few additional points and tips that may be of help:

1. Baskets come in a number of sizes but, within reason, the larger the better. I prefer the wire type but strides are being made with plastic, particularly in the area of self-watering, and these may be worth considering. The minimum size for really good results is 12 in (30 cm) diameter and above. Again, the larger wall baskets and mangers are, the better the display.

2. Stand the empty hanging or wall basket in the top of a large empty pot or bucket to aid the work of filling; mangers will require some similar support for filling them.

3. With hanging baskets, carefully remove the chain until filling is complete; this prevents damage, when the basket is fully planted, from trying to get the chain up and over the plants.

4. A $1\frac{1}{2}$–2 in (4–5 cm) layer of moss is my choice for lining baskets, wall baskets or mangers, but there are a number of alternative liners available and as long as the lining material absorbs water and allows plant roots to grow into it while keeping those roots cool in summer, the new materials are worth experimenting with.

When purchasing moss try to find retailers who will sell it loose or who have packaged it themselves, rather than buying prepacked, as it will often be better value for money.

5. After lining with moss and before filling with potting compost, place a saucer or appropriate-sized round piece of polythene in the bottom of the basket or other container to act as a reservoir for water that the plants roots can reach and use in times of need.

6. Both J. Arthur Bower's Standard Seed and Potting Compost and John Innes No. 2 are suitable potting composts. There are also specifically promoted basket composts, but these may not be cost-effective.

7. Before filling, mix with the potting compost, as recommended by the manufacturer, some biodegradable water storage granules to help retain moisture and plant food, reducing the need to water so often.

8. If using a wire basket, fill up to halfway with potting compost and insert between the wires trailing Lobelia or other suitable hanging plants about 5–7 in (12–17 cm) apart to hang down the sides when grown. This can also be done for wall baskets or mangers.

9. Finish filling the basket and plant selected plants in the top.

10. Top off the planting with a 1 in (3 cm) deep layer of cocoa shell to retain moisture further.

11. Feed and water as for a container, but once a month, or more frequently in dry weather, remove the hanging or wall basket from the wall and immerse in a container or bucket of water for thirty minutes, so that the moss or moss-substitute liner becomes fully soaked and can act as a supply of water.

Mixed plantings give colour or variety, and often the effect can be very rewarding, but solo or mono plantings can also be dramatic and should be considered.

Many nurseries and garden centres offer ready-filled baskets or a basket-filling service; these can be very cost-effective and because the plants have been grown in protected structures such as tunnel-houses, the display will be effective sooner in your garden.

ENJOY YOUR GARDENING

Index

Discover more about our forthcoming books through Penguin's FREE newspaper...

Penguin

Quarterly

It's packed with:

- exciting features
- author interviews
- previews & reviews
- books from your favourite films & TV series
- exclusive competitions & much, much more...

Write off for your free copy today to:
Dept JC
Penguin Books Ltd
FREEPOST
West Drayton
Middlesex
UB7 0BR
NO STAMP REQUIRED

READ MORE IN PENGUIN

In every corner of the world, on every subject under the sun, Penguin represents quality and variety – the very best in publishing today.

For complete information about books available from Penguin – including Puffins, Penguin Classics and Arkana – and how to order them, write to us at the appropriate address below. Please note that for copyright reasons the selection of books varies from country to country.

In the United Kingdom: Please write to *Dept. JC, Penguin Books Ltd, FREEPOST, West Drayton, Middlesex UB7 0BR.*

If you have any difficulty in obtaining a title, please send your order with the correct money, plus ten per cent for postage and packaging, to *PO Box No. 11, West Drayton, Middlesex UB7 0BR*

In the United States: Please write to *Consumer Sales, Penguin USA, P.O. Box 999, Dept. 17109, Bergenfield, New Jersey 07621-0120.* VISA and MasterCard holders call 1-800-253-6476 to order all Penguin titles

In Canada: Please write to *Penguin Books Canada Ltd, 10 Alcorn Avenue, Suite 300, Toronto, Ontario M4V 3B2*

In Australia: Please write to *Penguin Books Australia Ltd, P.O. Box 257, Ringwood, Victoria 3134*

In New Zealand: Please write to *Penguin Books (NZ) Ltd, Private Bag 102902, North Shore Mail Centre, Auckland 10*

In India: Please write to *Penguin Books India Pvt Ltd, 706 Eros Apartments, 56 Nehru Place, New Delhi 110 019*

In the Netherlands: Please write to *Penguin Books Netherlands bv, Postbus 3507, NL-1001 AH Amsterdam*

In Germany: Please write to *Penguin Books Deutschland GmbH, Metzlerstrasse 26, 60594 Frankfurt am Main*

In Spain: Please write to *Penguin Books S. A., Bravo Murillo 19, 1° B, 28015 Madrid*

In Italy: Please write to *Penguin Italia s.r.l., Via Felice Casati 20, I-20124 Milano*

In France: Please write to *Penguin France S. A., 17 rue Lejeune, F-31000 Toulouse*

In Japan: Please write to *Penguin Books Japan, Ishikiribashi Building, 2-5-4, Suido, Bunkyo-ku, Tokyo 112*

In Greece: Please write to *Penguin Hellas Ltd, Dimocritou 3, GR-106 71 Athens*

In South Africa: Please write to *Longman Penguin Southern Africa (Pty) Ltd, Private Bag X08, Bertsham 2013*

READ MORE IN PENGUIN

A SELECTION OF FOOD AND COOKERY BOOKS

The Fratelli Camisa Cookery Book   Elizabeth Camisa

From antipasti to zabaglione, from the origins of gorgonzola to the storage of salami, an indispensable guide to real Italian home cooking from Elizabeth Camisa of the famous Fratelli Camisa delicatessen in Soho's Berwick Street.

A Table in Provence   Leslie Forbes

In her latest culinary adventure the bestselling author of *A Table in Tuscany* captures the essence of French Provençal cooking. 'Gives a wonderful flavour of Provence through the recipes and the author's drawings' – *Country Living*

Far Flung Floyd   Keith Floyd

Keith Floyd's latest culinary odyssey takes him to the far flung East and the exotic flavours of Malaysia, Hong Kong, Vietnam and Thailand. And as ever, the irrepressible Floyd spices his recipes with witty stories, wry observation and a generous pinch of gastronomic wisdom.

Chinese Food   Kenneth Lo

'From a Chinese breakfast (*congee* rice, pickled eggs, meat wool, jellied and pickled meats, roasted peanuts and "oil stick" doughnuts) to a feast poetically called Autumn on the Lower Yangtze, Mr Lo takes us brilliantly through a cuisine which it is not frivolous to call a civilization' – *Sunday Times*

The Dinner Party Book   Patricia Lousada

The Dinner Party Book hands you the magic key to entertaining without days of panic or last minute butterflies. The magic lies in cooking each course ahead, so that you can enjoy yourself along with your guests.

Easy Cooking in Retirement   Louise Davies

The mouth-watering recipes in this book are delightfully easy to prepare and involve the least possible fuss to cook and serve.

READ MORE IN PENGUIN

A SELECTION OF FOOD AND COOKERY BOOKS

Traditional Jamaican Cookery Norma Benghiat

Reflecting Arawak, Spanish, African, Jewish, English, French, East Indian and Chinese influences, the exciting recipes in this definitive book range from the lavish eating of the old plantocracy to imaginative and ingenious slave and peasant dishes.

Cooking in a Bedsitter Katharine Whitehorn
Completely revised edition

Practical, light-hearted and full of bright ideas, *Cooking in a Bedsitter* will lure you away from the frying pan and tin-opener towards a healthier, more varied range of delicious dishes.

Simple Vegetarian Meals Rosamond Richardson

Vegetarian food offers an exciting range of flavours and textures. It can be light and summery or rich and warming, homely or exotic. In this inspired book Rosamond Richardson explores all these aspects of vegetarian cooking, emphasizing the simplest, freshest dishes that are imaginative, economical and easy to prepare for one or two people.

Jane Grigson's Fish Book Jane Grigson

A new edition of Jane Grigson's imaginative and comprehensive guide to the delights of cooking and eating fish. 'A splendid book ... Most Britishers are rather shy of fish and how to cook it ... This book will change all that' – *Evening Standard*

Flavours of Greece Rosemary Barron

From the sharp olives, the salty feta and the delicate seafood of the first courses to the fragrant honey pastries and luscious figs of the desserts, Greek food offers a feast of variety that changes with the seasons. With wit and enthusiasm Rosemary Barron shows us how to recreate them in our own kitchen, for family meals or when entertaining.

READ MORE IN PENGUIN

A SELECTION OF FOOD AND COOKERY BOOKS

Real Fast Puddings Nigel Slater

'Nigel Slater has produced another winner in *Real Fast Puddings* ...
Slater has great flair for flavour combinations and he talks much sense. The
book is snappy and fun' – *Financial Times*. 'Delectable ... Slater is an
unashamed spoon-licker' – *Daily Telegraph*

Floyd on Spain Keith Floyd

'The recipes in *Floyd on Spain* are *wonderful*. The smells of herbs and
onions, tomato sauce and grilled fish rise from the page and you want to
get out, buy a hunk of hake and cook it with potatoes and garlic' – Prue
Leith in the *Sunday Express*

Simple French Food Richard Olney

'There is no other book about food that is anything like it ... essential and
exciting reading for cooks, of course, but it is also a book for eaters ... its
pages brim over with invention' – *Observer*

English Bread and Yeast Cookery Elizabeth David

'Here is a real book, written with authority and enthusiasm – a collection
of history, investigation, comment, recipes' – Jane Grigson

The Chocolate Book Helge Rubinstein

'Fact-filled celebration of the cocoa bean with toothsome recipes from
turkey in chilli and chocolate sauce to brownies and chocolate grog' – *Mail
on Sunday*. 'Crammed with mouth-watering puddings, drinks, cakes and
confectionery' – *Guardian*

The Cookery of England Elisabeth Ayrton

Her fascinating and beautifully compiled history and recipe book of
English cooking from the fifteenth century to the present day is 'a lovely
book, which could restore pride in our English kitchens' – *The Times
Literary Supplement*

READ MORE IN PENGUIN

GARDENING

The Well-Tempered Garden Christopher Lloyd

A thoroughly revised and updated edition of the great gardening classic. 'By far the best-informed, liveliest and most worthwhile gardener–writer of our time ... There is no reasonable excuse for any gardener failing to possess Christopher Lloyd's books' – *Interiors*

The Country Diary of an Edwardian Lady Edith Holden

Edith Holden's exquisitely illustrated country diary has, since its rediscovery after seventy years, delighted thousands of readers. In delicate water-colour, poetry and personal entries, it captures the changing beauty of the English countryside through the course of one year and expresses a profound love of the natural world.

The Good Plant Guide Brian Davis

When you are buying plants for your garden there are facts you need to know before selecting and purchasing. *The Good Plant Guide* provides information on almost every type of plant that you may want to purchase, including trees, shrubs, flowers, fruit and vegetables. No keen gardener can afford to be without this indispensable book.

Organic Gardening Lawrence D. Hills

The classic manual on growing fruit and vegetables without using artificial or harmful fertilizers. 'Enormous value ... enthusiastic writing and off-beat tips' – *Daily Mail*

READ MORE IN PENGUIN

GARDENING

The Adventurous Gardener Christopher Lloyd

Prejudiced, delightful and always stimulating, Christopher Lloyd's book is essential reading for everyone who loves gardening. 'Get it and enjoy it' – *Financial Times*

Gardens of a Golden Afternoon Jane Brown

'A Lutyens house with a Jekyll garden' was an Edwardian catch-phrase denoting excellence, something fabulous in both scale and detail. Together they created over 100 gardens, and in this magnificent book Jane Brown tells the story of their unusual and abundantly creative partnership.

A History of British Gardening Miles Hadfield

From the Tudor knot gardens through the formal realities of Jacobean and Georgian landscaping and on to the Gothic fantasies of wealthy Victorian landowners, Miles Hadfield brings the British gardens of the past vividly alive. 'An extraordinarily rich harvest of valuable and entertaining information ... it is hard to see that it can ever be superseded' – *Journal of the Royal Horticultural Society*

Plants from the Past David Stuart and James Sutherland

As soon as it is planted, even the most modern garden can be full of history, whether overflowing with flowers domesticated by the early civilizations of Mesopotamia or with plants collected in the Himalayas for Victorian millionaires. 'A thoroughly engaging style that sometimes allows bracingly sharp claws to emerge from velvet paws' – *World of Interiors*